LAW, POLITICS, AND MORALITY IN J

THE ETHIKON SERIES IN COMPARATIVE ETHICS

—————————————— *Editorial Board* ——————————————

Carole Pateman
Series Editor

The Ethikon Series publishes studies on ethical issues of current importance. By bringing scholars representing a diversity of moral viewpoints into structured dialogue, the series aims to broaden the scope of ethical discourse and to identify commonalities and differences between alternative views.

TITLES IN THE SERIES

Brian Barry and Robert E. Goodin, eds.
*Free Movement: Ethical Issues in the Transnational Migration
of People and Money*

Chris Brown, ed.
Political Restructuring in Europe: Ethical Perspectives

Terry Nardin, ed.
The Ethics of War and Peace: Religious and Secular Perspectives

David R. Mapel and Terry Nardin, eds.
International Society: Diverse Ethical Perspectives

David Miller and Sohail H. Hashmi, eds.
Boundaries and Justice: Diverse Ethical Perspectives

Simone Chambers and Will Kymlicka, eds.
Alternative Conceptions of Civil Society

Nancy L. Rosenblum and Robert Post, eds.
Civil Society and Government

Sohail Hashmi, ed.
Foreword by Jack Miles
Islamic Political Ethics: Civil Society, Pluralism, and Conflict

Richard Madsen and Tracy B. Strong, eds.
*The Many and the One:
Religious and Secular Perspectives on Ethical Pluralism in the Modern World*

Margaret Moore and Allen Buchanan, eds.
States, Nations, and Borders: The Ethics of Making Boundaries

Sohail H. Hashmi and Steven P. Lee, eds.
Ethics and Weapons of Mass Destruction: Religious and Secular Perspectives

Michael Walzer, ed.
Law, Politics, and Morality in Judaism

LAW, POLITICS, AND MORALITY IN JUDAISM

EDITED AND WITH A PREFACE BY

Michael Walzer

PRINCETON UNIVERSITY PRESS   PRINCETON AND OXFORD

Copyright 2006 © by Princeton University Press

Published by Princeton University Press, 41 William Street, Princeton, New Jersey 08540

In the United Kingdom: Princeton University Press, 3 Market Place, Woodstock, Oxfordshire

OX20 1SY

Requests for permission to reproduce material from this work should be sent to Permissions, Princeton University Press.

Library of Congress Cataloging-in-Publication Data

Law, politics, and morality in Judaism / edited and with preface by Michael Walzer.
      p.   cm.   — (Ethikon series in comparative ethics)
   Includes bibliographical references (p.   ) and index.
   ISBN-13: 978-0-691-12507-7 (cl : alk. paper)
   ISBN-10: 0-691-12507-4 (cl : alk. paper)
   ISBN-13: 978-0-691-12508-4 (pb : alk. paper)
   ISBN-10: 0-691-12508-2 (pb : alk. paper)
   1. Jewish law—Moral and ethical aspects.   2. Public law (Jewish law)
   3. Judaism and state.   4. Law—Israel—Jewish influences.   I. Walzer, Michael.
   II. Series.

   KBM524.14.L39 2006
   296.3'6—dc22   2005051468

British Library Cataloging-in Publication Data is available

This book has been composed in Palatino

Printed on acid-free paper. ∞

pup.princeton.edu

Printed in the United States of America

10 9 8 7 6 5 4 3 2 1

Contents

Preface _____

MICHAEL WALZER

THERE ARE TWO MODERN ANSWERS to what used to be called "the Jewish question." I mean, two humane answers; we won't be talking in this volume about the other kind. The question itself might be phrased as follows: What political space is there for Jews in the modern world? The first answer points toward citizenship in inclusive democratic states; the second answer points toward sovereignty in "the land of Israel."

Both of these answers have now been realized; the process of emancipation brought Jews into the democratic state as equal members; a vote at the United Nations and a war for independence brought Jews a state of their own. These two achievements now require the revision and renewal of Judaism generally and of Jewish legal and moral discourse (halakah) in particular. For Judaism and its halakah are essentially the products of exile and exclusion. They reflect the experience of being ruled by the "others." They are shaped by a long and difficult adaptation to the harsh realities of homelessness. Now they must be reshaped to accommodate two different ways of being "at home" in the political world.

It is the normative system, the halakic order, that most requires revision and renewal. The resources available for this work are manifold: first of all, the long tradition of legal interpretation and controversy, and then the history of the Jews, the practice of ethical storytelling (aggadah), theological reflection, and, finally, secular philosophy. Interpretation has always been the dominant strategy of Jewish legal innovation, and many of our authors explore its uses here, but it is important to insist on the other possibilities also. In this volume, David Novak argues for the importance of theology, and Menachem Fisch for secular philosophy. As Maimonides appropriated Aristotle, so Fisch appropriates Karl Popper, it is a useful model.

The stress in all these essays is more on making the tradition usable (though some of our authors insist on the difficulties of doing that) than on learning from the tradition. There is, indeed, a lot to learn from the Jewish experience of sustaining a national identity and a common law without territory, sovereignty, citizenship, or, most of the time, coercive power. Some of that learning is visible here, but what is mostly on display in these essays is the effort to find features of Jewish experience that might be useful in thinking about how to live as citizens and sovereigns. The point is not to "negate the exile," as the first generation of Zionist writers wanted to do, but rather to pull exilic Judaism into the world of modern democracy. Whatever the value of medieval and early modern communal life, it was a sharply segregated life, and it did not prepare the Jews for two crucial features of modern citizenship and statehood. The first of these is voluntary association, where Jews and non-Jews coexist in civil society, with Jewish groups operating side by side with Christian, Muslim, and secular groups, all under the same set of rules—and where individual Jews and non-Jews often join together in the same association for some common purpose. The second feature of modern politics for which exile did not prepare the Jews is democratic responsibility: the sense of being committed, along with non-Jewish fellow citizens, to the well-being of the commonwealth—responsible for the "others" as they are for you. The *kahal*, the semiautonomous Jewish community of the exile, was radically homogeneous. In it, Jews were responsible only for their own well-being. They were denied any share in the larger political community and any role in its decision-making; there were a small number of Jewish ministers and even generals (in medieval Spain, for example), but the Jews generally were a pariah community. The common good belonged to the others, who often looked after it very badly, but who had at least some sense that it needed looking after. Jews today, in Israel especially, but also in every democratic setting, need to revise exilic law and moral sensibility so as to accommodate the idea of an extended common good.

These are some of the issues that we mean to take up in this book, joining a discussion already in progress, which will continue for a long time. The adjustment to exile took place over decades and centuries; the adjustment to citizenship and statehood will take place over a similar span. It isn't our intention to rush the adjustment along, only to participate in the work it involves. We are not collecting programmatic statements about how religious Jews should relate, here and now, to American democracy and secularism or about how Jews, as the majority religious community in Israel, should deal with the different minorities. With regard to questions like these, most of our contributors have classically liberal views. But what they are investigating here is the range of options for thinking about such questions within the religious tradition. What are the possibilities for innovative thought that builds on historically familiar elements and tendencies within Judaism? What are the possibilities for the criticism, revision, elaboration, and extension of halakah—and perhaps also of liberalism and democracy themselves— by scholars working from inside the tradition? We include, of course, a number of writers who think that the possibilities are limited, and who argue that help must be sought outside the tradition—and at least one writer who wonders whether the adaptation to modern politics is really worthwhile. It seems fair to say that the plurality of voices and the mixed messages in this book are themselves expressive of the very tradition that some of the voices criticize.

This last point leads me to a more personal reflection, with which some of my fellow authors might disagree. Years of reading and arguing about Jewish texts suggest to me a doubled view of Judaism over the centuries. On the one hand, it is a standard traditional orthodoxy, whose believers are very much like other orthodox believers with different histories and doctrinal commitments. Like Christian fundamentalists, say, they resist change, sometimes with great vigor. Recall the famous dictum of Moses Sofer, one of the founders of contemporary ultra-orthodoxy: "Everything new is forbidden by the Torah." But Judaism is also, at the same time, a premodern anticipation of modernism. There are many possible explanations for the remarkable argumentativeness, the ironical cast of mind, the deep-seated skepticism, and the tolerance for ambiguity that marked so many (not all) Jews in the early modern period and that facilitated their passage into modernity. Exile itself must be the paramount explanation, and the wandering it required, and the absence of coercive power, and the inability to establish stable hierarchical authority structures. But if that were the whole story, then the end of exile might enable the formation of a newly authoritarian Judaism; certainly, there are signs of this in the modern state of Israel. I suspect, however, that there is a deeper explanation of the Jewish "fit" with modernist culture and politics, which has to do with the earliest history of the religion—with slavery and deliverance, with the covenant, with the multiple and dissimilar law codes, with the prophets and the scribes standing alongside and sometimes against the priests. In any case, it is these features of Judaism, remembered over many centuries, that make me optimistic about the chances for revision and renewal.

The chapters in this book are divided into three parts, which reflect imperfectly the structure of the four volumes in The Ethikon Series in Comparative Ethics from which they have been drawn. Each of those volumes was devoted to a particular topic (civil society, boundaries, pluralism and international society, and war and peace) and brought together essays written from the perspective of different religions and philosophical/political positions: Christianity, Islam, and Judaism, and also liberalism, egalitarianism, and feminism. Each of these positions, and others too, was presented, analyzed, and criticized at a conference organized by the Ethikon Institute and then rewritten for the different

volumes. We have collected here the essays written from the Jewish
perspective or, better, from differing Jewish perspectives, added a few
closely connected pieces prepared for other occasions, and rearranged
them slightly in the interests of intellectual coherence. The point is to
display a range of Jewish responses to some of the hardest questions
posed by modern democratic politics.

The first set of chapters deals with the general shape of the social
and political orders—first, with the foundational question of rights
and obligations and then, more particularly, with the experience of living in civil society, where voluntary association is the rule, and individuals move (relatively) freely from one group to another. Was there
ever anything like this in Jewish experience? What might religious
Jews think about the wide toleration on which this kind of civility
rests, and that makes room for groups that would otherwise be called
heretical or wicked?

The second part of the book deals with the boundedness of state territory and the openness of international society. Jewish law has always
insisted on the connection of land and people, but what exactly is the
nature of, and the justification for, the specific connection of the land
and the people of Israel? And how might this connection be generalized
in a highly diverse and contentious world of lands and peoples? What
kinds of responsibility come with membership in the society of states?
What kinds of responsibility come with sovereignty in a single state?

The third set of chapters deals with questions of war and peace,
most centrally with the classification and judgment of wars by Jewish
writers over many centuries, including the centuries when there was
no Jewish state and no Jewish army. The dominant classification
scheme in the contemporary world is provided by the Catholic doctrine of just (and unjust) war. The Jewish scheme was different, though
our authors disagree about exactly how different it was. We conclude
the book with a chapter that continues the discussion of warfare but
also looks back to the issues of citizenship and obligation—seen now
from the perspective of the state in dire straits: what can it ask of its citizens when its own survival is at risk?

Our authors are Americans and Israelis; European Jewry is unrepre-
sented here. But it is America where emancipation has, arguably, been
most successful, and only in Israel is there a full engagement with political sovereignty. So the limitations of our contributors list is not necessarily a disadvantage. Many of the examples and texts discussed in
these chapters come from the European diaspora, and the discussion
of tolerance and diversity should be of interest to all the world's
Jewries—and also to the many different neighbors of the world's Jews.
It is, of course, Israel's experience of external war and internal division

that gives these chapters their special urgency, but the unusually extensive participation of American Jews in their country's civil society and politics invites democratic theorists everywhere to attend to these arguments.

The trustees of the Ethikon Institute join with Philip Valera, president; Carole Pateman, series editor; and the volume editor, in thanking all who contributed to the development of this book. In addition to the authors and original volume editors, special thanks are due to the Ahmanson Foundation, the Pew Charitable Trusts, the Sidney Stern Memorial Trust, the Doheny Foundation, the Carnegie Council on Ethics and International Affairs, Joan Palevsky and the Skirball Institute on American Values for their generous support of the various Ethikon dialogue projects from which most of these essays and other books emerged. Finally, we wish to express our thanks to Ian Malcolm, our editor at Princeton University Press; and Carolyn Hollis, also of Princeton University Press, for their valuable guidance and support.

Information on Sources

Chapter 1 was originally published in *The Journal of Law and Religion* (Catholic University of America Press, 1988).

Chapter 2 was originally published in *Alternative Conceptions of Civil Society*, eds. Simone Chambers and Will Kymlicka (Princeton: Princeton University Press, 2002), 151–70.

Chapters 3 and 4 were first published in *Civil Society and Government*, eds. Nancy L. Rosenblum and Robert Post (Princeton: Princeton University Press, 2002), 265–83.

Chapters 5 and 6 were originally published in *Boundaries and Justice*, eds. David Miller and Sohail H. Hashmi (Princeton: Princeton University Press, 2001), 213–48.

Chapters 7 and 8 were first published in *The Many and the One*, eds. Richard Madsen and Tracy B. Strong (Princeton: Princeton University Press, 2003), 195–225.

Chapter 9 was first published in *International Society*, eds. David R. Mapel and Terry Nardin (Princeton: Princeton University Press, 1998), 185–200.

Chapters 10 and 11 were originally published in *The Ethics of War and Peace*, ed. Terry Nardin (Princeton: Princeton University Press, 1996), 95–127.

Chapter 12 was originally published in the *Association of Jewish Studies Review* (1987).

Part I

POLITICAL ORDER AND CIVIL SOCIETY

1

Obligation: A Jewish Jurisprudence of the Social Order

ROBERT M. COVER

Fundamental Words

Every legal culture has its fundamental words. When we define our subject as human rights, we also locate ourselves in a normative universe at a particular place. The word "rights" is a highly evocative one for those of us who have grown up in the post-Enlightenment secular society of the West. Even those among us who have been graced with a deep and abiding religious background can hardly have escaped the evocations that the terminology of "rights" carries. Indeed, we try in this essay to take a little credit here and there for the luster that the edifice of rights reflects, perhaps suggesting now and again that the fine reflection owes something to some ultimate source of the light.

Judaism is, itself, a legal culture of great antiquity. It has hardly led a wholly autonomous existence these past three millennia. Yet, I suppose it can lay as much claim as any of the other great legal cultures to having an integrity in its basic categories. When I am asked to reflect upon Judaism and human rights, therefore, the first thought that comes to mind is that the categories are wrong. I do not mean, of course, that basic ideas of human dignity and worth are not powerfully expressed in the Jewish legal and literary traditions. Rather, I mean that because it is a legal tradition, Judaism has its own categories for expressing through law the worth and dignity of each human being. And the categories are not closely analogous to "human rights." The principal word in Jewish law, which occupies a place equivalent in evocative force to the American legal system's "rights," is the word *mitzvah*, which literally means "commandment" but has a general meaning closer to "incumbent obligation."

Before I begin an analysis of the differing implications of these two rather different key words, I should like to put the words in context— the contexts of their respective myths. These words are connected to fundamental stories and receive their force from those stories as much as from the denotative meaning of the words themselves. The story behind the term "rights" is the story of social contract. The myth postulates free and independent if highly vulnerable beings who voluntarily trade a portion of their autonomy for a measure of collective security. The myth makes the collective arrangement the product of individual choice and thus secondary to the individual. "Rights" is the fundamental category because it is the normative category that most nearly approximates that which is the source of the legitimacy of everything else. Rights are traded for collective security. But some rights are retained, and, in some theories, some rights are inalienable. In any event the first and fundamental unit is the individual, and "rights" locate him as an individual separate and apart from every other individual.

I must stress that I do not mean to suggest that all or even most theories that are founded upon rights are "individualistic" or "atomistic." Nor would I suggest for a moment that with a starting point of "rights" and social contract one must get to a certain end. Hobbes as well as Locke is part of this tradition. And, of course, so is Rousseau. Collective solutions as well as individualistic ones are possible, but it is the case that even the collective solutions are solutions that arrive at their destination by way of a theory that derives the authority of the collective from the individual. It is necessarily a theory that posits that that which was "given up" and therefore, at least implicitly, that which is desired, is a perfect freedom with all the alienated rights returned and the contradictions resolved.

The basic word of Judaism is "obligation" or *mitzvah*. It, too, is intrinsically bound up in a myth—the myth of Sinai. Just as the myth of social contract is essentially a myth of autonomy, so the myth of Sinai is essentially a myth of heteronomy. Sinai is a collective—indeed, a corporate—experience. The experience at Sinai is not chosen. The event gives forth the words, which are commandments. In all rabbinic and post-rabbinic embellishment upon the biblical account of Sinai this event is the code for all law. All law was given at Sinai and therefore all law is related back to the ultimate heteronomous event in which we were chosen—passive voice.

Now, just as the social contract theories generated by Hobbes and others who bore a monstrous and powerful collective engine from the myth of individualism, so the Sinaitic myth has given rise to countermyths and accounts that stress human autonomy. Indeed, the rabbinic accounts of law-making autonomy are powerful indeed, though they all conclude by suggesting that everything—even the questions yet to be asked by the brilliant students of the future and the answers to those questions—everything was given at Sinai. And, of course, therefore, all is, was, and has been commanded—and we are obligated to this command.

What have these stories to do with the ways in which the law languages of these respective legal cultures are spoken? Social movements in the United States organize around rights. When there is some urgently felt need to change the law or keep it in one way or another, a "rights" movement is started, civil rights, the right to life, welfare rights, and so on. The premium that is to be put upon an entitlement is so coded. When we "take rights seriously" we understand them to be trumps in the legal game. In Jewish law, an entitlement without an obligation is a sad, almost pathetic thing. There were, in ancient rabbinic Judaism, many obligations from which a blind person was excused. One of the great rabbis of the fourth century, Rabbi Joseph, who was blind, asked the great question of his colleagues: is it greater to do the commandments out of love when one is not obligated to do them or is it greater to do the commandments out of obligation? He had at first assumed that to voluntarily comply with the commandments though not obligated to do so entailed a greater merit. But his colleagues held that to do the commandments out of obligation—more correctly, to do them as obligated—was the act that entailed greater merit. He then offered a feast for the scholars if any could demonstrate that Rabbi Judah's position that the blind were not obligated to do the commandments was erroneous.

Indeed, to be one who acts out of obligation is the closest thing there is to a Jewish definition of completion as a person within the community. A child does not become emancipated or "free" when he or she reaches maturity. Nor does she/he become sui juris. No, the child becomes bar or bat mitzvah, literally one who is "of the obligations." Traditionally, the parent at that time says a blessing. Blessed is He that has exonerated me from the punishment of this child. The primary legal distinction between Jew and non-Jew is that the non-Jew is only obligated to the seven Noahide commandments. Where women have been denied by traditional Judaism an equal participation in ritual, the reasoning of the traditional legist has been that women are not obligated in the same way as are men with respect to those ritual matters (public prayer). It is almost a sure sign of a nontraditional background for someone to argue that women in Judaism should have the right to be counted in the prayer quorum, to lead prayer services, or to be called to the Torah. Traditionalists who do argue for women's participation (and there are some who do) do so not on the basis of rights. They argue rather that the law, properly understood, does or ought to impose on women the obligation of public prayer, of study of Torah, and so forth. For the logic of Jewish law is such that once the obligation is understood as falling upon women, or whomever, then there is no question of "right" of participation. Indeed, the public role is a responsibility.

The Uses of Rights and Obligations

The Jewish legal system has evolved for the past 1,900 years without a state and largely without much in the way of coercive powers to be exercised upon the adherents of the faith. I do not mean to idealize the situation. The Jewish communities over the millennia have wielded power. Communal sanctions of banning and shunning have been regularly and occasionally cruelly imposed on individuals or groups. Less frequently, but often enough, Jewish communities granted quasi-autonomy by gentile rulers have used the power of the gentile state to discipline dissidents and deviants. Nonetheless, there remains a difference between wielding a power that draws on but also depends on preexisting social solidarity, and wielding one that depends on violence. There is also a difference between controlling the violence that is wielded autonomously and being dependent upon a potentially hostile power for that force. The Jewish legal apparatus had not had the autonomous use of violence at its disposal for the two millennia that are, indeed, for all practical purposes the period in which Jewish law as we know it came to be.

In a situation in which there is no centralized power and little in the way of coercive violence, it is critical that the mythic center of the law reinforce the bonds of solidarity. Common, mutual, reciprocal obligation is necessary. The myth of divine commandment creates that web. It must also be pointed out that through most of the past two millennia there has been no well-defined hierarchy of law articulating voices in Judaism. There have been times when great figures have lamented the cacophony of laws, and have understood it to be a condition imposed upon us for our sins. But another strain has almost rejoiced in the plethora of laws and has drawn strength from the traditional solution given by the Talmud to the question of whether the School of Hillel or the School of Shammai was truly correct. "Both are the words of the Living God." The acceptance of the idea that the single great mythic event of lawgiving can issue in apparently inconsistent precepts and understandings but that the apparent inconsistency can, itself, be the product of two correct readings of a larger understanding—that way of looking at the normative world—was immensely useful to a people doomed to live without a hierarchically determined authoritative voice. It was a myth that created legitimacy for a radically diffuse and coordinate system of authority. But while it created room for the diffusion of authority, it did not have a place for individualism. One might have independent and divergent understandings of the obligations imposed by God through his chosen people, but one could not have a worldview that denied the obligations.

The jurisprudence of rights, on the other hand, has gained ascendance in the Western world together with the rise of the national state with its almost unique mastery of violence over extensive territories. Certainly, it may be argued, it has been essential to counterbalance the development of the state with a myth that (a) establishes the state as legitimate only insofar as it can be derived from the autonomous creatures who trade in their rights for security—that is, one must tell a story about the states' utility or service to us, and (b) potentially justifies individual and communal resistance to the Behemoth. It may be true as Bentham so aptly pointed out that natural rights may be used either apologetically or in revolutionary fashion, and there is nothing in the concept powerful enough analytically to constrain which use it shall be put to. Nevertheless, it is the case that natural rights apologies are of a sort that in their articulation limit the most far-reaching claims of the state, and that the revolutionary ideology that can be generated is also of a sort that is particularly effective in countering organic statist claims.

Thus, there is a sense in which the ideology of rights has been a useful counter to the centrifugal forces of the Western nation-state while the ideology of mitzvoth or obligation has been equally useful as a counter to the centripetal forces that have beset Judaism over the centuries. But, in a sense, this kind of speculation is beside the point. The primary function of basic words is not to be found in so simple a functional explanation. We must look to the internal organization of normative thought, not to the external political results in the first instance.

The Nature of the Jurisprudence of Mitzvoth

The leading Maimonides scholar of this generation, Professor Isadore Twersky, has attributed to Maimonides' philosophy of law a thoroughgoing teleological understanding of the mitzvoth. Maimonides is generally thought of as being at the rationalist end of the spectrum of Jewish thinkers, so perhaps this attribution is natural. In any event, the position of Twersky is that Maimonides understood the rationale for the obligations of mitzvoth not only in terms of the bases for each of the commandments understood alone, but more important as a system with a systemic telos as well. In particular, Maimonides' system contrasts the normative world of mitzvoth with the world of vanity—*hebel*. It seems that Maimonides, in this respect, as in so many others, has hit the mark. A world centered upon obligation is not, really cannot be, an empty or vain world. Rights, as an organizing principle, are indifferent to the vanity of varying ends. But mitzvoth because they so strongly bind and locate the individual must make a strong claim for the substantive content of that which they dictate. The system, if it's content be vain, can hardly claim to be a system. The rights system is indifferent to ends and in its indifference can claim systemic coherence without making any strong claims about the fullness or vanity of the ends it permits.

Maimonides' claim is more specific than the above. In the Epistle to Yemen he writes:

> If he could only fathom the inner intent of the law, he would realize that the essence of the true divine religion lies in the deeper meaning of its positive and negative precepts [mitzvoth], every one of which will aid man in his striving after perfection, and remove every impediment to the attainment of excellence.

It is difficult in the light of such a claim to apply certain familiar categories of jurisprudence such as the distinction between a morality of duty and one of aspiration. It is certainly true that Judaism like every other normative system recognizes degrees of attainment in moral or legal excellence. However, the mitzvoth generally do not distinguish between precepts of duty and those of aspiration. And, indeed, the element of aspiration comes into the picture in part as a natural growth from the discipline of the duty imposed upon all. In any event, purpose and divine purpose are located in the basic word.

The Natural Domains of Rights and Mitzvoth

There are certain kinds of problems that a jurisprudence of mitzvoth manages to solve rather naturally. There are others that present conceptual difficulties of the first order. Similarly, a jurisprudence of rights naturally solves certain problems while stumbling over others. It seems interesting to me that these dissimilarities have not been much explored. The claim I am making is not a very strong one. It is not, I will stress, that particular problems cannot be solved, in one system or the other—only that the solution entails a sort of rhetorical or philosophical strain.

The jurisprudence of rights has proved singularly weak in providing for the material guarantees of life and dignity flowing from the community to the individual. While we may talk of the right to medical care, the right to subsistence, the right to an education, we are constantly met by the realization that such rhetorical tropes are empty in a way that the right to freedom of expression or the right to due process are not. When the issue is restraint upon power, it is intelligible to simply state the principle of restraint. Of course, whether the restraint will be effective depends on many things, not least of which is the good faith of those restrained. However, the intelligibility of the principle remains because it is always clear who is being addressed—whoever it is that acts to threaten the right in question. However, the "right to an education" is not even an intelligible principle unless we know to whom it is addressed. Taken alone it only speaks to a need. A distributional premise is missing that can only be supplied through a principle of "obligation."

In a system of mitzvoth this problem does not arise. Jewish law is very firm in its guarantee of an education. Something approaching universal male schooling was pursued perhaps two millennia ago. In any event, it is clear that throughout the Middle Ages it was the obligation of families and communities to provide schooling to all male children. I do not mean to imply that this principle was not often honored in the breach. But it was a principle and a clear one. And it did give rise to a system of schooling unrivaled in its time for educational opportunity. Yet, it is striking that the Jewish legal materials never speak of the right or entitlement of the child to an education. Rather, they speak of the obligation incumbent upon various providers to make the education available. It is a mitzvah for a father to educate his son, or grandson. It is a mitzvah for a teacher under certain circumstances to teach even without remuneration. It is a mitzvah for the community to make certain provisions for education and its institutions. It is a mitzvah for householders to board poor scholars and support them, and so forth.

Now, of course, in the United States with its rhetoric of rights, we too have statutes and provisions that allocate the responsibilities, fiscal and administrative, for the provision of education to children. As I said at the outset, we are comparing rhetorics not results. What is the case, however, is that these provisions concerning school districts and property taxes carry very little in the way of rhetorical freight. They do not move us or provide slogans or organizing ideologies. The provisions exist because if we are to carry on certain functions we need them. They neither move nor dignify in themselves. If we want to leap forward providing a kind or degree of education heretofore unprovided, we usually gravitate to the rhetoric of rights—declaring, for instance, a campaign for the rights of the retarded to special education. "For every child has a right to an education." Then, the evocative force of the rights rhetoric having done its work, we leave to the technicians the allocation of fiscal responsibility. If past experience is any indication, there will be a series of attempts to foist the responsibility off on someone else.

In a jurisprudence of mitzvoth the loaded, evocative edge is at the assignment of responsibility. It is to the parent paying tuition, the householder paying his assessment that the law speaks eloquently and persuasively. It is for him/her that the myth resonates. This is true for all welfare functions and for ritual ones as well.

There are procedural issues as well in which the rhetorical edge of mitzvoth as opposed to rights seems to make a difference. Consider for example the problem of the dress of litigants before a tribunal. In *Estelle v. Williams* the Supreme Court held that the defendant had a right to appear at his trial (a jury trial) dressed in civilian garb of his choice rather than the convict garb in which he had spent the previous days in jail. But, the Court concluded, in the absence of timely objection by counsel the right was deemed waived or not exercised. Now contrast Maimonides' treatment of a very similar though not identical issue:

> **1.** A positive commandment enjoins upon the judge the duty to judge righteously . . .
>
> **2.** If one of the parties to a suit is well clad and the other ill clad, the judge should say to the former, "either dress him like yourself before the trial is held or dress like him, then the trial will take place." (Mishneh Torah, Laws of Sanhedrin, c. 21)

It is, of course, the case that the rights-centered system of jurisprudence does frequently place affirmative obligations upon a judge to see to the protection of the "rights" of the parties. In that sense, the kind of obligation evoked in Maimonides' code is not completely strange. Moreover, the ethics of certain roles, like the roles of judges or even lawyers, do carry with them an evocative capacity associated with obligation and responsibility. Nevertheless, it is the case that even with respect to these areas we tend to have a system that is almost uniquely dependent upon parties and their representatives asserting their "fairness rights" rather than upon judges fulfilling their fairness obligations.

If there is a comparative rhetorical advantage to mitzvoth in the realm of communal entitlements, there is, it seems to me, a corresponding comparative rhetorical advantage to rights in the area of political participation. The myth of social contract is a myth of coequal, autonomous, voluntary acts. It is a myth that posits participation because the legitimacy of what is generated depends upon the moral force of participation. The argument, for example, for the equal participation of women in political affairs or for their legal equality is very straightforward under a rights jurisprudence, once the parties to the argument accept the moral or biological equality of the sexes. However, in a jurisprudence of mitzvoth, one must first create an argument for equality of obligation and only as a result of that come to equality of participation. The fact is that there might be important reasons for justifying distinctions in obligations (e.g., the capacity to bear children) that nonetheless do not in any straightforward way mitigate against complete equality of participation. The rights rhetoric goes to the nub of this matter because it is keyed to the projection of personality among indifferent or hostile others. The reality of such indifference, hostility, or oppression is what the rhetoric of responsibility obscures. At its best it obscures it by, in fact, removing or mitigating the causes. At its worst it is the ideological mask of familiar oppressions.

Conclusions

The struggle for universal human dignity and equality still proceeds on many levels all over the world. There is no question that we can use as many good myths in that struggle as we can find. Sinai and social contract both have their place. Yet, as I scan my own—our own—privileged position in the world social order and the national social order, as I attend the spiritual and material blessings of my life and the rather obvious connection that some of these have with the suffering of others, it seems to me that the rhetoric of obligation speaks more sharply to me than that of rights. Of course, I believe that every child has a right to decent education and shelter, food and medical care; of course, I believe that refugees from political oppression have a right to a haven in a free land; of course, I believe that every person has a right to work in dignity and for a decent wage. I do believe and affirm the social contract that grounds these rights. But more to the point, I also believe that I am commanded—that we are obligated—to realize those rights.

2

Judaism and Civil Society

SUZANNE LAST STONE

THERE IS NO term for, much less a theory of, civil society in classical Jewish texts.[1] Rabbinic writers do not produce theories; they produce commentaries on a biblical or talmudic text, codes of law, and legal responsa. These sources, moreover, are extremely diverse, covering over two millenniums of history, and were for the most part generated in premodern exile, when Jews lacked a state of their own; lived in compact, internally autonomous, and religiously homogenous communities scattered across continents; and were segregated from general society legally, politically, and socially. Without a state of their own, and with little sense of belonging to the host states in which they live, rabbinic writers do not discuss the role of society in relation to the state. So, the Jewish tradition has little to contribute to the civil society/state debate. If one understands civil society, instead, as "an ethical vision of social life,"[2] concerned with the conditions for establishing bonds of social solidarity between diverse members of society and shaping rights of association to promote such bonds, then Judaism has much to contribute to the discussion.

The topic of forging and maintaining overlapping bonds of social solidarity not only among the community of Jews but also in a pluralistic social world appears throughout Jewish literature, beginning with the biblical portrayal of the terms and conditions of Israelite associational life with other groups living in the biblical polity. This discussion is continued in rabbinic sources that reconstruct Israel's biblical past and messianic future, although without reference to any actually existing Jewish polity. The rabbinic tradition developed a theory of what constitutes not a "civil society" but, rather, a "civilized society." The Jewish tradition thus offers its own ethical perspective on the criteria necessary to establish trust, bonds of social solidarity, and duties of association in a pluralistic world, which I shall describe in the first part of this chapter.

Whether this particular ethical vision of social life can be applied meaningfully today is a difficult and pertinent question. Although the traditional rabbinic division of time views all history between the destruction of the Temple in the first century and its hoped-for rebuilding in the messianic age as an undifferentiated time of exile, modernity fundamentally altered the background conditions to which the classical sources respond. The extension of civil society itself to include Jews raises new questions about the terms of such inclusion. What rights of association do Jews require in order to thrive in a manner continuous with the Jewish tradition, and what does the rabbinic tradition say about the participation of Jews in the pluralistic, associational life of the nation? Moreover, the changes wrought by the "Jewish emancipation and self-emancipation"[3]—the breakup of homogenous religious communities, the rise of secularism, and the consequent fragmentation of Jewish society—raise new questions for the rabbinic tradition about intragroup associational life itself. The most dramatic change is the creation of the state of Israel. Several Jewish intellectuals view the construction of a "Jewish" theory of civil society, one capable of encompassing the diverse groups, both Jewish and non-Jewish, that constitute Israeli society, as an urgent need—even though they are not at all sure how to connect such a theory to the rabbinic sources.

There are no developed answers to these questions. The rabbinic process is one of gradual adaptation, the search for legal responses to new problems through the slow accretion of consensus, and the use of the traditional talmudic categories developed in the earliest centuries. With respect to Israel, in particular, historical events have far preceded rabbinic legal development. So, in addressing these questions in the second part of this chapter, I shall speculate as much as report.

The Ideal Jewish Social Order

Ingredients, Society

The Bible begins with the story of the creation of humans in God's image, endowing humanity with special worth and dignity. This idea embodies an ethical ideal of social harmony among humans, one that the prophets envision as the goal of the end of days. Humanity is not intended to be a universal human order, however, nor "one fellowship and societie," as Locke wrote.[4] Nor are humans made a community by any common enjoyment of natural rights. The lesson of the biblical story of the Tower of Babel is that a universal human order is potentially dangerous. Instead, humanity is divided into unique collectivities, each with its own language and laws, and each capable of attaining independent moral significance.

The biblical election of Israel at Sinai creates an immediate division within humanity between Israel and the other nations of the world.

The community or nation of Israel comes into being through the covenant, a historical social contract between God and Israel at Sinai (described in most rabbinic sources as grounded in consent), which establishes the Torah as the law of the Israelites. What gives Israelite society its identity, without which it would cease to be a society or would become a different one, is the law. The Torah, the written and oral law given at Sinai, is the particular inheritance of Israel, and only Israel is bound by the 613 commandments contained in it. The law is permanent and binding on all future generations of Jews, because God included in the covenant all who stood at Sinai and those who are "not here with us this day" (Deut. 29:14). As an original member of the covenant, each Jew continues to be obligated to perform the law even if he or she disassociates from the community. Although the concept of chosenness is sometimes linked, especially among mystical thinkers, to the idea of a distinctive Jewish soul, for most, chosenness is a societal concept, referring to the national community's obligation to become a religious community by observing the law.

The unity of Jewish society derives from a common subjection of all its constituent parts—political organs, the family, and the individual—to the exclusive authority of the law. All aspects of life are governed by the law, including private individual conduct, private family relations, social relations, and market activity. The organs that wield coercive power are similarly parts of the community that the law addresses. The monarch does not exemplify divine law. He is essentially a magistrate who applies the law in concrete circumstances such as in conditions of war, just as the judges apply the law to concrete cases.

Nor is the individual a distinct unit possessed of individual rights that separate him from other individuals and society itself. Covenantal obligations are imposed on the individual not as a singular human being but, rather, as a member of the community. One cannot ignore one's obligations without endangering others. This is the meaning of the talmudic legal principle that "all Jews are responsible [literally, sureties] for one another."[5] Each Jew is held accountable for the preventable transgressions of another and is responsible for the other's fulfillment of the commandments. Ritva glosses this further: "All Jews are responsible for one another. They are like [parts of] one body and like a guarantor who repays the debt of a friend."[6] Such a system may, and does, respect individual rights of personhood and property, but it cannot confer on its members the kind of freedom or autonomy presupposed by civil society. In the Jewish conception, the individual is neither sovereign over his or her own life and experience nor a fully independent source of moral values. Freedom is not defined in terms of subjective rights or the choice of one's aims and desires. Freedom means individual accountability, the free will to obey or disobey the law.

Judaism thus lacks the building blocks, drawn largely from Christian conceptions of society and the individual and the experience of European Christendom, that gave rise to the idea of civil society in the West.[7] Given the comprehensiveness of the law, Judaism could not develop a picture of society as independent of its political organization, as did the Church; nor a concept of independent realms of experience, separate domains such as the household, the state, the economy, and society itself, each arranged according to its own logic or laws; nor even a sharp distinction between public and private spheres. Nor could it develop a notion of the individual as an equal moral agent possessed of rights that separate him from society as a whole.

Civil society, it is worth underscoring, is a historical and culturally specific model, an outgrowth of and corrective to the Western tradition of individualism. The problem that the idea of civil society first sought to solve, how to synthesize individualism with community, cannot arise in a tradition that views the individual as heteronomous, not autonomous, and as located firmly in a particularist community. Nor does the ancillary problem that the idea of civil society seeks to solve, the development of a society strong enough to resist state hegemony and the concentration of power in the state, arise. Because power belongs properly to God, in the Jewish tradition power is dispersed throughout society. The law places limits on the accumulation of property and land, equalizing material resources, and on the accumulation of power by the monarchy or other coercive institutions. The Jewish tradition offers, then, precisely the kind of historical model that should be contrasted to civil society: what Ernest Gellner has called the "segmentary community which avoids central tyranny by firmly turning the individual into an integral part of the social sub-unit."[8] The individual is protected from central dictatorship but is subject instead to the dictatorship of friends and neighbors, for "the collective responsibility of members of the covenant invites mutual surveillance and pressure to conform to divine norms, as oppressive to the individual as any tyranny."[9]

The Jewish tradition provides not only an alternative historical option to civil society, but also an alternative ethical model of how associational life should be structured and concretized in a pluralistic society. The rabbinic vision reaches beyond the Jewish social structure. It contemplates a world populated by morally corrupt societies, on the one hand, and civilized societies, on the other—societies that adhere to the moral order given by God to humanity, according to the biblical account, prior to the Sinaitic election. The rabbinic tradition codifies this order as consisting of seven basic human obligations: to refrain from

idolatry, blasphemy, homicide, incest and adultery, robbery, and eating
the flesh of a live creature, and to establish a system of justice.[10] The nations of the world thus also potentially constitute societies of moral
significance whose basic purpose is to establish justice in the social
sphere; they are not merely aggregates of individuals. Only those who
do not adhere to the (Jewish) universal moral code are not members of
a true society. They live, instead, in a state of moral chaos.

So, there are other societies that overlap the covenantal one. The rabbinic tradition stipulates criteria, quite different from those proposed
by other political traditions for adjudicating which associations in a
pluralistic society should be supported and which should not, which
associations are mandatory and which impermissible. Communal
bonds, social proximity, political and material dependence, and moral
character determine the level of social solidarity owed to society's diverse members.[11]

I begin with the covenantal community, in which the strongest
bonds of social solidarity are owed. Covenantal fellowship, unlike the
friendship of citizens in the liberal state, is not voluntary. The law im-
poses a duty to associate with other covenantal members. It is not only
that many legal obligations, from the cultic to the mundane, can only
be performed within a group setting. Rather, as Maimonides summa-
rizes, "one who diverges from communal paths, even if he commits no
transgression but merely separates himself from the congregation of Israel, and does not participate in their sorrows, loses his share in the
world to come."[12] The social solidarity that the law stipulates for
covenantal fellows is regulated by two interrelated principles: to "love
one's neighbor as oneself" (Lev. 19:18) and to "hate" evildoers (Psalms
139:21). The tradition is less concerned with the problem of commanding the emotions of love and hate and more concerned with concretizing
these obligations in specific acts, such as visiting the sick, comforting
mourners, and assisting in burials,[13] and with "interpreting and restricting the object of love" and hate.[14] Some acts of benevolence are so
extraordinary that they are obligatory only among covenantal fellows:
extending interest-free loans, redeeming captives, sabbatical cancella-
tion of debts, just-pricing, rebuking fellows to prevent transgression,
and special forms of charity. Certain objects of love cannot be subsumed
under the general category of reciprocal love. It is not sufficient to love
the unfortunate reciprocally, as one loves oneself; they require special
protection.[15] Similarly, specific provisions are made for those one may
view with hostility. The biblical ideal of a social bond among all Israelites assumes that social relations are a site not only of natural amity
and affection but also of personal jealousy and conflict. The concrete
obligations of fellowship extend to personal enemies.[16]

It is forbidden to extend social solidarity and assistance to the undeserving, however, for to do so implies a failure to employ critical judgment. In a society defined by common allegiance to the law, the undeserving are rebellious sinners, heretics, and apostates, who show through their actions that they reject the authority of the law.[17] Such rebellious sinners are no longer "fellows" to whom mutual social obligations are owed, and they no longer enjoy rights of association with covenantal members. Social contact with them is forbidden, they are neither mourned nor eulogized, and intermarriage with them is forbidden. The wish to preserve the historic community, which overlapped with the religious community, no doubt accounted for increasingly narrow definitions of what constitutes deliberate defiance of the law and thus abdication of community membership.[18] But the core concept remained and was enforced. Thus, one may be a Jew for purposes of incurring an obligation to God to observe the law, yet not a Jew for purposes of asserting rights of fellowship.[19] The status of covenantal fellow turns on conduct, and not ascription, a concept that plays a critical role in defining who is included in Jewish society, one that has assumed critical significance in modern conditions of Jewish social fragmentation.

An additional model of social solidarity overlapping the covenantal is provided by the biblical portrayal of the associational life that Israelites share with non-Israelites residing in the polity. The biblical concept of social solidarity among diverse ethnic members of the polity bears a resemblance to the fellowship of citizens in the modern nation. The Bible speaks of three types potentially within the polity: the heathen, the stranger, and the resident stranger. The heathen is an idolater who is not to associate with Israelites. Idolatry is not only an absolute falsehood; it is linked in biblical thought with moral corruption. The Bible repeatedly commands the community to rid the territory of idolatry and idolaters—pagan and Israel alike.

In contrast, Israelites are enjoined in the Bible to love the stranger as oneself (Lev. 19:33–34), to provide one law for the stranger and the Israelite alike (Exod. 12–49), and to provide the stranger with food, clothing, and agricultural charity (Lev. 23:22; Deut. 24:19). The Hebrew word stranger, *ger*, connotes both foreignness and residence. In its original biblical setting, the stranger is an individual of non-Jewish birth living in the land in close proximity with Jews, who accepts Jewish political authority, and obeys some, though not all, of the covenantal law. The social solidarity that Israelites owe to the stranger is ascribed specifically to the stranger's material and political dependence. The stranger does not have an allotted portion of the land and is therefore associated with the Levite, the widow, and the orphan (Deut. 10:17–18), to whom special consideration must be shown. The Bible also appeals to history to ground the obligations of social solidarity owed to those who are politically dependent on others. Israelites, too, were once strangers in Egypt (Deut. 10–19).

This sense of social obligation, rooted in political and material dependence and in social proximity, is muted in the rabbinic reworking of the biblical model. The biblical stranger was gradually assimilated into the covenantal community and reconceived as a convert, who became a full member of the covenant upon assuming the obligations of the law. The rabbinic tradition equates the biblical stranger with the resident stranger, which it identifies as a non-Jew who formally accepts the Noahide laws as a condition of living in the land.[20] Social solidarity owed to those who are dependent and proximate is replaced by a more abstract ethical commitment to those who accept the Jewish teaching of justice and morality.

The category of resident stranger had no practical application in exile. The early talmudic discussion of the obligations owed by Jews to non-Jews with whom they lived assumes that non-Jews are pagan idolaters and erects encumbrances against any association with them. The Talmud also discriminates against non-Jews with respect to juridical rights and obligations. Whether the legal inequality of non-Jews posited in the Talmud is based on their status as idolaters or, rather, reflects the mutual alienation between Jews and non-Jews or even a perception of an ontological division between the two groups is unclear.[21] Even in the talmudic period, however, the differential rules were sometimes held inapplicable, not because non-Jews were analogized to "strangers" but, rather, because other halakic principles intervened. The principle of *darkhei shalom*, pursuing paths of peace in social life, was often invoked as a legal basis for supporting the pagan poor, visiting the sick of both groups, and burying their dead with Jews.[22] This principle reasserts the importance of extending social solidarity to those with whom one lives in close proximity.

In the medieval period, rabbinic jurists began to apply the concept of Noahides to Muslims and Christians. Menahem ha-Me'iri, a thirteenth-century French decisor, presented an original synthesis of the entire talmudic system of discriminatory rules and exceptions, essentially rendering most obsolete. He held that juridical discrimination against non-Jews refers to non-Jewish idolaters who lived in the culture of the ancient world, who "were not bound by proper customs," and not to the people of the medieval era, who are disciplined by enlightened religion.[23] The latter are owed full charitable, legal, and ethical reciprocity.[24] Ha-Me'iri's formulation is of particular importance for two reasons. Although other jurists reached similar legal conclusions, they did so through the traditional talmudic, casuistic method and confined their rulings to the practical needs of the community. Ha-Me'iri, as Jacob Katz points out, formulated his distinction between the two periods as a "principle," and thus "transcended the conventional methods of halakhic thinking."[25] Moreover, although ha-Me'iri compares religiously enlightened non-Jews to resident strangers who observe Noahide law, he does not equate them. Rather, ha-Me'iri creates a new intermediate category between paganism and Judaism. This category consists of "nations that are restricted by the ways of religion." Societies that fear God are lawful, disciplined societies. As Moshe Halbertal points out, ha-Me'iri emphasizes the functional aspect of all religions in creating a well-ordered society.[26] As Katz earlier suggested, ha-Me'iri had in mind all societies that maintain legal institutions and enforce moral standards in society.[27]

The system of social solidarity that Judaism proposes is the product of its peculiar blend of particularism and universalism. Minimal obligations are owed to all humanity. Social solidarity is owed to civilized societies who adhere to universal criteria of morality. The deepest bonds of solidarity are reserved for covenantal fellows. "To renounce this distinction," as Gordon Lafer writes, "is not to extend the intimacy and commitment of communal relations to the world at large, but rather to reduce even familial and communal bonds to the level of our relations with strangers."[28]

Values, Responsibility

Maimonides identifies the command to love one's fellow and its corollary, to love the stranger, as the second cardinal principle of the Torah. For Maimonides, social solidarity is not a good in itself; it is linked to the first principle, love of God. It is through love of God that one comes to understand that social solidarity is based not on self-interest but, rather, on reciprocity, that those who obey the different sets of duties God has charged them with are "normatively interchangeable" in the eyes of God.[29]

In contrast to the Christian tradition, Judaism does not view sociality and solidarity as grounded in human nature. Human nature, in the traditional Jewish viewpoint, is too fragile a basis for ordering political, legal, and ethical obligations, for humanity is capable of moral corruption. Social bonds are a product of culture, of law. They are created and molded by the concrete obligations imposed by the law, mandating some associations and forbidding others. The legal principles regulating associational life are thus part and parcel of the larger purpose of the law: in biblical terminology, to mold a holy nation; in the philosophic

language of Maimonides, to provide for the well-being of the community. In the Bible, holiness is defined as separation, both physical separation of Israelites from idolaters and social separation from general
society. Such separation is designed to preserve cultural distinctiveness and prevent the infiltration of foreign norms. As Jacob Katz notes,
even ha-Me'iri refused to suspend various segregative laws that
served to separate Jews from non-Jews.[30] The obligation to show social
solidarity with all civilized societies cannot efface the biblical plan to
create a unique national collectivity.

For Maimonides, the fellowship created by the social commandment
assures general human well-being. The law does not take into account
individual interests, however, as the individual is not a sufficient judge
of his own well-being. Nor need individuals agree about the general
justness of the law. A divine law addresses objective human well-being.
Human well-being consists in the well-being of the body, that is, the human need for physical security and material sustenance. But human
well-being consists, more importantly, of the creation of conditions that
allow persons to perfect their moral character and their intellect. These
laws are not only cultic. They include the obligation of fathers to educate their children, the obligation of children to care for parents, economic restrictions on maximizing profits designed to protect weaker
parties and redistribute resources according to need, and the like. In
short, the law is responsible for assuring human well-being, and it is
the law that determines who is to do what.

Responsibility for performing the law and thus providing for the
well-being of oneself and others rests on each individual community
member in the first instance. The social organization of Judaism,
which includes extensive education of children and adults as well as
periodic public recitation of the law, is designed to promote self-
governance, to enable persons to perform the law themselves. The
pedagogic form in which the law is cast invites willing adherence to
the law, although coercive institutions are also provided. But there is
a marked tendency to devalue coercion. Many laws, particularly
those that involve no public act, entail no public sanction. Even major
criminal offenses are often unpunished by human authorities, as a result of the well-known biblical procedural rules that make conviction
unlikely.

The principal function of judges (later, rabbinic authorities) is to determine the law that the individual community member is obliged to
perform. In contrast to the natural law tradition, which posits that humans can discern their obligations through reason, or the Confucian
tradition, which combines affective and cognitive modes of knowing
one's obligations, in Judaism, the innate moral capacities of humans

are developed within the context of revelation, the source of genuine moral knowledge. The law itself specifies the good, while human reason is employed to interpret the law so that its moral and ethical import is realized. The law is assumed to contain the principles for its own elaboration, serving as a broad mandate for judicial legislation and interpretation, including extending or adding to its provisions and restricting or annulling others.

Conspicuously absent from the biblical model is any assignment of responsibility for human well-being to private or communal associations. Communal associations first emerged in the talmudic period. According to the Talmud, the "townspeople," a legally recognized partnership, provided for local public needs, such as synagogues, schools, ritual baths, and police protection.[31] They also acted as labor unions, with the right to fix weights and measures, prices and wages.[32] The medieval *kehillot*, lay representative associations that legislated for the public good, were viewed as extensions of this talmudic model. The communal associations had the right to tax and to subject individuals within their geographic jurisdiction to their authority, subject to rabbinic review, a right medieval jurists justified as grounded in the consent of their membership.[33] They also became the vehicle for fulfilling various fellowship obligations, such as dispensing charity and redeeming captives. It is unclear whether the communal associations are properly classified as mediating institutions or political institutions. In a society without a state, the distinction is, needless to say, elusive. Genuinely private voluntary associations, organized for religious, charitable, educational, and occupational purposes, proliferated in the late-medieval period.[34] But these associations were not endowed with any legal or theoretical importance. From the tradition's perspective, these associations were the natural consequence of the law's social orientation.

Post-Enlightenment Judaism and Contemporary Pluralism

Risks, Freedom

I have already suggested that the Jewish tradition has few resources from which to build a modern, liberal conception of civil society. Indeed, from the rabbinic perspective, liberal civil society, defined as a realm of voluntary association and free entry and exit, is the problem of modern Jewish existence because it liberates individuals from the group, enabling them to discard traditional forms of life, express their identity in nontraditional terms, or put aside the question of identity altogether. Liberal civil society encourages sectarian divisions to multiply

and overlapping associations to proliferate, and interprets this fragmentation as benign because "plural memberships and divided loyalties make for toleration."[35]

The main risk that the rabbinic vision of associational life poses for
its members in contemporary conditions of freedom is self-isolation
and estrangement, both from general society and from nonconforming
Jews. This isolation, although often seen by members as an intensifica-
tion of the principle of holiness as separation embodied in the remnant of the faithful, is an abdication of rabbinic Judaism's historic role
of assuring the survival of the religio-national community. In order for
rabbinic Judaism to play a positive role in the drama of Jewish life, especially in Israel, it needs to develop a mode or theory of associational
life in an ethically pluralistic society existing under modern conditions
of freedom and equality—a new synthesis akin to that developed by ha-
Me'iri in the medieval period. No such theory has yet emerged. Instead,
rabbinic authorities resort to casuistic reasoning, cast in a language that
is, at best, strange to modern eyes, which has been only partially successful in accomplishing this goal.

The critical questions of associational life in Israel concern the place
of secular Jews and non-Jews in a Jewish polity and the role of religious legislation. Rabbinic discussion of these issues sheds some light
on what form of civil society the Jewish tradition could, at least, support or tolerate in a modern Jewish state.

Given the traditional definition of Jewish society as excluding deviants, including public desecrators of the Sabbath, the question arises
whether secular Jews are, from the rabbinic perspective, within Jewish
society. This question arose immediately on the heels of the Jewish Enlightenment, well before the creation of the state, when nontraditional
denominations and secularist movements began to proliferate. As ex-
pulsion or banning was not an option, several traditional communities
self-separated themselves from general Jewish society and formed segregated communities of the faithful.[36] The early settlement community
in Israel raised the question in its most acute form but also spurred efforts at accommodation because the very fact of the individual's continued attachment to the idea of a Jewish nation softened the rabbinic
category of rebellious sinners who reject the law.

Although one still can find contemporary rabbinic opinions holding
that those who deny the divinity of Jewish law or publicly desecrate the
Sabbath are no longer a part of the covenantal community,[37] most rabbinic authorities hold otherwise. These opinions, for the most part, continue earlier talmudic and medieval patterns of restricting the category
of rebellious sinners by viewing sinners as not fully responsible for
their actions. External factors, and not individual autonomous decision,

cause the sin.[38] Rabbi Abraham Yeshayahu Karelitz, the Hazon Ish, argues more broadly, however, that the times have so changed that the traditional categories no longer even apply. Modernity is different because it is "a time of God's concealment."[39] Such rulings are motivated, however, by communitarian concerns, and not by respect for the value of diverse forms of Jewish life or of individual choice. As such, they create a virtual fellowship, in which the primordial obligation of social solidarity exists only on one side. An equally nettlesome issue for the rabbinic tradition is the place of the non-Jew within the state. Does the halakah provide an adequate "model of mutuality as a basis for stable group relations"?[40] Social reciprocity does not present a serious legal issue, given the norms of mutuality achieved even in the earlier talmudic model through invocation of the principle of pursuing paths of peace. (Political realia is a far greater impediment.) The more critical issue is the extension of full citizenship rights. According to Maimonides, non-Jews (and Jewish women) are forbidden to hold positions of political authority in the Jewish polity.[41] The exilic models of reciprocity do not resolve this issue because they address only sharing acts of benevolence.

The admission of non-Jews (and Jewish women) as equal partners in the polity would seem to require a bolder theory, one that affirms the equality of all persons under the law. The Jewish philosopher Hermann Cohen claimed that the biblical injunction to provide one law for the citizen and the stranger (who obeys Noahide law) was, in fact, the precursor of this emancipation ideal. "The Noahide," he writes, "is a citizen," a person whose equal moral worth is recognized, triggering full equality under the law.[42] Cohen seems to have no followers within the halakic community, however, for the talmudic understanding of the laws of the resident stranger hedge the concept with restrictions that make it far less amenable to such uses. Rabbinic adoption of the approach of ha-Me'iri, who equalizes the juridical rights of Jews and non-Jews "restricted by the ways of religion," would provide an alternative basis for a theory that affirms the equality of all persons under the law. But ha-Me'iri's work, which was lost for centuries, has only now begun to penetrate mainstream rabbinic thought. Moreover, the application of ha-Me'iri's view to members of secular societies, in which the empirical instantiation of a just and ethical society substitutes for adherence to religion that generates lawfulness, remains at issue.

The more common rabbinic strategy is to retain the differential rules in theory but to make them inapplicable to the issue at hand. Thus, Chief Rabbi Isaac Herzog argued that the ban on non-Jews holding political authority refers to the exercise of nonelective, life-tenure powers because it had in mind the office of the Jewish king.[43] Rabbi

Shaul Yisraeli proposes to circumvent the ban by conceiving the state itself as no more than a partnership, modeled on the talmudic partnership of the "townspeople." He analogizes the holding of office in the state to holding office in a business, which a non-Jew may do.[44] The disturbing feature of these opinions is not their result but their rationales, which highlight the paucity of resources in the tradition for developing a comprehensive theory of equal citizenship.

The most controversial issue in Israel today is religious coercion. Must an authentic Jewish civil society incorporate religious law? Here rabbinic writers have been far bolder, drawing on a persistent tension in the halakah with respect to the validity of coercion in general and religious coercion in specific. Performance of the commandments is ideally undertaken freely. At the same time, the law was imposed both to preserve the character of the community as a whole and on the assumption that compelled observance produces "inner consent." More recent rabbinic writings seriously question whether coercion is valid in circumstances where it is unlikely to produce such inner consent.[45] Such inner recognition of the ultimate justice of coercion, possible in a religious age, does not exist in the modern era.

Although the roots of this view go back to talmudic debates about the validity of coercing religious behavior, the growing shift away from coercion suggests a genuine penetration of modern modes of thought into the halakah. Rather than lamenting the decline of a religious worldview, several rabbinic writers assign a positive value to the contraction of opportunities for religious coercion and attribute this contraction to the providential progression of Jewish and human history. Not only was the course of Jewish history providentially guided to limit the scope of coercive powers;[46] the progression of human history toward a maximizing of individual human freedom is a precursor of the messianic age, enabling the law to be performed under ideal conditions of free choice.[47] Thus, a political structure that protects autonomous decision making is superior to the political structure of the past, once a given society attains "intellectual and moral maturity."[48]

The far-reaching implication of this reconception of the value of religious coercion is that religious legislation in the secular state would have no halakic justification if its purpose is to compel observance of Jewish law. Such legislation must be justified on other grounds, such as the will of the people—a return to the talmudic partnership model of the "townspeople" and its medieval successor, the *kehillah*, which legislated for the common good of the geographic community on the basis of consent. Thus, the critical question is what the communal will is at a given time. That religious legislation is still acceptable to various segments of

Israeli society suggests that some form of consensus still exists about the form a Jewish civil society should take.

Debates about religious jurisdiction over marriage and divorce illuminate the differing reasons underlying such consensus. Pursuant to a political compromise between religious and secular parties entered into at the creation of the state, the state retains the Ottoman millet system, ceding matters of personal status to the jurisdiction of recognized religio-ethnic groups. Although it is fashionable to view the political arrangements as purely instrumental, the compromises are best understood as tentative agreements, subject to revision, about what a Jewish society that does not define its identity exclusively in terms of the halakah should entail. Religious parties advocate religious jurisdiction over marriage and divorce, not primarily in order to impose religious standards of behavior on individuals, but because they fear that civil marriage and divorce will produce two exogamous groups, which will lead to a rupture in the unity of the Jewish people living in close proximity in the state. For secular Zionists, religious jurisdiction over marriage and divorce is still largely viewed as in the interests of the collective to preserve a Jewish national identity as well as an expression of Jewish national and cultural norms. Zionism views the laws of society as reflections of the collective self, and not merely convergences of interest between individuals, and thus is also willing to subordinate individual rights (such as freedom from religion) for the welfare of the collective society.

A new "post-Zionist" group has entered this debate. This group wishes to establish a liberal democratic society in which rights are located in the individual and not in the collectivity that constitutes society and in which "the individual is freed from the burden of a priori duty to a collectivity in which he was born 'by chance' and not of his own free choice."[49] They stress the heterogenous character of Israel, which includes other ethnicities and religious groups, and urge a liberal vision of civil society as one in which people freely enter and exit groups—a vision that requires civil marriage and divorce. So far, this perspective has not led to a call for complete reform of religious jurisdiction over marriage but rather for adjustments, the establishment of an alternative structure for those individuals who cannot be accommodated by the halakah.

These debates open a window onto what a distinctively "Jewish" form of civil society might look like. Both the rabbinic tradition and Zionism would be philosophically opposed to a model of society in which voluntarily chosen groups form and dissolve at the pleasure of their membership, as both stress the critical role of the community in defining individual identity and as both affirm nationhood, ethnicity, and peoplehood as ways to organize society. Both link the value of individual diversity to the uniqueness of human collectivities, which is valued over any abstract universal human order, and both see associational rights as lodged in the community or culture itself, not in individuals. Finally, both might claim that voluntarist groups are "parasitic" on cultural or religious communities, using their insights. If these communities disappeared, the intellectual resources of ad hoc groups would be diminished, nor could voluntary groups form around their traditions.[50] Thus, a distinctively "Jewish" form of civil society ideally should support a collectively held right of cultural and religious groups to cultural perpetuation.

On the question whether a liberal version of civil society could be tolerated, however, the rabbinic tradition and Zionism might part ways. The nationalist imagination is unconstrained by texts and traditions. In the rabbinic tradition, however, the issue is invariably a legal question, to be determined by the halakah. If there is no halakic validity to religious legislation under modern conditions of freedom other than that rooted in consent, any model of civil society could be tolerated so long as it would not impinge on the halakic practices and institutions of those desirous to observe the law. Whether a liberal version of civil society does indeed present such difficulties for the halakah is best analyzed by looking briefly at the problems traditional Judaism faces in the liberal West.

The transformation of Judaism from a corporate body enjoying group rights of religio-legal autonomy into a private, voluntary religious association within civil society, whose freedoms are protected through individual rights of free exercise and association, does not pose an insuperable obstacle for traditional Judaism. The particularity of Judaism means that the non-Jewish state is under no obligation to conduct itself in accordance with Jewish precepts or to impose such precepts on non-Jewish society. Nor does rabbinic Judaism contain any theories about state obligation to support or refrain from interfering with the activities of the smaller associations within its midst, akin to the Christian idea of subsidiarity. Rabbinic Judaism never entertained the possibility of dictating terms to its host states; it searched for legitimate halakic ways to survive under conditions of foreign rule. The early talmudic principle that "the law of the state is the law," whether understood as a pragmatic concession to alien state power or as a principle of recognition of the legitimacy of all political governance, exemplifies the kinds of accommodation the halakah made.[51]

The relegation of religion to the private domain is not conflict free, however. The halakic principle that "the law of the state is the law" cannot serve to legitimate state incursions on matters of religious prohibition or permission; its application is confined to fiscal matters.[52] Thus, it is axiomatic that halakic Judaism cannot thrive in exile if the state prevents Jews from fulfilling their religious obligations, whether requiring Jews to perform acts that are forbidden or forbidding Jews from performing acts that are required.

Other effects of the reorganization of Judaism as a private religion within civil society present a different level of conflict because they bear on the question of cultural distinctiveness. One of the most intractable social problems within the Jewish community today is the dilemma of the Jewish woman unable to secure a Jewish divorce. Because marriage and divorce are matters of religious prohibition and permission, a Jewish divorce is required to dissolve a marriage valid under Jewish law. Such divorces must be initiated by the husband. Jewish law developed strategies that enabled the Jewish court to secure a bill of divorce from a recalcitrant husband in order to free a woman from the union. But the ability to do justice from within is difficult to achieve when the Jewish court lacks autonomy and when the husband can divorce and remarry under civil law, despite the failure of the husband to furnish a Jewish divorce. In the absence of comprehensive halakic solutions, rabbinic authorities have sanctioned resort to the state for assistance, urging it either to recognize the authority of the Jewish court over parties who have evidenced a prior commitment to its jurisdiction or to enact special legislation to offset cultural disabilities unique to Jewish women, such as conditioning the grant of a civil divorce on removing barriers to the remarriage of a spouse.[53] But the argument for juridical recognition or for nonneutral legislation is not easily accommodated within the liberal individualist model of rights.

Education of children is another sensitive topic within the traditional Jewish community. May the state compel private associations to teach particular values that are seen as critical to the maintenance of a healthy civil society or that are based in comprehensive liberal principles, such as individual autonomy? Can sexual inequality or illiberalism within the associations comprising civil society be permitted in a democratic state? Michael Walzer, for example, proposes that "associational policies and practices that radically curtail the life chances of members" or that "limit the rights or deny the responsibilities of citizenship" should be resisted by the state, offering a hypothetical refusal by the Catholic Church to educate Catholic women as one example. These practices cannot be justified on grounds of free choice, for, as he points out, "voluntary associations are often in part involuntary: children are enrolled by parents and membership is tied up with fundamental aspects of identity that are powerful constraints on rights of exit."[54] If rights of association may be shaped by an ideal conception of civil society, liberal features of education could be imposed in the private sphere. Even in a liberal regime that regards civil society solely as a by-product of rights of association, associational rights, because of an a priori commitment to individual autonomy, may be limited in cases where it can be argued that group practices conflict with the production of an individual capable of selecting among alternative life choices.

The most traditional segments of halakic Judaism are particularly vulnerable to this critique because they routinely curtail the life chances of their members for economic success or social integration by imposing restrictions on secular education. They believe that the development of integrated halakic personalities, of individuals who internalize the Jewish system of obligation and who will embody its values both in their personal lives and in their role as transmitters of the tradition, requires near exclusive immersion in the intricate content and value system of the halakah, particularly at an early age. The Jewish tradition is thus more comfortable with the classically liberal position that views rights of association as independent of any ideal model of civil society and that seeks to avoid a comprehensive liberalism. It would also argue that it is a harm to prevent people from perpetuating a way of life of enormous significance to them and that toleration "based on the harm argument" is a more inclusive concept for those groups that do not themselves value autonomy.[55]

So far I have concentrated on what Jews require from civil society. But what do they owe to civil society? The existence of universals within Judaism, the Noahide commandments, raises the question whether Jews have a halakic obligation to assure a civilized society by actively promoting observance of Noahide law. Although nominally seven, each Noahide principle is the subject of extensive rabbinic juridical elaboration so that Noahide law potentially covers a large variety of topics, including international human rights, euthanasia, abortion, and capital punishment. So far, the concept has been far less useful than one might suppose. Most rabbinic authorities hold that Jews are not legally obliged to promote observance of Noahide law.[56]

Noahide law aside, there is a constellation of halakic principles that could be interpreted to impose an obligation on Jews to collaborate with other members of society in projects that better the ethical, moral, spiritual, and material condition of general society.[57] The intuition that such an obligation exists sustains those who interpret Judaism nontraditionally in terms of a Jewish mission to pursue justice in the social sphere and who define Jewish identity "associationally," as participation in "sub- or extracommunal voluntary social organizations."[58] The more traditional segments of religious Judaism have generally avoided this topic, in part out of reluctance to bolster non-traditional understandings of Judaism as a mission. But there is a growing, if tacit, acknowledgment that religious sources do obligate Jews to collaborate with others in projects designed to better the moral and material climate of society, even if the exact contours of this obligation are unclear. That observant Jews have failed to turn their energies in this direction, favoring projects that advance the interests of Jews to the exclusion of those involving humanity, is not surprising. This group was the most affected by the Holocaust, which led to despair over common projects of social solidarity and a pouring of energies into the reconstruction of Eastern European Jewry. Given time and stable political conditions, one may expect to see developments on this front.

Concluding Note

The most glaring deficiency in the tradition that I have been reporting on is the lack of a model for the extension of equal citizenship rights in the Jewish polity. The biblical exhortation to provide one law for the citizen and stranger alike cannot bear this weight, given the restrictions that talmudic and medieval jurisprudence impose on the institution of the resident stranger. Although several rabbinic sources offer other pragmatic solutions to this issue, their rationales are unsatisfying. Resort to casuistic reasoning and other technical means of problem solving is, of course, a traditional rabbinic method. Such methods also often are accompanied by a genuine shift in consciousness about the justness of an institution. The abolition of slavery, for example, was accomplished through a series of technical restrictions, clearly motivated by a deep abhorrence to the institution. Whether such methods can do this work today is unclear.

It is time, Gerald Blidstein writes, to attempt a new position, based on the candid acknowledgment that Jews relate to the non-Jew, for example, as "fully human possessors" of the divine image.[59] Blidstein asks whether "the divine image of man" can "become a more powerful halakhic concept than it seems to be at present or than it has been historically."[60] To draw this question out: can the idea that man is created in the image of God provide a new universal category of membership in the Jewish polity and a new universal category for the creation of social bonds with all members of society, by virtue of their humanity alone? This is no easy task in a tradition that has as its centerpiece the idea of the distinctiveness of human collectivities, that eschews the creation of a universal human order, and that values the particular over the general.

The tense coexistence of universalism and particularism within one tradition is both the problem of Judaism and its definition.

Further Reading

Gerald J. Blidstein. "Halakha and Democracy." *Tradition* 32, no. 1 (1997).

Jacob Katz. *Jewish Emancipation and Self-Emancipation* (Philadelphia: Jewish Publication Society, 1986).

Gordon Lafer. "Universalism and Particularism in Jewish Law: Making Sense of Political Loyalties." In *Jewish Identity*, ed. David Theo Goldberg and Michael Krausz (Philadelphia: Temple University Press, 1993).

Eliezer Schweid, " 'Beyond' All That—Modernization, Zionism, Judaism," *Israel Studies* 1, no. 1 (Spring 1996).

David Shatz, Chaim I. Waxman, and Nathan Diament, eds. *Tikkum Olam: Social Responsibility in Jewish Thought and Law* (Mountvale, N.J.: Jason Aronson, 1997).

Notes

1. Although the Jewish viewpoint on any given subject is no longer identical with the classical rabbinic viewpoint, until modernity the latter provided the intellectual framework within which all Jewish thought was set. Any understanding of how Judaism views a topic must begin with the rabbinic tradition, which still provides the primary intellectual constraint on the adoption of any political theory represented in this volume.

2. Adam B. Seligman, *The Idea of Civil Society* (Princeton: Princeton University Press, 1992), p. 10.

3. Jacob Katz, *Jewish Emancipation and Self-Emancipation* (Philadelphia: Jewish Publication Society, 1986).

4. John Locke, *The Second Treatise of Civil Government* in *Locke's Two Treatises of Government*, ed. Peter Laslett (Cambridge: Cambridge University Press, 1967), p. 401.

5. Sifra on Lev. 26:37; Babylonian Talmud, Shevuot 39a.

6. Ritva, Babylonian Talmud, Rosh Hashanah 29a.

7. See Charles Taylor, "Modes of Civil Society," *Public Culture* 3, no. 1 (Fall 1990): 95–118.

8. Ernest Gellner, *Conditions of Liberty: Civil Society and Its Rivals* (London: Penguin Books, 1996), p. 8.

9. Moshe Greenberg, *Studies in the Bible and Jewish Thought* (Philadelphia: Jewish Publication Society, 1995), p. 57.

10. On Noahide law, see David Novak, *The Image of the Non-Jew in Judaism: An Historical and Constructive Study of the Noahide Laws* (New York: Edwin Mellen Press, 1983); Suzanne Last Stone, "Sinaitic and Noahide Law: Legal Pluralism in Jewish Law," *Cardozo Law Review* 12 (1991): 1157–214.

11. For a fuller discussion, see Greenberg, *Studies in the Bible and Jewish Thought*, pp. 369–94; Gordon Lafer, "Universalism and Particularism in Jewish Law: Making Sense of Political Loyalties," in *Jewish Identity*, ed. David Theo Goldberg and Michael Krausz (Philadelphia: Temple University Press, 1993), pp. 177–211.

12. Maimonides, Mishneh Torah, Hilkhot Teshuvah 3:11.

13. Maimonides, Mishneh Torah, Hilkhot Evel 14:1.

14. Steven Harvey, "Love," in *Contemporary Jewish Religious Thought*, ed. Arthur A. Cohen and Paul Mendes-Flohr (New York: Charles Scribner's Sons, 1987), p. 558.

15. This point is made by Lenn Evan Goodman, "Maimonides' Philosophy of Law," *Jewish Law Annual* 1 (1978): 88–89.

16. See Goodman, "Maimonides' Philosophy of Law," pp. 89–90.

17. For an analysis of these categories, see Samuel Morell, "The Halachic Status of Non-Halachic Jews," *Judaism* 18, no. 4 (Fall 1969): 448–57.

18. See Aviezer Ravitzky, "The Question of Tolerance in the Jewish Religious Tradition," in *Hazon Nahum: Studies in Jewish Law, Thought, and History*, ed. Yaakov Elman and Jeffrey S. Gurock (New York: Yeshiva University Press, 1997), 378–85.

19. For a fuller treatment of the topic, see Norman Lamm, "Loving and Hating Jews as Halakhic Categories" in *Jewish Tradition and the Nontraditional Jew*, ed. Jacob J. Schacter (Mountvale, N.J.: Jason Aronson, 1992), pp. 150–57.

20. Babylonian Talmud, Avodah Zarah 69b; Maimonides, Mishneh Torah, Hilkhot Melakhim 8:10.

21. See Moshe Halbertal, *Bein Hokhmah Le-Torah* [Between Torah and wisdom] (Jerusalem: Hebrew University Magnes Press, 2000), p. 84.

22. Babylonian Talmud, Gittin 61a.

23. Menahem ha-Me'iri, Beit Ha-Behira, on Avodah Zara 22a.

24. Menahem ha-Me'iri, Beit Ha-Behira, on Baba Qama 113b.

25. See Jacob Katz, *Exclusiveness and Tolerance* (New York: Schocken Books, 1961), p. 118.

26. See Halbertal, *Bein Hokhmah Le-Torah*, pp. 102–3.

27. See Katz, *Exclusiveness and Tolerance*, p. 121.

28. Lafer, "Universalism and Particularism," p. 195.

29. Goodman, "Maimonides' Philosophy of Law," p. 101.

30. See Katz, *Exclusiveness and Tolerance*, pp. 125–28.

31. See *Encyclopedia Talmudit*, vol. 3, s.v. "bene ha'ir."

32. Babylonian Talmud, Baba Bathra 8b.

33. See Martin P. Golding, "The Juridical Basis of Communal Associations in Mediaeval Rabbinic Legal Thought," *Jewish Social Studies* 18, no. 2 (1966): 67–78.

34. See Derek J. Penslar, "The Origins of Modern Jewish Philanthropy," in *Philanthropy in the World's Traditions*, ed. Warren F. Ilchman, Stanley N. Katz, and Edward L. Queen II (Bloomington: Indiana University Press, 1998), pp. 197–201.

35. Michael Walzer, "Rescuing Civil Society," *Dissent* (Winter 1999): 65.

36. See Judith Bleich, "Rabbinic Responses to Nonobservance in the Modern Era," in Schacter, *Jewish Tradition and the Nontraditional Jew*, pp. 37–115.

37. For examples, see Lamm, "Loving and Hating Jews as Halakhic Categories," p. 158 n. 22.

38. See Ravitzky, "The Question of Tolerance in the Jewish Religious Tradition," pp. 381–84.

39. Hazon Ish 13:16, cited in Lamm, "Loving and Hating Jews as Halakhic Categories," pp. 160–61.

40. Gerald J. Blidstein, "Halakha and Democracy," *Tradition* 32, no. 1 (1997): 28.

41. Maimonides, Mishneh Torah, Hilkhot Melakhim 1:4–5.

42. Quoted in David Novak, "Universal Moral Law in the Theology of Hermann Cohen," *Modern Judaism* 1 (1981): 105.

43. The opinion is discussed in Blidstein, "Halakha and Democracy," pp. 25–27.

44. Rabbi Shaul Yisraeli, Ha-Torah ve-ha-Medina, again discussed in Blidstein, "Halakha and Democracy," p. 27.

45. Rabbi Meir Simha of Dvinsk, Or Sameakh, Hilkhot Gerushin 2:20; Hilkhot Mamrim 4:3.

46. This is the view of Rabbi Yosef Eliyahu Henkin, Ha-Darom 10 (Elul 1959), pp. 5–9, cited in Blidstein, "Halakha and Democracy," p. 37 n. 22.

47. This is the view of Rabbi Abraham Isaac Kook, according to Tamar Ross, "Between Metaphysical and Liberal Pluralism: A Reappraisal of Rabbi A. I. Kook's Espousal of Toleration," *AJS Review: Journal of the Association of Jewish Studies* 21 (1996): 82, 101–102.

48. Ross, "Between Metaphysical and Liberal Pluralism," p. 82.

49. Eliezer Schweid, " 'Beyond' All That—Modernism, Zionism, Judaism," *Israel Studies* 1, no. 1 (Spring 1996): 240.

50. Diana Tietjens Meyers, "Cultural Goals: Rights, Goals, and Competing Values," in Goldberg and Krausz, *Jewish Identity*, p. 21.

51. For a systematic treatment of the doctrine, see Shmuel Shilo, *Dina De-Malkhuta Dina* (Heb. 1974).

52. See Shmuel Shilo, "Dina de-Malkhuta Dina," *Encyclopaedia Judaica* (1972), 6:53–54.

53. For a full treatment of this issue, see Irving Breitowitz, *Between Civil and Religious Law: The Plight of the Agunah in American Society* (Westport, Conn.: Greenwood Press, 1993).

54. Walzer, *Alternative Conceptions of Civil Society* (Princeton: Princeton University Press, 2002), chap. 2.

55. For a fuller articulation of this position, see Moshe Halbertal, "Autonomy, Toleration, and Group Rights: A Response to Will Kymlicka," in *Toleration: An Elusive Virtue*, ed. David Heyd (Princeton: Princeton University Press, 1996), 110–13.

56. See J. David Bleich, "Tikkun Olam: Jewish Obligations to Non-Jewish Society," in *Tikkun Olam: Social Responsibility in Jewish Thought and Law*, ed. David Shatz, Chaim I. Waxman, and Nathan Diament (Mountvale, N.J.: Jason Aronson, 1997), pp. 61–102.

57. This issue is discussed extensively in a collection of essays appearing in Shatz, Waxman, and Diament, 170 *Tikkun Olam: Social Responsibility in Jewish Thought and Law*.

58. See Penslar, "The Origins of Modern Jewish Philanthropy," pp. 205–8.

59. Blidstein, "Halakha and Democracy," p. 29.

60. Blidstein, "Halakha and Democracy," p. 33.

3

Civil Society and Government

NOAM J. ZOHAR

DOES THE Jewish tradition have anything to say about civil society? The answer depends as much upon how *civil society* is defined as upon any investigation into Judaic sources. According to one rather strict conception, the entire notion of civil society—and the ideals, problems, and solutions attributed to it—is situated within the framework of modern ideologies of individualism and liberty. Insofar as traditional Judaism does not adopt this democratic stance, with its emphasis on individualism and liberty, it must regard the project and problematics of "civil society" as inherently alien.[1]

Now in fact I believe that the distance between traditional Judaism and democratic thought is smaller than is often suggested; the notion of individual rights, for example, finds expression in classical halakic discussions, as will be illustrated below. But my exposition in this chapter will not be built upon this contested ground. Instead, I will seek to apply Judaic sources and insights to the issues of civil society, arguing by extension and analogy. In so doing, I will adopt a broad notion of "civil society," covering the entire set of institutions and associations that stand between the individual and the overarching state.

In discussing these matters from the perspective of the Jewish tradition, it is essential to distinguish between three main periods. First, there is the biblical period, when Israel existed as a sovereign kingdom (or rather, mostly, two parallel kingdoms). Then, there is the long period of exile, when disparate Jewish communities lived within gentile states or empires, often exercising some degree of autonomy. And finally, there is the modern state of Israel, proclaiming itself a "Jewish and democratic state."

This division into periods is meant as no more than a rough sketch. For in the biblical narrative Israel begins its history, as it were, in a state of exile, from the Patriarchs' residence in Canaan to the Israelites' sojourn in Egypt. Then too, during the last centuries of the period of the Hebrew Bible, most of the people lived again in exile, with only a small segment returning to found the Second Commonwealth.[2] And even though the Jewish population in the land of Israel later grew larger, most of the time they were not a sovereign kingdom. It seems best, then, to speak of three *phases* of Jewish historical existence: *monarchy*, *exile*, and *statehood*. My remarks will therefore refer specifically to the context of these distinct phases as appropriate.

It was the phase of exile that prevailed throughout most of Jewish history. In the exilic situation, the affairs of state and society were addressed predominantly from the perspective of a Jewish group living within an alien state. When we consider the idea of a "civil society" distinct from the state, an analogy may be drawn to the Jewish exilic paradigm of an autonomous community within the gentile state.

From another perspective, however, the Jewish community might itself be likened to a state, particularly in those times and places in which it enjoyed greater autonomy and extensive powers over its members. Issues akin to those that interest us here may thus be raised with regard to the intracommunal arrangements: What proportion of the group's affairs was conducted centrally, and how much was left for smaller associations and organizations?

Working with these different perspectives, the application of the state/civil society distinction becomes relative. The exilic phase is marked by the fact that political society is nested: group within group. Some of our questions can best be illuminated, from the Jewish tradition, by thinking of the entire Jewish community as a component of civil society within the larger state; others, by thinking of smaller units within Jewish society in their relations to the self-governing community.

Boundaries: Torah versus State Law

"The Law of the Kingdom Is Law"

How did Jews in exile perceive the proper division of power between their community and the host state? It might be thought that there would be no principled acceptance of *any* division of power, since in principle the Torah—God's teaching—is supposed to govern all aspects of life, private and public. The state might thus be regarded merely as an alien force, which must be accommodated even while we try to maximize the extent of communal self-government. The crucial question can be put in terms of *law*: Can a community committed to God's revealed law recognize as valid the laws of a human state?

In fact, *halakah* (the Jewish tradition of normative discourse) adopted the dictum, first formulated in the third century, that "The law of the kingdom is law" (BT Bava Kama 113a–b). This meant that "the kingdom," as distinct from just anyone wielding brute force, can issue edicts that get recognized as "law" and thus *ought* to be obeyed. Now the crucial question was, what is the legitimate realm of state legislation—and what realm should be preserved, as far as possible, to be governed by the Jewish community under its internal halakic norms?

A characteristic statement can be found in a medieval commentary on a talmudic ruling concerning the validity of legal documents, signed by gentile witnesses and issued under the auspices of state courts. Such deeds effecting various transactions are generally valid, "except for writs of divorce" (BT Gittin 9b). The distinction is explained in terms of the difference between the universal norms of justice, which (rabbinic tradition teaches) are binding upon all "Noahides" (i.e., all of humankind),[3] on the one hand, and particular Jewish norms, such as those defining matrimonial law, on the other hand. Rashi (eleventh century, France) in his classical commentary writes that non-Jews "are not [deemed effective agents for] severing [a halakic marriage] since they are not party to [halakic] matrimonial law. Noahides were, however, commanded to institute justice—[therefore all other legal transactions are valid]."

Universal norms are properly administered by the common state. The Jewish community—and by the same token, other communities as well—should autonomously administer its particular norms, such as those pertaining to marriage. This division assumes that individuals belong to, and marry within, distinct ethnic/religious communities.

Torah Law and Religious Communities in the Modern State

In modern times, such communal autonomy has been greatly curtailed by the state's assertion of jurisdiction in all areas. It is not surprising, perhaps, that the state of Israel has retained a system of special jurisdictions in "personal law," under which each person belongs to a particular religious group and is subject to its religious courts. But even in liberal democracies that refuse to authorize such jurisdiction, religio-cultural groups have shown significant capacity for surviving via voluntary adherence. A crucial question here is whether group autonomy is in fact consistent with the universal demands of justice, considering especially the vulnerable members of the group, whose adherence may in fact be far from truly voluntary.[4] In Israel, moreover, individuals have no real option but to belong to a group and be (with regard to "personal law") its legal subjects.

The injustices inherent in the Israeli system invite the conclusion that the boundary between state and ethnic/religious groups should be pushed firmly to the point of excluding such groups from wielding any legal power over their members. Against this, it is plausible to evoke, from within the biblical tradition, opposition to having the power to make and enforce the law reside fully and exclusively in the state.

Unlike other monarchs in the ancient Near East, the Israelite king was not a promulgator of laws; these were given in God's Torah.[5] Popular loyalty to a law above any royal decree is an important element in resistance to injustice propagated by the state. In the history of the Israelite monarchy, this is exemplified in the story of Naboth's vineyard (1 Kings 21:1–20). Naboth at first successfully resisted the king's pressure to yield or sell his vineyard, clearly relying on an accepted notion of his legal rights. Finally, the king had to resort to fabricated charges and a false trial in order to overcome this resistance and have Naboth killed; the fierce critique, led by the prophet Elijah, eventually led to a popular revolt.

This aspect of the biblical tradition is continued in the notion, prevalent among traditional Jews, that the supreme law is Torah law; a state law that fundamentally conflicts with it is thus invalid. In this sense, religious society can be seen as an important source of resistance to state-sponsored evil. "The *law* of the kingdom is law"—but some decrees are not "law" at all, and should be opposed.

Torah Study and Educational Institutions

The centrality of adherence to Torah is expressed in the fact that its study is the most highly valued practice in Jewish traditional society. Education in the Torah is seen as the personal duty of every parent (traditionally, primarily every *father*), though its exercise is commonly achieved through the services of a professional teacher, engaged jointly by the parents—or, in the traditional community, by the communal officers.

Hence, care should be taken with regard to the claim that Judaism has an ancient ideal of public education. This is true in the sense that Torah education was offered to all (male) children; but it was not an education for future *citizens* offered by the state, but rather education of the next generation of the *covenant*, overseen by the covenantal community.

Accordingly, in the wake of emancipation, Jewish communities were concerned over the state's intervention in education even more, perhaps, than over its intervention in marriage or divorce. And in contemporary Israel, the educational system is one of state-sponsored parochial schools. At full parental discretion, children are educated in any of a great variety of schools, so that each kind of religious (or secular) community can replicate itself. There is little appreciation—particularly in traditional circles—for any suggestion that the state has a crucial stake in the content of education. The boundary between the concerns of the state and those of the spiritual community is delineated with Torah—and education—outside the purview of the state.

Liabilities (and Needs)

The State as Liability: Religious Anarchism

There is a strand in the biblical tradition that views the very existence of the state—specifically, in those days, the monarchy—as a major liability. The book of Judges portrays what might be termed a "civil society" *without* a state, governed by local elders. When Gideon leads the Israelites to military victory, we are told that

> the men of Israel said to Gideon, "Rule over us—you, your son, and your grandson as well; for you have saved us from the Midianites." But Gideon replied, "I will not rule over you myself, nor shall my son rule over you; the Lord alone shall rule over you." (Judg. 8:22–23)[6]

It might be argued that the regime upheld by the pious Gideon—clearly endorsed by the author—amounts not to anarchy but to theocracy: there is a king, albeit not human but divine. But since no human institution is legitimized as God's agent, the actual picture is best defined, I think, in terms of (religious) anarchism.

Here there is a sharp contrast between the message of these chapters in the book of Judges (6–9) and the message of the book as a whole, and especially its concluding chapters with their plaintive refrain: "In those days there was no king in Israel; everyone did as he pleased" (Judg. 21:25, and cf. 18:1, 19:1). The centralized state mechanism of the monarchy is established in the wake of the failure of stateless civil society. The monarchy, though endorsed by God, is promoted against the prophetic protest that, in demanding a king, the people were rejecting their divine king (1 Sam. 8–12).

Arguably, then, it was only the Davidic dynasty, directly elected by God, that could wield legitimate power in His name. A strand of religious opposition to any other human claim of state power has persisted throughout Jewish history. The fundamental critique of state power extended with even greater force to the great empires, as in the prophet Habakkuk's classical litany about the looting Chaldeans (Hab. 1; although even on this there was a rival prophetic vision—cf. Jer. 27).

The other side of this same coin is, of course, that a community with such a tradition will be seen as posing a liability to the state. During the last decades of the Second Commonwealth, the so-called Zealots

led the rebellion against Rome, and in their efforts to subdue the repeated revolts the Romans sought to repress the Jewish religion.

In the exilic phase, Jewish teaching had come to accept the rule of the
alien state (cf. above, the section "Boundaries"), yet the state was seen
as a constant threat to the community's integrity. Jews were generally
expected to resolve any conflicts or complaints internally; those who
turned to gentile courts or rulers were deemed traitors and—where circumstances allowed—treated quite harshly.

The Community and Voluntary Associations

As indicated above in the introductory section, an alternative analogy
might be drawn: the Jewish community as a whole might be compared
to a state, containing elements of civil society in the form of certain
functional subgroups within it. In the medieval Jewish community,
we find a "burial society" (called *hevra kaddisha*—literally, "the holy
association"), a sick-care society, and so forth. The members' time is
volunteered, and necessary funding supplied mainly by votive contributions. The community certainly needs these societies, not only in the
sense that its members rely on their services, but also in the sense that
the societies are seen as discharging collective obligations.

These voluntary associations, in turn, tacitly rely on the community.
The burial society takes care of the dead, but it is the community that
provides the cemetery. The sick-care society undertakes visiting the
sick, which also involved ministering to them; but payment for feeding
and care of the destitute is provided by the basic welfare system of
Tzedaka, funded by communal taxation.

Groups and Individuals

Taxation in a Corporate Society

For the community in exile, it was deemed very important that individual members not deal directly with the state. This may be easily explained in terms of the community's vital interest in maintaining its
authority over members. In the context of medieval corporate society,
this authority rested first and foremost on the premise that the state authorities deal only with the corporate community.

Nevertheless, kings and princes often considered it advantageous to
deal directly with individuals. This was a thorny issue, especially
when it involved taxes. The standard procedure was for the prince to
demand a certain sum from the community as a whole; its officers then

proceeded to assess each member according to his wealth. The community sometimes stood to lose much if a separate arrangement was allowed for a wealthy member. What is interesting for us is not communal opposition to such an arrangement in itself, but rather the arguments offered in disallowing it.

Most often it could be assumed that the prince's profit from the separate taxation lay in the fact that the individual's direct payment was not deducted—at least, not in its entirety—from the collective levy. This was criticized in terms of fairness: whatever total sum was due to the prince, it was the community who knew best how to justly divide the burden among its members. The individual making his separate arrangement was in fact unfairly transferring some of his due burden to his fellows.

What places the community, rather than the prince (or state), in a better position to determine a fair distribution among its members? The answer is far from self-evident, for after all, the community officers are often themselves powerful and wealthy individuals who have a personal stake in the distribution of the tax burden. Indeed, several medieval discussions record concern over the officers' possible partiality, and require a sacred oath of good faith. Still, the traditional view is that insiders have both more information and a better sense of the communally accepted values and notions of fairness.

In contemporary states, the powers of taxation reside in the government and not in associations constituting civil society. Yet perhaps a similar rationale can apply to other activities that require special knowledge and an intimate sense of specific values and norms. I have in mind practices like self-regulation by members of a profession. For this to be effective, of course, there must exist at least as much trust in the integrity of the profession's officers (e.g., its ethics committee) as that engendered in the past through a sacred oath.

Families and Individuals in the Bible

Overall, the Hebrew Bible does not speak univocally on the relative importance of individuals versus groups; and scholars offer rival reconstructions of the history of ideas concerning these matters in biblical Israel. I cannot hope to offer here any compelling summary. Instead, let us look briefly at two examples pertaining to the standing of individuals in relation to their families—immediate and extended.

Paraphrasing Aristotle, it might be said that the smallest unit of civil society is the family. A basic tenet of biblical criminal law is that "Parents shall not be put to death for children, nor children be put to death for parents: a person shall be put to death only for his own crime" (Deut. 24:16)—a rule clearly seeking to contest prevalent norms of collective punishment: each member of the family must be judged alone.[7] Yet this principle, promulgated in the context of retributive justice, does not extend as clearly to the context of distributive justice, the setting of our second example.

The primary distribution in biblical Israel was that of the land—apportioned to all males of mature age. A distribution to these males, evidently as heads of households, leaves all others—primarily all females—as dependents. Presumably, the land's yield is subject to secondary distribution within the family. It is worth noting that the primary distribution is conducted by lottery, with a concomitant emphasis on quantitative equality (see Num. 26:52–56). But no procedural mechanisms of fairness are established for intrafamilial distribution.

Against this background, it is striking that the daughters of Zelophehad were able to gain recognition of their claim to a stake in the land in lieu of their deceased father, who had no sons. In these (atypical) circumstances, each of the five women was granted the status of individual landowner. Yet even as individuals, they remained also part of their tribe, and were not freed from the tribesmen's control of individual landholdings. As females, their land might be lost to the tribe when they married and their holdings eventually passed on to their sons (whose tribal affiliation would be determined paternally). An effort to strike a balance between individual and tribal rights is evident in the compromise ruling, delivered by Moses:

> This is what the LORD has commanded concerning the daughters of Zelophehad: They may marry anyone they wish, provided they marry into a clan of their father's tribe. No inheritance of the Israelites may pass over from one tribe to another, but the Israelites must remain bound each to the ancestral portion of his tribe. Every daughter among the Israelite tribes who inherits a share must marry someone from a clan of her father's tribe. (Num. 34:5–9)

Here, as in numerous other contexts in biblical law and practice, great importance is granted to family and tribe. Against this background, what stands out is the emphasis—evidently rather revolutionary—on the individual standing of each person in any administration of justice, whether human or divine.[8]

Citizenship?

Townsmen as Neighbors and Partners

If it is far from clear what, in the Jewish tradition, should be called "state" and what "civil society," it is even less clear what in this tradition is the corollary of "citizen." The word *ezrah*, used in modern Hebrew for "citizen," is adapted from biblical usage, where it means "native," as distinct from a resident (alien)—as in the command, "The stranger that sojourneth with you shall be unto you as the home-born [*ezrah*] among you" (Lev. 19:34).[9] In the Mishnah, the core document of rabbinic Judaism,[10] the statement that touches most closely upon this issue is found in a rule about compelling an unwilling resident to share in certain expenditures for security:

> They compel him [to share] in [the cost of] building a wall and gates for the town, and a bolt for the gates. R. Shimon ben Gamaliel says: Not every town requires a wall. How long shall one reside in town to be considered a townsman? Twelve months. If, however, one acquires a residence there, one is considered a townsman immediately. (Bava Batra 1:5)

Even here, I have taken some liberty in translation with the phrase "to be considered a townsman," for the Hebrew lacks such a term. Literally, the sentence reads: "How long shall one reside in town *so as to be like the men of the town*?" Indeed it might be said that in the posing and answering of this question, we witness the *birth* of a (rudimentary) notion of citizenship. The context is instructive: this chapter of the Mishnah begins with rules about the wall between two neighbors (called "partners" because they share a courtyard), and the fifth clause (cited above) opens with a rule about relations between several house owners who share a courtyard—"They compel him [to share] in [the cost of] building an antechamber and door for the courtyard. R. Shimon ben Gamaliel says: Not every courtyard requires an antechamber"—and moves on from this directly to the rule about a town. The town is conceived, it seems, simply as a supercourtyard, requiring more elaborate defenses. And the thinking appears very libertarian: the majority cannot compel a minority to contribute to any project, but only to these specific measures, recognized as "requisite." Now, since the wall and gates take long to build and are expected to endure for many years, there is a need to determine who is a "man of the town" (this can be contrasted with the rabbinic discussion elsewhere about how much each traveler in a caravan must contribute for emergency rescue).[11]

To be precise, it seems the issue here is one of determining *residence* (for tax purposes) rather than *citizenship*. Even in the alternative account of the Tosefta,[12] which presents a richer view of the townsmen's mutual obligations (e.g., building an aqueduct, buying a Torah scroll for the synagogue, and more), belonging to a town consists simply in sharing in the provision of public goods. Of "citizenship" in a moral sense, as the function or condition of special virtue, there is scarce evidence in any of the rabbinic texts.

"The Community of Israel"

Having said all the above, it is worth emphasizing that the Judaic tradition is by no means radically individualistic. Great value is placed upon belonging to a collective; Jewish identity lies in belonging to the People Israel (*am yisra'el*), who constitute the covenantal community. The core of the covenant is a commitment to live according to God's commandments, and it has a dual character; every Israelite is obligated individually and is also responsible for the collective obligation. The rabbis express the idea of mutual responsibility by saying that each Israelite became a "guarantor" for each and every of his fellows.[13]

Thus great moral/spiritual significance is attached to membership in the covenantal community. But is this membership akin to citizenship? The answer hinges upon the function and focus of this community; and, since the Torah's commandments are numerous and pertain to many things, upon that which is identified as their central concern.

On one view—which I shall call "priestly"—the central issue in fulfilling the covenant is maintaining the temple ritual. This is the least "political" conception of the People Israel: they are primarily a community of worship, and whatever earthly affairs they may conduct are significant mainly in the support they provide for the temple cult. This is how the Second Commonwealth was conceived at its inception (see Ezra 1:1–6, 7:11–28).

A second view, which I shall call "prophetic," holds the opposite, pronouncing the temple ritual as decisively secondary in relation to interpersonal morality and social justice. Now, if the crucial challenge of the covenant is in protecting the vulnerable and "redeeming Zion in Justice" (cf. Isa. 1:27), it might be argued, perhaps, that membership in the covenantal community amounts to membership in a political community. But this seems something of an overstatement; for the focus is on relations between persons—or even between social classes—rather than on political roles and institutions or on the governance of the city or state. An important exception here is the explicit concern with the honesty of the judiciary. According to the prophets, the entire society is held to account for suffering the perversion of justice. So in this specific sense, every Israelite has a citizen-like stake in the polity's judicial institutions.

Another perspective on covenant and citizenship grows out of the third view, pervasive in many biblical books but most clearly associated with the message of Deuteronomy. On this view, the most crucial aspect of the covenant is the prohibition of idolatry. According to many interpreters, the underlying idea has a political character: God is Israel's (divine) sovereign, and idolatry constitutes high treason. Being an Israelite thus means being a member of a religious collective dedicated to the eradication of idolatry. For Maimonides, who (many years later) came to explain a large part of the Torah's commandments in terms of the battle against idolatry, being Jewish is defined as being a citizen of a monotheistic polity.[14]

It is important to note that this community, the People Israel, is not necessarily coextensive with any actual political community. This is true especially in the exilic phase, when Jews belong politically to a *local* Jewish community or to the host non-Jewish state or to both.[15] But it is true also in contemporary Israel, which as a political community has many citizens who are non-Jewish (as well as many who see their Jewish identity in ethnic, rather than religious, terms)—and whose Jewish population in any case includes only a minority of the covenantal People Israel.

It is true that the medieval *kahal* (Jewish community) was conceived and experienced as a concrete instantiation of the greater whole, *knesset Yisrael* ("congregation of Israel"). Thus for example, the *kahal*'s ultimate sanction was the ban (*herem*), under which a person would be completely shunned by all members of the community. This was perceived as being separated from "all of Israel," and indeed Jews of other localities were required to abide by the ban pronounced by the culprit's own community.[16]

Membership was attributed, as it were, from the top downward: one was a Jew, a member of the People Israel—and then, by virtue of this Jewish identity, one was (derivatively) also a member, together with other local Jews, of the *kahal* of a particular town.[17] In the terms of our present discussion, the morally significant membership was in the "civil society" of the (dispersed) People Israel. This affiliation then determined the scope of the local, more mundane political community, and the parameters for its operation.

In the modern state of Israel, the political community encompasses numerous non-Jews. Israeli citizenship, then—unlike belonging to a medieval *kahal*—is not dependent upon membership in the Jewish people. Nevertheless, the two are connected through the "Law of Return," under which Israeli citizenship is granted to any Jewish immigrant. Moreover, Israeli law, in a system taken over from the Ottoman Empire, places individuals under the jurisdiction of religious courts for purposes of "personal law" (chiefly, marriage and divorce), and each person's affiliation must therefore be determined. Hence state officials (and, in disputed cases, state courts) have been called upon to decide whether particular individuals are Jews. There has been a string of controversies, whose theme is often labeled the Who is a Jew? question.

If Israeli law turns to the Jewish tradition, it is not for defining the notion of "citizenship"—which does not fit easily into the traditional discourse—but for defining the notion of "Jew." Due to the major changes in Jewish history and society in modern times, this definition is a matter of deep ideological struggle—particularly between those adhering to a religious conception of Jewishness and those opting instead for a national or ethnic conception.[18] Moreover, opting for a religious conception opens the door to further controversies, as each of the various religious movements within Judaism has its own standards and procedures for conversion, whereby a non-Jew may become a Jew. If these movements are seen as components of civil society, then the state finds itself curiously—and perhaps unhappily—depending on them for defining a crucial element in its constitutive institution of citizenship.

Conflict

According to the tradition, a Jew's primary commitment is to the Torah. No local *kahal* may act contrary to Torah, and it should not be obeyed if it does so act.[19] Likewise in the Jewish monarchy (according to the retroactive pronouncements of halakic discourse),[20] if the king issues commands countervening Torah law, they must be disobeyed. And in the streets of Jerusalem (less often in Tel Aviv) one can see bumper stickers proclaiming, The laws of Torah have priority over the laws of the state!

How far must one carry this commitment? In general, whenever disobeying state law might entail danger, the requirements of Torah law are set aside. This does not apply, however, to three issues. If anyone—including the state—requires a Jew to transgress the prohibition of bloodshed, incest, or idolatry, he must "be killed rather than transgress" (BT Sanhedrin 74a). Significantly, the duty of martyrdom is extended to cover the commandments in conditions of state persecution against the Jewish religion. In any direct test of allegiance, the covenantal commitment must reign supreme.

In many traditional circles today, a similar attitude finds expression in less dramatic, everyday circumstances. As indicated above, the realm of Torah study is seen as belonging to the religious community rather than to the state. But Torah study is much more than the stuff of children's education. The traditional ideal is that everyone should engage in the study of Torah for as much of his time as possible. Jewish communities have supported a class of Torah scholars who devote their lives to study and teaching. Moreover, even individuals who end up pursuing other careers often spend their formative adolescent and young-adult years as students at a *yeshivah* (talmudic academy).

All this produces what we might call a "Torah society," a formally voluntary network of religious culture, learning, and practice. The normative claims of this network are felt to have clear priority over those of the larger society or of the state, which are seen as wholly external. Allegiance to this "civil society" is potentially detrimental to the development of a civic spirit with respect to the state or to fellow citizens. Of course, this need not be so; in certain traditional circles, a duty of loyalty to the state has been posited and promoted in the internal terms of traditional halakic discourse. But unless this is expressly worked out, the state will tend to be regarded with indifference, at best, and with a cynical, exploitative attitude, at worst.

Such an attitude, where prevalent, can produce sharp conflicts. In contemporary Israel, advocates of nascent notions of citizenship find themselves in bitter confrontation with many adherents of Torah society. The main contested issues are, first, massive state support for those engaged in Torah study and, second, a perception of double loyalty. Members of the "Torah society" are perceived—often rightly—as being more loyal to the claims of that society than to those of the state as a whole.

Moreover, the question of loyalty arises poignantly in the context of the Israeli educational system. Israel's system of public education is in principle pluralistic: the Ministry of Education operates several so-called streams. In addition to the "general" stream, these include, for example, the Arabic school system and a religious-Zionist system.[21] The latter is distinguished from the schools of the non-Zionist ultra-Orthodox. The ultra-Orthodox educational arrangements are themselves quite varied, ranging from complete separatists who refuse all state funding and are completely free from any state supervision, to so-called recognized schools, which the state partly funds, requiring in return that certain subjects (such as arithmetic) be taught in addition to Torah study. In recent years, the Ministry of Education has also listed an officially sanctioned class of "nonrecognized" schools, which get state funding with virtually no supervision.

The sources of conflict lie not only in what the non-Zionist schools do not teach—for example, history or civics courses—but in what they do teach: a fundamental allegiance to Torah and to rabbinic leaders rather than to the state or its laws. Admittedly, allegiance to Torah is also taught in the religious-Zionist schools; but in the past, this was perceived as nonproblematic, as their ideology has always held the state and its authority in positive regard. In the 1980s and 1990s, however, religious Zionist ideology commonly took a radical bent, strongly opposing any withdrawal from the territories conquered in 1967. In the context of political negotiations over prospective withdrawals, students and graduates of this stream often experience an intense internal struggle between the two commitments that they internalized without realizing their potential for coming into conflict. Their revered rabbis might pronounce a particular government policy illegitimate—without denying that, in principle, the halakah itself requires also obedience to state authority.

For the non-Zionist groups, there is much less of an internal conflict: subject to considerations of prudence, their ideology clearly places rabbinic authority above whatever authority (if any) is accorded to the state's laws or officers. The conflict for them, then, is external; and for the state, the question is, arguably, not only whether to continue to fund schools fostering such ideology, but whether to tolerate them altogether.

I began this chapter by noting the three distinct phases of Jewish history. It seems fair to say that the condition of exile has not only been the longest, but has also had a formative effect with regard to the state/civil society dichotomy. In a crucial sense, Jewish experience is that of a society striving (often with difficulty and tension) to maintain its integrity as distinct from the surrounding political domain. Hence the essential challenge to this tradition in the modern setting is this: To what extent can a Jewish perspective embrace the vision of a full-blown state, transcending the particular interests of a defined religious community?

Notes

1. Suzanne Stone's essay in this volume tends to adopt this stance.

2. Since these Jews chose not come to live in the land of Israel, it may be more appropriate to describe them as "diaspora" rather than "exile"—echoing the preferred self-description of many contemporary Jews.

3. Talmudic discussions define a set of norms binding upon all humankind, akin to natural law and called the Noahide Code. For an extensive discussion, see David Novak, *The Image of the Non-Jew in Judaism: A Historical and Constructive Study of the Noahide Laws* (New York: Edwin Mellen Press, 1983). See also *The Jewish Political Tradition, Volume 2: Membership* (eds. Michael Walzer et al., New Haven: Yale University Press, 2003), 441–71. Regarding the law of the kingdom, see *The Jewish Political Tradition: Volume 1: Authority* (eds. Michael Walzer et al., New Haven: Yale University Press, 2000), chapter 9: "The Gentile State," 430–62.

4. I have in mind here primarily issues of gender hierarchy, as discussed cogently by Susan Moller Okin in "Feminism and Multiculturalism: Some Tensions," *Ethics* 108 (1998): 685–701.

5. See M. Noth, *The Laws in the Pentateuch* (London: SCM Press, 1984), 14.

6. The translation here, and in most biblical citations below, is from the New JPS version, *Tanakh, The Holy Scriptures* (Philadelphia and Jerusalem: Jewish Publication Society, 1985).

7. In 2 Kings 14:6 we are told, with some admiration, of a king who actually lived up to this rule, and did not put to death the sons of those who had slain his father.

8. For an extended polemic in this spirit, see Ezek. 18:1–20.

9. This is the Jewish Publication Society (JPS) old translation (Philadelphia, 1917). Similarly, the King James version reads "one born among you"; the new JPS offers, anachronistically, I think, "The stranger who resides with you shall be to you as one of your citizens."

10. Compiled in the Galilee by Rabbi Judah the Prince around 200 c.e. An English translation by H. Danby was published by Clarendon Press, Oxford, 1933, but the text here is in my own translation.

11. Such a scenario is discussed in the Talmud, BT Bava Kama 116b.

12. A complementary compilation, redacted soon after the Mishnah in the third century. The reference here is to Tosefta Bava Metzia 11:17, 23.

13. See BT Sotah 37a–b, where this is computed to produce a staggering number of covenants.

14. See Maimonides, *The Book of Knowledge* ("MT") "Laws Concerning Idolatry," chap. 1, and *The Guide of the Perplexed*, trans. S. Pines (Chicago: University of Chicago Press, 1963), pt. 3, chapters 29ff., and particularly in explaining circumcision, 3:49 (pp. 609–10).

15. Spinoza therefore argued that after the fall of the ancient Israelite kingdom, Torah law—the law of the Jewish polity—had become obsolete. There were no more people to whom it could apply, for the Jews had, in exile, become citizens of other states. B. Spinoza, *Tractatus Theologico-Politicus*, trans. Samuel Shirley (Leiden: E. J. Brill, 1991), chap. 5.

16. The theoretical and spiritual links between the local *herem* and the powers inherent in the people as a whole are set forth in the classical medieval treatment of these matters, Nahmanides' "Mishpat ha-Herem."

17. A similar hierarchy of membership obtains in the United States. One is primarily a citizen of the United States, and by virtue of that has the right to reside in—and thus become a citizen—of any particular state.

18. A famous instance of this struggle was the 1968 Shalit case, decided in the Israeli Supreme Court; see *Select Judgments of the Supreme Court of Israel*, special vol., ed. Asher Felix Landau and Peter Elman (Jerusalem: Ministry of Justice, 1971), 48–191.

19. It was recognized, however, that political necessity—"the needs of the hour"—might require temporary deviation from Torah law. Moreover, according to certain prominent medieval halakists (e.g., Rabbis Solomon ibn Adret and Nissim Gerondi), mundane legislation must quite generally leave aside the utopian requirements of talmudic law, especially in the realm of criminal justice (and cf. the discussion of "the law of the kingdom" above). See Menachem Lorberbaum, *Politics and the Limits of Law: Secularizing the Political in Medieval Jewish Thought* (Palo Alto: Stanford University Press, 2001).

20. See Maimonides' formulation in MT, "Laws Concerning Kings" 3:9.

21. The adjective I rendered "general" is actually *mamlakhti*, a term harking back to the state's first prime minister, David Ben-Gurion. A central theme of Ben-Gurion's ideology, the word suggests a civic consciousness or public-spiritedness grounded in the commitment of citizens to the state. It is used also in the caption of the religious-Zionist section of the public education system, called *mamlakhti-dati*.

4

Autonomy and Modernity

DAVID BIALE

THE RELATIONSHIP between state and civil society in the Jewish tradition is complicated by the factors that make Jewish history in many ways unique. Like Islam, the Jewish tradition is political in nature: its laws are intended to be the laws of the state. On the other hand, since Jews did not possess a state for most of their history, the political character of the tradition was necessarily circumscribed. As Noam Zohar argues in his excellent excursus, the semiautonomous communities in which Jews lived as early as the Greco-Roman Diaspora up until the nineteenth century combined many of the features of a quasi state with features of voluntary communities. The modern state of Israel, which represents an unprecedented development, is riven by tensions that derive from this twofold, contradictory character of Jewish political history.

There is, however, an inherent problem in trying to locate categories like "the state," "citizenship," and "civil society" in historically remote contexts. The very concept of a civil society—a realm of voluntary, noncoercive associations made up of individuals and distinct from the state—is the creation of modern political theory; put differently, it is the rise of the modern state that generated civil society. As Zohar notes, the regnant political concept in the Jewish tradition is not citizenship, but the covenant with God that constitutes the "community of Israel"(*knesset yisrael*). Although the sources at times seem to recognize the autonomous status of the individual, as in Zohar's example of when a person becomes a "townsman," the individual is most commonly defined as a member of a collectivity that in turn is defined by its covenantal relationship to God. Thus, the premise of modern political theory that the state is created by a compact of individuals comprising civil society reverses the fundamental premise of the Jewish tradition according to which it is the collective that defines the individual. In this regard, the Jewish tradition does not dramatically differ from other premodern political theories. For all of these, the source of an individual's identity was his or her corporate, tribal, or familial affiliation, even if these affiliations were not described in the religious language of covenant. It is evident that a "civil society" consisting of voluntary associations is utterly foreign to such a theory as is the social contract conceived as the source of the state.

Thus, the difficulty with Zohar's argument lies in applying categories from modern political theory to historically anachronistic cases. Several examples, taken from Zohar's chapter, will illustrate my point. Zohar characterizes the period of the Judges as "civil society without a state" and as a condition of "(religious) anarchism." But, in fact, the charismatic system of leadership constituted something like a state (although not in the modern sense), or at least like a form of tribal governance. Moreover, the early kings of Israel (Saul and David) were themselves charismatic judges as much as kings. The two categories overlap, and it was only the redactors of the biblical texts who tried to make them completely distinct: thus, the statement in Judges 21:25 that "in those days there was no king in Israel; everyone did what he pleased" is the ideological judgment of an editor from the Davidic court who wished to justify the system of monarchy against its predecessor. We cannot presume to learn anything historical from this statement about the true nature of politics in the period of the Judges. But in neither the period of Judges or of Kings can one speak of civil society as we understand it.

Zohar is quite correct in identifying a kind of oppositional strain—from the biblical prophets to the Second-Temple Zealots—to the power of the state. This tradition is based on the notion of the Torah as potentially superior to the law of the state. Yet this opposition comes from a messianic perspective: only in the end of time will the Torah become the fully realized law of the state. The degree to which one might oppose the state in favor of the Torah typically hinged on whether one believed the *eschaton* to be imminent. It was their apocalyptic mentality rather than some fundamentally anarchistic impulse that explains the Zealots' opposition to the Romans in the first century of the common era. In any case, it must be emphasized that this messianic stance has nothing to do with choosing civil society over the state.

A second example is medieval associations such as the burial society (*hevre kadisha*), which Zohar characterizes as "elements of civil society." But here, too, the categories are fuzzier. In some communities, such as Prague, the burial society sometimes assumed many of the functions of the communal government, such as the giving of charity. Communal governments (the so-called *kehillah*), whose powers were sanctioned by the non-Jewish state, often look to modern eyes like voluntary associations of the wealthy. In fact, they functioned as semiautonomous, quasi governments in political entities in which power was not centralized. The self-governing Jewish communities were neither states in the

modern sense nor were they voluntary associations. For the Middle
Ages in general—and not only for the Jews—the diffusion of power
among many "corporations" makes it harder to speak of a sharp dichotomy between "state" and "society." The categories themselves do
not work.

This kind of fluidity of (modern) categories applies to concepts of
citizenship as well. The Bible itself insists on the same law for the *ger*
(resident alien) and the *ezrah* (native), as Zohar points out. But the very
categories remain substantially unclear, as one example will demonstrate: Uriah the Hittite, a general in David's army, who was married to
an Israelite, Bathsheba. Was David's Hittite general a citizen or an alien?
Was his marriage an intermarriage (a violation of Deut. 7)? And what are
we to make of his name, which suggests that he was a worshiper of the
Israelite god? Is this an ancient case of citizenship encompassing several
ethnic groups, or was identity understood very differently than in modern terms?

Zohar suggests that the Torah was understood to be a kind of ideal
constitution. This contention is definitely borne out for certain
thinkers. Moses Maimonides, for example, evidently understood the
Davidic kings as something like constitutional monarchs, since their
actions were constrained by a divine law. Maimonides distinguished
the Davidic kings from the Hasmonean kings, whom he treated as absolute monarchs beholden to no higher law. In this sense, a "theological" regime based on the Torah would be far more constricted than a
"secular" regime. Yet, not all traditional Jewish commentators have
necessarily understood the Torah to have this political meaning. For
example, the contemporary Orthodox Jewish philosopher Yeshayahu
Leibowitz adamantly denied that the Torah ought to be used as a political blueprint.

The doctrine that "the law of the Kingdom is the law" was originally
circumscribed to the right of the non-Jewish state to levy taxes on the
Jews. By the Middle Ages, the dictum had become the foundation of a
political theory in which the Jews might justify in their own legal terms
their status as a minority community and that would explain the division of political power between the Jewish community and the gentile
state. In modern times, certain Reformers took the doctrine to an unintended extreme: the non-Jewish state ought to possess full political and
legal authority, and the Jewish community ought to exercise none at
all. This new stance reflected the attempt by these critics of the medieval Jewish community to dismantle what they regarded as a "state
within the state." Note, however, that "the state within the state" formulation does not recognize the medieval Jewish community as a voluntary association or as composed of voluntary associations. This very

category of civil society did not exist and, indeed, it might be argued that the Reformers were trying to introduce it.

Curiously enough, certain Orthodox authorities in modern times have themselves adopted the dictum that "the law of the Kingdom is the law" to turn the Torah into the codebook for a purely voluntary Jewish association within the non-Jewish state. Faced with the loss of communal authority, some Orthodox sought to salvage a measure of power by embracing the new realm of civil society.

It is in the state of Israel that these shifting relationships between the Jewish community and the state took an entirely different turn. In the earlier years of the state of Israel, most Orthodox Jews such as the Agudat Yisrael (the ultra-Orthodox political party formed in 1912) understood the state in the same terms as a non-Jewish state: its law was the law. In recent years, though, another point of view has emerged, which seeks to turn the state of Israel into a theocracy with the Torah as its constitution. The phenomenon that Zohar mentions of Orthodox Jews threatening to disobey the laws of the state in favor of "higher" laws is curiously only to be found in Israel and not in any of the other, non-Jewish countries in which Orthodox Jews live. Only in Israel, it would seem, do some Orthodox Jews refuse to accept the dictum "the law of the Kingdom is the law." Precisely because Israel defines itself as a Jewish state, the categories that the legal tradition developed over centuries to regulate relations between Jewish communities and the non-Jewish state no longer seem to apply.

Israel has, in fact, become the battleground for conflicting ideas about the relationship between religion and state, perhaps more than any other country in the democratic world (Turkey is another case that comes to mind). Medieval concepts of empowered corporations compete with modern concepts of civil society. On the one hand, religion in Israel has the status that it inherited from the Ottoman Empire in governing personal status (marriage, divorce, and inheritance). On the other hand, since Israel is a democracy, with all power residing in the legislature, this status was conferred on religious authorities by an act of a secular parliament. So those who argue for the Torah as the constitution of the state and who wish to redefine the source of the state's legitimacy must do so using the instruments of democracy. Religious parties and institutions in Israel therefore function at once as part of civil society and as competitors for and beneficiaries of state power. Biblical models appear utterly irrelevant to the present reality, for nowhere can we find there either modern notions of democracy or of civil society. Neither are medieval models particularly useful, since they are drawn from quasiautonomous minority communities rather than from a state in which Jews held political power. It is therefore both this confusion of categories and the lack of real historical precedents that suggest the great difficulties that Israel has experienced and will no doubt continue to experience in creating the autonomous civil society that most liberal theorists would argue is necessary for a healthy democracy.

Part II

TERRITORY, SOVEREIGNTY, AND INTERNATIONAL SOCIETY

5

Land and People

DAVID NOVAK

THE QUESTION of territorial boundaries has been ubiquitous in political discourse throughout history. That is because human life is inconceivable outside of a finite community and its structures. Those who do not need such a defined community are either gods or beasts, as Aristotle so well put it.[1] Now one of the structures of any such defined human community is the place that it occupies. One could very well say that even when a human community does not regard its present place of occupation as permanent (as has been the case with the Jewish people for much of her history in exile), it nevertheless aspires to eventually occupy its own place in the world (as in the Jewish doctrine of the return to Zion).

The political question of territorial boundaries that has always been with us is the question of defining the proper limits between one place and another, and then determining just how the inhabitants of one such defined place are to interact with those who dwell within their own boundaries, as well as with those who dwell outside these same boundaries. The question of these boundaries is ubiquitous because it is historically inescapable. None of us are either from nowhere or on our way to nowhere. We are all both historical and geographical beings. Indeed, just as time and space cannot be separated in physics, as Einstein taught us, so it would seem that history and geography cannot be separated in political discourse. Even in the version of the Jewish messianic vision that sees one world polity as the goal of all human history, such a world polity is still oriented around Zion as the *axis mundi*.[2] We can no more intelligently conceive of ourselves outside of a particular place than we can conceive of ourselves outside our own bodies. (Indeed, it is significant that the Jewish doctrine of the return to Zion is closely connected to the Jewish doctrine of the bodily resurrection of the dead.)[3]

As we can already see, for Jews, the question of territorial borders cannot be addressed outside of the whole issue of Zionism, not only Zionism (taken in the broadest sense of the term) as a doctrine of Jewish tradition, but Zionism as a historical reality that has led to the presence of the state of Israel among the nation-states in the world in which we now live. Territorial borders are usually seen as a practical political question. However, they are also a theoretical one: the ontological question of *place*, which seems to underlie the political question of territory.

Now there are those who would deny the validity of ontological questions altogether, or the relevance of ontological questions to real political concerns. For them, law (even religious law) and politics require no more fundamental grounding. They are simply to be posited as such. But for any Jewish reflection on the political question of territory, such positivism becomes indefensible. For even though one need not engage in ontology before beginning coherent political discourse, the fact is that the Jewish tradition has certainly taken itself to be theologically grounded. Ultimately, even if not immediately, deeper theological issues cannot be intelligently avoided. And, theology (usually called "revealed theology," namely, a theology constituted out of a historical revelation), like metaphysics (inevitably culminating in what is usually called "natural theology," namely, a theology constituted out of that which is taken to be universal nature), is a way of engaging in ontology: the reflection on being. For Judaism, the connection between politics and theology is unavoidable, so much so that even that quintessential modern defector from Judaism, Baruch Spinoza, entitled his deconstruction of Judaism *Tractatus Theologico-Politicus*. (Spinoza knew Judaism very well from the inside, and then attempted to answer the theologico-political question differently from the outside, but with respect for the validity of the question nonetheless).[4]

Ownership

Territorial boundaries are essentially connected to the question of ownership. If I have a right to be in a certain place and you do not have such a right, or only the right to be there because I have invited you in as my guest, then it seems that my right is one of ownership. In modern times, with the rise of a commercial class of individual property owners, a theorist like Locke could develop a whole political philosophy based on the notion of individual possession of property and the rational principles to govern its development and transfer.[5] But this philosophy seems to assume that money and property are interchangeable terms. In fact, though, they are only interchangeable when property is primarily conceived of as movable goods, which are detached from any particular place. In this case, property and its ownership come down to being that which an individual can move around at will and trade for anything anywhere. The essence of money is its anonymous transferability; as we often say, it has no "earmarks."[6] Nevertheless, movable property originally is derived from a particular place on earth and must ultimately be set down somewhere on earth. Therefore, the question of ownership is still fundamentally one of territory, however less apparent it is now than was the case in pre-commercial society.[7] But it is still territory, much more than movable goods and money, for which peoples have been willing to risk the own lives and especially the lives of their most able-bodied sons and daughters in war.

One can see the legal and political question of ownership inevitably leading into the ontological question of creation. Thus the modern concern with the individual or collective ownership of property reflected in capitalist and socialist theories respectively is primarily concerned with the greatly expanded role of human creativity that came with the commercial-then-industrial revolution in history. But as the various ecologies that have been emerging of late well remind us, this exaltation of the human creation of "goods" (hence the equation of "good" and "value" in much modern ethical theory) has been at the increasingly heavy price of the abuse of the earth and its limits, which certainly precede all of our own creative efforts and which these efforts can ultimately never transcend. The question, though, is whether the crisis of our human relationship with the earth is one that can be solved by eliminating the institution of ownership altogether, or whether its solution requires a correction of our presently flawed notions of ownership. This latter option seems to assume that the issue of ownership cannot be avoided in any human relationship with the earth. The attempt of all socialisms, ancient and modern, to solve the problem of ownership by transferring it from individuals to collectives simply begs the real question altogether. Indeed, to simply avoid it means that it will come back inadequately resolved like any other "return of the repressed." Clearly, though, if we regard what has been called the "territorial imperative" as an essential aspect of human political nature, then correction and guidance of it as it has been manifest in history are our only rational options.

In the Jewish tradition, beginning with its sources in scripture, the question of ownership and the question of creation are seen in tandem. Thus Eve, upon the first human birth in the world (she and her husband having been fully made by God and placed in the world as adults), that of her firstborn son Cain (*Qayin*), calls him by this name because "I have acquired/made (*qaniti*) a manchild (*ish*) with (*et*) the Lord" (Genesis 4:1). What she is acknowledging is that she has become the co-creator of a child with God.[8] The question is just what the moral/political significance of any co-creation/acquisition is. This is very much connected with our issue of territory inasmuch as our original connection to anyplace is that of our being heirs of our ancestors, now preparing a heritage to pass on to our children. It is the necessary

connection between the particular historical time and the particular lo-
cation that lies at the core of human experience and action in the
world. Thus when this firstborn child finally settles down as the
builder of the first city, he dedicates (that is, perpetuates) it by calling
the city by his son's name Enoch (Genesis 4:17), which itself (*Hanokh*)
means "dedication." The perpetuity of the city and the perpetuity of
the family/clan are the subject of the very same word.[9]

The question of ownership is the question of the right relationship
between God as the absolute owner/creator of everything in the world
and humans as limited participants in what is to be seen as creation,
which is an ongoing process rather than a once and for all event. Thus
providence (*hashgahah*) is not an addition to creation but a property of
it. God does not lose interest in anything He has made. God never
transfers true ownership of anything. For without God's continual care
and concern, the world would revert to primordial chaos. "If My
covenant (*briti*) is not there day and night, then I have not put in place
the laws (*huqqot*) of heaven and earth" (Jeremiah 33:25).[10] This truth requires that God's ownership be continually emphasized by a number
of practices, both communal and individual. When it comes to the relation to landed property, at most, various creatures are given leases on
certain areas of the created order, and these leases require regular renewal. The basis of the renewal procedure is whether the continuing
surveillance of the true owner has determined that the tenants are
treating His property properly or not.

This point comes out quite clearly in the legislation of the Pentateuch that deals with the acquisition of the Promised Land by the people of Israel and their continuing domicile therein. Thus the Torah
rules out any permanent transfer of the agricultural real estate that is
considered the original patrimony of the tribes of Israel to whom it has
been *given* by God conditionally. Land is only a relative commercial entity, which can only be leased to a tribal outsider for a maximum of
forty-nine years from one Jubilee year to the next. (The rent was to be
prorated based on the number of years left at the time of the "sale" before the next Jubilee year, when all such real estate would be returned
to its original tribal owners.) Unlike most of the legislation of the
Torah, a reason is supplied for this whole institution of removing agricultural land from the realm of commercial transfer: "For the land shall
not be sold into perpetuity (*la-tsmitut*), since the earth is Mine, hence
you are sojourners and tenants with Me (*gerim ve-toshavim immadi*)"
(Leviticus 25:23). This theological reason is surely that "the earth is the
Lord's and the fullness thereof, the world and all who dwell therein"
(Psalms 24:1).[11] And, although it is taught "and the earth He has given
(*natan*) to humans" (Psalms 115:16), this only means that God has

allotted various parts of His earth to various peoples.[12] All of these peoples are to be aware of the fact that it is God who both moves peoples
from one place to another and settles them therein, and all of them are
to be aware that their domicile is conditional, that it is for the sake of
their obedience to the law of God. "Are you not unto Me like the
Ethiopians, children of Israel. . . . Have I not brought up Israel out of
Egypt, and the Philistines from Caphtor, and Aram from Kir? Behold
the eyes of the Lord God are on the sinful kingdom, and I shall destroy
her from the face of the earth" (Amos 9:7–8). But, since the Torah is primarily concerned with the people of Israel, it is the various laws which
have been given to her and for her, such as the restrictions of the Sabbatical and Jubilee years, that enable us to see just how divine ownership is practically emphasized in her national life.

To lose sight of this truth, and the practical results it entails, is a form
of the primal sin, which for scripture is idolatry. Thus the Torah warns
the Israelites not to make the same mistake in the land of Israel because
of which God transferred its tenancy from the earlier Canaanite residents to them. "You shall not practice all these idolatrous acts (ha-
to'evot). . . . For all these idolatrous acts were practiced by the people of
the land before you, and the land became defiled (va-titma). Let not the
land vomit you out because of your defilement of it as it vomited out
the nation before you" (Leviticus 18:26–28). The idolatry for which the
Canaanites forfeited the land is closely bound up with sexual license
and bloodshed (sins that later rabbinic tradition saw as unconditional
prohibitions for both Jews and non-Jews).[13]

This does not mean, though, that the displacement of the Jewish
people from the land of Israel by another people is that other people's
moral/political entitlement from God. Indeed, in history, such dis-
placements by other nations have been for purposes of their own
political/military conquest pure and simple, and these nations have
been castigated by the prophets, speaking in the name of God, as severely as they castigated Israel for her sins. "O Assyria the rod of My
anger; my wrath is a staff in their hand. . . . But he does imagine it and
in his heart he does not consider it, for to destroy is what is in his heart
and to annihilate not a few nations" (Isaiah 10:5, 7). Those nations have
been used and discarded by God without their knowledge and consent
of what their aggression against Israel means theologically. They have
only temporarily displaced Israel. To borrow words from T. S. Eliot,
they did "the right thing for the wrong reason."[14] Hence, Israel's precarious situation in the land can only be understood in the context of
the covenant with God. The threat of displacement is because Israel
must be aware that her right to unique domicile in the land is contingent on the purposes for which such domicile is to be conducted.

Unlike the election of Israel itself, which the preponderance of scripture and rabbinic tradition see as unconditional and hence irrevocable by either Israel or even God, the presence of the Jewish people in the land of Israel must be recognized as a contingent matter by them. That is why the people could survive with their identity intact even when exiled from the land, but could not survive without the Torah, which is the constitution of the irrevocable covenant between God and the people. And, whereas God has no covenantal justification for rejecting Israel, God does have covenantal justification for exiling Israel from the land when she has grossly violated the precepts of the Torah. Hence Israel's domicile in the land and her taking possession of it is for the sake of the covenant. As Martin Buber saw with great insight, the Zionism that emerges out of the Jewish tradition itself is no ordinary nationalism.[15]

Distribution

The right to live within the boundaries of the land of Israel is one that must be seen differently before and after the destruction of the First Temple in 586 B.C.E. Before the destruction of the First Temple, it is assumed that all twelve tribes of Israel are living intact upon the portions of the land that were assigned to them in the days of Moses, and of which possession was taken in the days of Joshua. Although the boundaries of the land expanded during the reigns of David and Solomon due to their successful military campaigns, the essential tribal pattern of domicile was taken by the rabbinic tradition to be intact before the destruction of the Northern Kingdom of Israel by the Assyrians and the destruction of the Kingdom of Judah (along with the much smaller tribe of Benjamin) by the Babylonians, of which the destruction of the Temple was the main defining event.[16] Thus the Torah speaks of the process of taking possession of the land as an essentially tribal undertaking. While still waiting on the plains of Moab, poised to enter the Promised Land, the people of Israel are told, "You shall inherit (ve-horashtem) the land and dwell therein, for to you have I given the land to inherit it. You shall apportion (ve-hitnahaltem) the land by lot for your clans (le-mishpehoteikhem): to the larger ones you shall apportion more of a share, and to the smaller ones less of a share" (Numbers 33:53–54).[17]

This tribal apportionment of the land had important distributional consequences for both Jews (at that time, more accurately, "Israelites") and non-Jews. For Jews, it meant that no one was allowed to permanently sell or purchase their tribal inheritance. So, when the daughters of Zelophehad successfully petitioned Moses for the right to inherit their deceased father's land, as they would have automatically had they been males, their request was approved by God. However, this caused a problem for the members of their tribe, Manasseh, which their leaders expressed as follows: "If they become the wives of members of one of the other tribes of Israel, then their portion will be subtracted (*ve-nigra'ah*) from the portion of our ancestors and added to the portion of the tribe they have married into" (Numbers 36:3). The compromise finally effected is that "the daughters of Zelophehad may become the wives of whomever they please, but they must become the wives of a family of the tribe of their father" (Numbers 36:6).[18] From this we see that even "personal" matters such as marriage were ultimately matters of tribal identification within tribal territory. Full political personhood was only possible for those men—and women—who had claims to tribal land.

For non-Jews, this meant that their status in what might be seen as this "landlocked" society would at worst be that of foreign slaves, either purchased from other nations or captured in war, or at best that of resident-aliens (*gerim*). In both statuses, non-Jews had some rights clearly defined, although they occupied an inferior status in the polity. In the case of slaves, they were entitled to their bodily integrity: they were not to be mutilated or raped. They were, also, to be included in a number of cultic observances such as the celebration of the Sabbath and Passover, which were certainly the most important communal religious celebrations in ancient Israel. In the case of non-Jewish free men and women in ancient Israel, they had the right to the full protection of civil and criminal law. Thus after the Torah prescribes capital punishment for a man who was the son of an Egyptian father and an Israelite mother, which would have meant that he was at least like a gentile resident-alien in having no claim to an ancestral portion in the land of Israel, a number of laws are set down pertaining to interhuman relations. Foremost among these laws is the requirement to execute the murderer of "any human person (*kol nefesh adam*)" (Leviticus 24:17). The general principle behind these laws is that "one judgment (*mishpat*) shall there be for you: the sojourner (*ka-ger*) and the native-born shall be treated alike" (Leviticus 24:22).[19]

From this we do see that even those who were not permanent property owners in the land of Israel were not totally disenfranchised in the national covenant. Indeed, the experience of landlessness, which was that of the resident-alien, is seen to be a reminder of Israel's own state during her sojourn in Egypt, hence "You may not oppress the sojourner, for you know the life of the sojourner (*nefesh ha-ger*) having yourselves been sojourners in the land of Egypt" (Exodus 23:9). Since Israel's experience in Egypt was indeed one of oppression, one where all her rights were eliminated, she is now commanded to treat sojourners in her own land differently. This is clearly an example of the later rabbinically formulated norm that "what is hateful to you, do not do to any fellow human being."[20] Thus the land of Israel is not to be a place that is ever to be "ethnically cleansed."[21]

The tribal form of land distribution was only effective when the society as a whole was constituted as a tribal confederation. In this political system, one's primary identification was tribal and only secondarily national. However, already before the First Temple was even built, military vulnerability caused the people of Israel to adopt a centralized monarchy, primarily because only such a centralized form of government could maintain the standing army necessary to defend Israel from the threat of highly organized Philistine aggression. (The Canaanites, Israel's earlier enemies, on the other hand, seem to have been as decentralized as were the tribes of Israel.) This was to have very important ramifications for the whole issue of territoriality in ancient Israel. For the power of the king very much included his redistribution of property. As such, even before the first king is actually selected, scripture tells of how the prophet Samuel, at the time the highest religio-political official in Israel, warned the people of the high price they would have to pay for the new institution of monarchy. Part of that overall price was territorial. "And your fields and your vineyards and your good olive trees he will take, giving them to his servants. Your produce and your vineyards he will tax [literally, 'tithe'], giving it to his officials and his servants" (I Samuel 8:14–15).[22]

The monarchy, with its greater centralization of political power and authority, also led to a greater urbanization of society. One of the main features of a more urban society as opposed to a more rural society is the greater role that money plays in it. And the very anonymity of money reflects the greater anonymity of urban society in general, but especially as pertains to the question of territorial domicile. Already in the Torah, one notes there is a fundamental difference between urban property (specifically, property held in a walled city) and property held in rural fields or villages. Property in rural fields or villages cannot be permanently purchased because it must return to the original tribal owners in the Jubilee year; hence it can only be leased. But concerning urban property, it is stated that if it is not redeemed within the year of its sale, then "it is permanently (la-tsmitut) the purchaser's" (Leviticus 25:30), which means that he or she can pass it on to heirs, or sell it to someone else. Only in cities does land become a truly commercial entity. And that reflects a different relationship of people to their territory than in a rural setting, which is in many ways closer to the earth.

By the time that the Jewish people returned from the Exile beginning around 516 B.C.E., the old tribal territorial divisions were no longer in effect. For it was only the Judeans (hence the name "Jews," now the "remnant of Israel") who came back to the land of Israel, and the territory they occupied was not the same as that of the old twelve tribes.[23] Thus, as it were, the whole society became urbanized, at least in the legal sense, even though the physical presence of agriculture was obviously still in place. The political impact of this changed geographic and economic reality is not to be underestimated.

First, it led to the gradual obliteration of the old distinctions between those who owned land and those who were landless. Thus the Levites, who were only assigned a number of villages that could not support sufficient agriculture for their needs and thus had to live off of the tithes that the rest of the people paid them, were eventually integrated into the rest of the population. That seems to be the case because in what has been called by historians the "Second Jewish Commonwealth," the Levites no longer had their old villages, and because most of the people had ceased to pay them the old tithes. To be sure, some of this may have been due to the assimilation of many of the Levites into Babylonian society, thus preventing very many of them from returning to the land of Israel under Ezra and Nehemiah.[24] But it seems more likely that their status had largely depended on the role they had played *among* all the tribes of Israel when they were all living on their old ancestral territories. But the new political realities could not restore that *ancien régime*, however much it remained a messianic hope. Aside from their secondary role in the service of the Temple, which only involved a minority of them anyway, the Levites had lost the unique territorial role they had formerly played in the covenantal society. And this might well explain why only the most exceptionally pious people felt it necessary to continue to support them with their tithes, especially when during the Second Temple period the people were paying taxes to the various empires (Persian, Macedonian, Ptolemaic, Seleucid, Roman) under whose rule (sometimes distant; sometimes quite immediate) they had to live.[25]

The most radical social change that came in the wake of the territorial changes during the Second Temple period was that possessing rural land or living in rural areas, which had alone given one full social status in the pre-exilic period, by the time of at least the Roman occupation actually became a sign of social inferiority, for the urbanization of society had greatly increased the opportunities for learning, and learning took on a new importance in the very governance of society. In many ways, the portability of sacred texts and their rabbinic expositors took on the importance that had formerly pertained to the landed gentry and the institutions that depended on their support.

This seems to have been the result of the Exile itself, where the identity of the now landless Jewish people was dependent on the centrality of the Book in their communal life. Thus, when the people were being reestablished in the land again, the central feature in their celebration of this great event was that Ezra the Scribe (and not, significantly, Nehemiah the territorial governor) had the people "read the law of God that was explicit in the book (*ba-sefer*), and they intelligently understood the reading (*ba-miqra*)" (Nehemiah 8:8).[26] From that time on, where the leadership of the people would lie became a struggle between those who had political power based on territory and those who had political power based on learning (viz., the scribes and sages). After the time of the destruction of the Second Temple in 70 C.E. (the final loss of their own place by the Jewish people), the political victory was that of the scribes and sages. Only they, through their mastery of the Book, had not lost the basis of their authority. In fact, based on that authority, these scribes and sages conceived what the return to national sovereignty in the land of Israel would be like, even including the rebuilding of the Temple.[27]

But those who lived in rural areas were rarely able to take advantage of the newer social institutions of the synagogue (*bet ha-keneset*), whose main function was the public reading and exposition of scripture, and the academy (*bet ha-midrash*), whose main function was the development of post-scriptural forms of normative teaching (what came to be called the "Oral Tradition").[28] Thus the old scriptural term *am ha'arets* (literally, "people of the land"), whose original meaning was probably the name of a council of local landed gentry, became by the time of the Pharisees a name designating an ignoramus, who would be called today a "country bumpkin."[29] Organized learning is very much a result of greater urbanity; only cities have the number and variety of people to enable learning to function on an institutional level. So, even though the overall sacred status of the land of Israel was continually emphasized in rabbinic jurisprudence and theology, the fact was that its distributional significance had radically changed.

Now, in an unprecedented manner, the entire Jewish people had an equal share in the land of Israel, and the old differences between the various types of landowners and non-landowners became less and less significant. Furthermore, even though there probably was some sort of Jewish diaspora already in the time of the First Temple, the reality of the Jewish diaspora was not fully established until the time of the Second Temple. This was due to the fact that many Jews did not return to the land of Israel when Cyrus the Great had permitted them to do so under the leadership of Ezra and Nehemiah. Although some of this was because of gradual assimilation, more of it seems to have been because large numbers of Jews believed that their religious and social identity did not depend on their physical presence in the land of Israel. And, although some of these Jews do seem to have cut off their ties altogether to the ancestral homeland (as evidenced, for example, by the construction of a temple to rival the one in Jerusalem by Egyptian Jews in Leontopolis sometime in the second century B.C.E.), the vast majority of diaspora Jews seem to have maintained their connection to the land of Israel.[30] This is especially evidenced by the pilgrimages many of them made regularly to the Temple in Jerusalem, and the offerings that were regularly sent there even by those who could not come in person.[31]

Of course, tensions did arise from time to time between Israeli and non-Israeli Jews. Frequently, the tensions were over issues of political sovereignty that occasionally erupted when diaspora communities balked at the idea of being treated as mere colonies of the motherland. Nevertheless, at least from what we know from rabbinic sources, even at the time of such political tensions, the religious uniqueness of the land of Israel was not challenged. What was challenged, especially after the demise of the Israel-centered Sanhedrin as the central legislative-juridical body in Jewry, was the notion that all authority was to be contained within the borders of the land. But the diaspora communities refused to surrender their own authority even when there was a politically viable community in the land of Israel.[32] And they were able to do this without cutting off their ties to the land and their hopes for its messianic redemption. We shall examine this idea of a land encompassing more than its actual inhabitants when we deal with the question of national autonomy.

Diversity

The breakdown of the old tribal system as well as the development of Judaism as a basically urban phenomenon also led to a different mode of relationship between Jews and non-Jews, both in the land of Israel and in the Diaspora.

In the land of Israel during the pre-exilic period, non-Jews were related to Jews as either foreigners (*nokhrim*) or resident-aliens (*gerim*). Foreigners were those who occupied what was taken to be essentially gentile space. Their territorial integrity was to be respected, however. Even in the event of imminent war, the people of Israel were commanded to "offer peace terms" (Deuteronomy 20:10) before entering into any acts of conquest. But here the distinction was made between the lands of the Canaanite tribes, which God entitled Israel to conquer, and the lands whose "cities are far away from you" (Deuteronomy 20:15). Yet even that distinction was also broken down in the development of the rabbinic tradition.[33]

The resident-aliens, as we have already seen, were those people living among the people of Israel in a subordinate capacity, although one having definite rights and duties and enjoying the protection of the due process of law. The only way they were able to gain full status in that landed society was to somehow or other assimilate with the people of Israel. The process seems to have taken a number of generations in order to be complete. It was usually done through intermarriage, especially the marriage of gentile women with Israelite men.[34] At least in the explicit norms of scripture, intermarriage was only prohibited with the sons and daughters of the Canaanite nations.[35]

The changed situation of the post-exilic Jewish community in the land of Israel, with its new relationship to territory, made the relationship of the Jews with the non-Jews living among them different. Not only were the old tribal distinctions between the Jews themselves largely a thing of the past, but the distinctions between the non-Jews themselves that the Torah had recognized in its legislation, especially as pertains to marriage, were also regarded to be a thing of the past. Thus, whereas in the past some non-Jews had been more privileged than others in their right to live in the land of Israel as resident-aliens, after the Exile these distinctions were considered impossible to detect. As the Mishnah put it, "And are the Ammonites and the Moabites still in their [original] locales? [After all] Senacherib the king of Assyria ascended and mixed up (u-bilbel) all the nations."[36] Indeed, the very process whereby the people were exiled—first the Northern Kingdom of Israel by the Assyrians and then the Kingdom of Judah by the Babylonians—was the same process that led to what seemed to be universal disruption of territorial and ethnic boundaries; just as the Jewish people had now become more of a homogeneous people, so were the nations of the world whom they faced as "others" now, at least for them, more homogeneous. For this reason, the old distinctions pertaining to intermarriage could no longer apply. But, instead of becoming more lenient because of this, the distinctions became stricter. Ezra's strictures against intermarriage applied across the board to all gentiles. And these strictures were promoted at the time that the people of Israel were retaking the land of Israel (albeit, in effect, as Persian colonists). The connection between marriage, domicile, and territory is integral.[37] As Ezra is reported to have put it, "the officials approached me saying that the people of Israel and the priests and the Levites had not separated themselves from the peoples of the lands . . . for they have taken their daughters for themselves and for their sons, and they have assimilated (*ve-hit'arvu*) the holy stock with the peoples of the lands" (Ezra 9:1–2).

The lack of full Jewish sovereignty in the land of Israel during the entire period of the Second Temple made the question of non-Jewish domicile within traditionally Jewish territory one that was essentially out of the hands of the Jews. Non-Jews were living in close proximity to Jewish settlements in the land, and that was a fact of life that the Jews had to face in a way other than by exercising the kind of control they formerly had over non-Jews under the pre-exilic monarchy.[38] Thus the Talmud assumed that the formal institution of the resident-alien (*ger toshav*) could have only been in force when all the tribes of Israel were intact in their respective ancestral territories.[39] This situation had a number of important ramifications as regards the diversity of population in the land of Israel.

First, it meant that the Jews had to recognize that in their own land (that is, their own land by virtue of their own theological-legal criteria) there was a permanent non-Jewish presence. Although by messianic criteria this may have been a situation to be ultimately overcome, in the present political reality it was a factor that had to be taken into serious consideration in communal policy decisions. For example, the Talmud notes:

> In Ammon and Moab the tithe for the poor is to be given even during the Sabbatical year, as an earlier authority indicated: Many towns were captured by those who left Egypt but were not captured by those who left Babylonia. For the sanctification of the land in the first instance was only established in the first instance for that time (*le-sha'atah*) but not for the future. They excluded these towns from the latter conquest in order that the poor might rely on them during the Sabbatical year.[40]

Whether any such exclusion was intentionally made at that earlier time is somewhat questionable. But what this passage does show is that Jewish policy decisions, having important economic and social consequences, were more likely made on the assumption that the non-Jewish presence within the larger historical borders of the land of Israel was a factor that could be accepted, and a factor that could be usefully employed in making policy decisions for the common good of the Jewish people herself.

Second, the disappearance of the old resident-alien status, for reasons we have seen above, also made any non-Jewish integration into the Jewish community and its territories harder, yet at the same time more immediate. For it is during the Second Temple period that we see the whole phenomenon of conversion to Judaism emerge as distinct from gradual assimilation into the Jewish people and her territories. By "conversion" I mean an event whereby one who is formerly a gentile becomes a Jew. That is quite different from the process of becoming either a permanent or temporary (a process of several generations) resident-alien that seems to have been in effect in earlier times.[41]

With the institution of conversion (*gerut*), a gentile had the opportunity to become a full member of the Jewish people by his or her own choice. Of course, the conversion itself was not done by converts themselves but, rather, by a tribunal, which functioned very much on behalf of the entire people if not, in effect, on behalf of God (since conversion seems to be based on the theological doctrine that the covenantal election of Israel by God can extend to individuals who are not themselves literal descendants of Abraham and Sarah).[42] Nevertheless, the consent of the convert himself or herself is a necessary, if not sufficient, condition for the conversion itself to be legally valid.[43] (This latter qualification may have been the result of the disastrous results the Jewish people experienced from the forced conversion of the people of Edom by the Hasmonean king, John Hyrcanus, in the second century B.C.E.)[44] Although a more immediate way to become part of the Jewish people and whatever territory they inhabit or control at the time, it is harder inasmuch as converts are required to demonstrate their willingness to adopt the full regimen of Jewish law.[45] To be sure, native-born Jews are also required to observe it, but their status as permanent members of the Jewish people is not dependent on any such prior commitment. At least in the Diaspora, becoming part of Jewish polity requires one's full religious integration into the life of the Jewish people.

The return of the Jewish people to national sovereignty in the land of Israel brought about by the state of Israel has raised some important new issues for the question of diversity in a Jewish polity. That is largely the case, it seems to me, because the new Jewish state (forty-eight years is a very short period of time in relation to the more than four-thousand-year history of the Jewish people) as a *secular Jewish state* is unprecedented in history. (The fact that the state of Israel does not have a written constitution makes the legal ramifications of its undefined character often quite problematic.) The main issue centers around the question of the status of non-Jews in a Jewish polity; indeed, how their very presence therein is to be designated politically and legally.

In ancient Israel, the status of the resident-alien, at least as the rabbinic sources retrospectively defined that status, partakes of both religious and secular aspects. This status has a religious component inasmuch as the rabbinic view is unanimous in presuming that the right to resident-alien status in ancient Israel required that the candidate for this status agree not to engage in any public idolatry (*avodah zarah*).[46] That, in effect, meant that resident-aliens were proscribed from practicing their native religion in the land of Israel. (The notion of a "private" religion is a peculiarly modern fiction that would have been unintelligible until very recent times.) This did not mean, though, that they had to adopt Jewish religious practices. (The scriptural sources do mention such "sojourners" being able to observe some Jewish cultic celebrations, but whether there was any actual legal pressure for them to do so is unclear.) The status has a secular component, too, inasmuch as the positive requirements of resident-aliens and the positive rights they enjoyed are all taken to be within the realm of interpersonal relations, such as the right to be protected from harm to one's person or one's property. In fact, the predominantly secular aspect of this institution very much impressed the great German Jewish philosopher Hermann Cohen (d. 1918), so much so that he saw it as a precedent for modern notions of citizenship that are meant to be unconnected to religious or ethnic origins.[47]

Nevertheless, as we have seen, this type of citizenship (or, at least, the idea of this type of citizenship) presupposes a basically religious polity, which also includes within itself the fully intact presence of all twelve tribes of Israel dwelling on their respective ancestral portions. And, even if the latter criterion is effectively a messianic one, the former criterion—the presupposition of a basically religious polity—does not hold in the land of Israel at present or in the foreseeable future. Accordingly, a peculiar paradox pertains to the way distinctions involving citizenship are made in the state of Israel. The paradox can be seen as follows: On the one hand, if the state of Israel is a secular, democratic polity, then there should be no ethnic or religious distinctions made between one group of *Israelis* or another. However, were this to be so, the essentially *Jewish* character of the state, including its significance for the majority of Jews who still live in the Diaspora, would no doubt be lost. (And there are, indeed, radically secularist Israelis who would like to see Israel as a state for Israelis in the same way, let us say, that Canada is a state for Canadians—of whatever religious or ethnic background.) On the other hand, if the state of Israel is to be a state for Jews governed by traditional Jewish law, then the only full citizens should be those Jews willing to live under the rule of this law. As for secular Jews, or liberal religious Jews, let alone non-Jews, their obviously second-class status would have to be determined by the rabbinical interpreters of that law.[48]

The fact is, though, that despite the officially secular character of the state of Israel, secular Jews, liberal religious Jews, and non-Jews all live at some sort of political disadvantage there. Secular Jews are required to submit themselves to Orthodox religious authorities in all matters pertaining to marriage and divorce. Liberal religious Jews do not have the government support for their institutions, and their leaders have no official clerical status. (Thus they may not officiate at marriage or divorce procedures.) As for non-Jews, although their religious institutions are officially recognized, they are not the subjects of the most basic right to which Jewish Israelis are entitled: the "Law of Return" (*hoq ha-shevut*), which entitles any Jew from anywhere to immediate citizenship upon arrival in Israel. (The passage of this law was the first official act of Israel's parliament, the *Kenesset*, after the establishment of the state in 1948.) And as for Arabs living on the West Bank (as distinct from Arabs living within Israel's pre-1967 borders), their whole political status is still very much in limbo.

Israel's problem of diversity within her territory, like several other such matters of identity, lacks a satisfactory solution because Israel has had neither the time nor the energy so far to more clearly define the character of her own society. But such a definition is surely a desideratum: first, for Israeli Jews themselves; second, for Israeli non-Jews; and third, for diaspora Jews, the overwhelming number of whom see the state of Israel as a Jewish polity to which they are connected politically, even if not in the strictly legal sense of citizenship. Being such a desideratum, the quest for clearer definition calls for theoretical reflection whenever possible.

This problem partakes of the inherent paradox of a secular state enforcing religious criteria of identity. It is best illustrated by a landmark decision of the Israel Supreme Court in the late 1960s. The case involved the petition of an Israeli naval officer, Binyamin Shalit, for his wife and children to be given Jewish citizenship in Israel. The problem was that Mrs. Shalit was a Scottish-born gentile. Their children, by virtue of the rabbinic principle of matrilineal descent (the mother's identity determines that of her children), are therefore gentiles.[49] The only solution would have been for Mrs. Shalit and her children to have converted to Judaism. However, such a "conversion" is by definition a religious act, involving full acceptance of the universal kingship of the God of Israel and the commandments of the Torah and Jewish tradition. That proved to be an insuperable impediment for Mrs. Shalit, since both she and Mr. Shalit are committed atheists who refused on principle to submit themselves to religious standards and rites which they could not in good conscience accept. Their argument was that their *Jewishness* was a secular matter, evidenced by their choice to live in the secular, Jewish state of Israel and raise their children in that society. They, in effect, requested a secular means for affirming the Jewishness of Mrs. Shalit and their children. But the problem was, of course, that no such means exists. The only way for one to become a Jew, even in this secular state, is through religious—and in Israel that means Orthodox—auspices. The Shalits' petition was thus denied.[50] The status of Mrs. Shalit and the Shalit children could only be that of gentiles (*goyyim*) living in the Jewish state as gentile citizens.

Now as is well known, the political reason for this secular concession to religious standards, indeed only one kind of Jewish religious standard, is that no secular party in Israel has ever been able to win its own majority in the Kenesset and thus be able to form a government (a *memshalah* as distinct from the state itself: *medinat yisrael*) by itself. All Israeli governments since 1948 have been formed by coalitions, coalitions that have always included Orthodox religious parties. The price these religious parties have exacted for their participation in these coalition governments has been their increasing control of such areas of society as familial and personal status. But what many Israelis—and non-Israelis—have argued is that this emphasizes the paradox of confusing religion and secularity, the result being that the worst elements of both worldviews emerge. For what we have is, in effect, a secular contract as the basis of religious coercion.

More and more people are becoming increasingly aware of just how unsatisfactory this approach to the question of diversity, both among Jews themselves and with respect to Jews and non-Jews, really is. The approach has heretofore been unable to deal with dangerous tensions between Jews themselves and the even more dangerous tensions between Jews and non-Jews. This grave practical problem seems to be very much with us for, at least, the near future. However, theorists should, whenever possible, attempt to imagine some way out of it, because intelligent public policy requires a basis in coherent theory. Thus let me make a suggestion here.

Although every society has to employ coercion from time to time to protect public order from those whose disrespect for the rule of law would endanger it, no society can hold the moral allegiance of its members if coercion is the very basis of that public order. One need not be an advocate of any sort of social contract theory as the basis of society to appreciate this point. It also pertains to a society that is based on a covenant between God and a people, which is the way Judaism has consistently constituted any Jewish polity. A covenantal society is based on God's initiation of a political relationship between Himself and a people. Unlike a contract, it is not the coming together of equal parties, nor do the people have any right of initial refusal or subsequent termination of the covenant. (Indeed, the only basis for any such termination would be the permanent absence of God or Israel from the world.) Both possibilities are in fact precluded by the very divine promises that founded the covenant in the first place. Thus only God has the right—the autonomy—to initiate the covenant, and God has promised away any right He could have had to terminate it.[51] At that level, then, the covenant could be said to be forced upon the people by God. Yet, however valid the covenant might be on the ontological level as an act of divine coercion (the rights of the Creator over any of His creatures), on the practical level it would be inoperative. In what might very well be one of the most theologically striking discussions in the entire Talmud, it is emphasized that although at Mount Sinai God "suspended the mountain over them [Israel]," it was only during the Exile, when Israel finally accepted the covenant and its Torah out of inherently free love, that the whole covenantal system—including its law—became truly effective.[52]

The upshot of all this is that the Jewish religious system of law and polity cannot operate coherently unless it is based on a continually renewed covenant between God and the people. To base it on a contract between religious political parties and a secular state, as is the case now in Israel, where the interpreters of religious law derive coercive power from secular authority, can only lead to widespread contempt for what is being presented by them as "the Torah." The contempt of the secular (or, at least, non-Orthodox) majority is due to their being forced to live under a law they do not wish, in good conscience, to accept. Moreover, there are a number in the religious communities as well who suspect this political situation, being pained to see what they love become the object of hate by so many others. And they see that this unnatural marriage between secular authority and religious enforcement leads to numerous compromises with secularity that threaten the very integrity of Jewish religious law itself.[53] Thus, for example, if matters of personal status and their legal ramifications, which could well be considered the most important aspect of a religion that is a communal covenant, are the subject of the legislation of the Kenesset, then these matters are being practically determined by a body whose majority consists of religiously nonobservant Jews—as well as its non-Jewish, Arab members. One need not be a religiously observant Jew to be troubled by all this.

The reemphasis of the covenantal basis of Judaism itself requires due (albeit critical) appreciation of the modern experience of democratic pluralism. For it is from this type of polity that Jews have derived such enormous political benefits wherever it has been in force. (It would be very hard to find a Jew who could make any sort of politically convincing argument for the political alternatives to democracy today, primarily because Jews have been so victimized in those societies where they have been operative.) That reemphasis has some rather direct implications for the problem of diversity in a society where political power and authority are constitutionally Jewish. (However vague that Jewish basis has been constituted heretofore, the state of Israel, by virtue of its Declaration of Independence, designates herself as a *medinah yehudit*, a "Jewish state.") These ramifications apply to both Jewish and non-Jewish diversity.

As for Jewish diversity, which in practice means the differences between Orthodox and non-Orthodox Jews as well as the even greater differences between religious and secular (better, "secularist") Jews, the question is how to find sources in the tradition itself for the employment of an absolute minimum of coercion by religious authorities. This is the only way, I think, that a rationally persuasive case could be made for a truly religious foundation for a Jewish polity, especially at this point in history. (And how could anything but a rational case be persuasive rather than intimidating?) The case could be made that such a religious foundation would alone be able to provide enough continuity with Jewish tradition to justify calling the polity a "Jewish state," and it would have enough in common with modern democratic notions of a minimum of coercion and a respect for individual rights to prove attractive to the vast majority of Jews who have, quite understandably, grown attached to these notions.

As regards Jewish diversity, there would have to be a reliance on authoritative sources within the classical literature that indicate that the use of coercion is often a matter of judicial or legislative discretion. For example, there is a principle that laws which are the result of rabbinic legislation should not be enforced if they prove to be practices which the majority of the community have already quite clearly neglected.[54] (Needless to say, any such reticence could not be cogently advocated when the sin to be committed, or which has just been committed, involves physical harm to persons or property.) Of course, all these procedural principles need to be very carefully nuanced when we reach the level of legal application.[55] All I am saying now is that the tradition has within it the potential for their development to meet the moral/political needs of the present.

The problem of diversity in a Jewish polity that includes non-Jews is harder to approach, let alone resolve, because the classical rabbinic sources, upon which we always have to draw, were all written during the very long period of time between the close of scripture and the reestablishment of the state of Israel when Jews had no real political power over any group of non-Jews. At most, they sometimes did have power over individual non-Jews whom they held as slaves; however, considering the scarcity of this institution in the world today due to virtually universal moral revulsion, we should not look to it for any precedents or parallels. Fortunately, there is no legal obligation (*hovah*) for Jews to impose themselves (or allow themselves to be imposed) over any non-Jew in this way.[56] Furthermore, that the Jewish experience of slavery in Egypt and redemption therefrom surely provided much of the historical inspiration for the outlawing of slavery in the English-speaking (and scripture-reading) world in the nineteenth century is a fact that should not be lost on Jews today when contemplating what their newly regained political power over others means.

Fortunately, though, real political solutions do come out of theoretical imaginings. One such theoretical imagining is the rabbinic concept of the "Noahide Laws," which were taken by the ancient rabbis to be those laws that God requires both Jews and non-Jews to accept and obey (although Jews are required to accept and obey much more because of the covenant at Sinai). They are theoretical because they did not arise out of any real juridical authority of Jews over non-Jews actually in operation in history.[57] The core of these laws concerns what we today would consider proper political matters, such as prohibitions of murder, robbery, and incest. There are many ramifications of this concept, which has played an important role in Jewish thought since rabbinic times. One such ramification is that it provided the rabbis with the means to imagine (since there seem to have been no explicit records extant) just what was required of the resident-alien (*ger toshav*) in the days when all Israel was living intact in the land of Israel.[58]

However, the question eventually arose as to who was to administer and enforce these laws for the gentiles living under Jewish rule. (Since the concept of the "Noahide" was taken to pertain to all of humankind universally, it is wider than the concept of the resident-alien, which only pertains to the land of Israel under optimal political conditions. Therefore, it is clear that in the absence of Jewish political authority, there is no question that it is the gentiles themselves who are to administer and enforce these laws for themselves among themselves.) Since the question was hypothetical in his day, there being no real precedents to cite, Maimonides (d. 1204) offers the following imaginative answer:

> The Jewish court [the Sanhedrin] is obligated (*hayyavim*) to appoint judges for those who are resident-aliens (*ha-gerim ha-toshavim*) to adjudicate for them according to these [Noahide] laws. This is to be done so that civilization (*ha'olam*) not be destroyed. If the court decides it is appropriate to appoint judges from among them (*me-hen*), it may do so; but if it decides it is appropriate to appoint Jewish judges for them (*la-hen*), it may do so.[59]

Now the question is just how much political and legal autonomy Maimonides is willing to allow to the non-Jewish residents of a Jewish polity. It seems that, at best, they are to be allowed some sort of subordinate status of partial internal rule over themselves. However, one of the most perspicacious students of Maimonides' jurisprudence, and himself a distinguished jurist in the same Egyptian community Maimonides had served three centuries earlier, the late fifteenth-century authority Rabbi David ibn Abi Zimra, in his notes *ad locum*, opines: "if they themselves did not [already] appoint a court for themselves, or there was no one among them fit (*ra'ui*) for the task, then (*az*) the Jewish court is obligated to appoint judges for them."[60] Whether he is actually interpreting Maimonides' own statement here, or is in fact emending it, is arguable either way.

Nevertheless, one can derive from his note that a Jewish polity may grant total juridical authority to a group of non-Jews living under its control, which suggests political sovereignty as well. The only proviso would be that the Jewish authorities be assured that the Noahide laws would be respected by this newly empowered juridical entity. In the case of Christians and Muslims, this would be so ipso facto inasmuch as we could rely on the widely influential opinion of the fourteenth-century Provençal jurist, Rabbi Menahem ha-Me'iri, who judged both Christians and Muslims to be "nations bound by the ways of [religiously acceptable] law (*ummot ha-gedurot be-darkhei ha-datot*)."[61] The question is, though, how closely one can connect juridical authority to what we would call political sovereignty today. (We shall return to this question in the last section of this chapter.)

Mobility

The question of the right of passage of nonresidents through the territorial boundaries of a polity, for Jews, goes back to the time when Moses and the Israelites requested passage through the land of the Edomites and the land of the Amorites on their way to the Promised Land. "I wish to pass through your land. . . . We shall go by way of the royal road (*be-derekh ha-melekh*) until we will have crossed your border" (Numbers 21:22). (The "royal road" seems to have been some sort of international highway that was to be open to all peaceful travelers.) Since they requested this right, with the qualification that they would be careful not to take what was not theirs or cause any damage during their passage to the land they were to be passing through, it would stand to reason that they could not in all fairness deny such a right to others passing through their own land. In fact, one rabbinic *midrash*

(exegesis) connects Moses' request for passage through the land of the
Amorites with the commandment "to offer peace terms to her [a foreign city]" (Deuteronomy 20:10). In fact, this rabbinic exegete imagined
God to have congratulated Moses for reminding him of His own commandment here.[62] Following this analogy, it would seem that just as
peace terms are to be both offered and accepted, so is the right of safe
passage through one's land for nonresidents something that can be requested and is to be fulfilled. So it would seem that no one could argue
against the right of passage—that is, under normal peacetime conditions. Like the negative experience of slavery in Egypt, so the negative
experience of being refused the right of passage through the land of
the Edomites and the land of the Amorites should cause Jews to infer
the positive from the negative, thus seeing what was denied them to be
a universal human right.

Autonomy

As we have already seen, one cannot argue for modern notions of autonomy within the Jewish tradition, for "autonomy" has come to mean
a law made by myself for myself, but that is a property that belongs to
God alone, not to any creature, not even the human creature created in
His image. This is so, whether one means "autonomy" in the Kantian
sense (the power to legislate duty for oneself and anyone else in one's
same general situation) or in the liberal sense (the right to do whatever
I want, so long as no one else is harmed thereby). Because of this, the
closest we can come to affirming a notion of "autonomy" is to affirm
"sovereignty," that is, when a community has the power to govern itself based on the law it has accepted for itself.[63]

Jews have always aspired to a maximum of such sovereignty in the
world. They have often had to settle, though, for the minimum of simply being able to govern their "religious" life, which is how they
conduct their relationship with God within their own community.
(Anything below that minimum makes Jewish life impossible as a public phenomenon, as witnessed by the *Marranos*, the "secret Jews," who
continued to practice Judaism in absolute privacy after it had been
banned in Spain and Portugal at the end of the fifteenth century. Their
inability to publicly practice Judaism led to the demise of virtually all
of them as Jews after a few generations.) But this sovereignty is relative
even when maximal. Even the sovereignty of a king in Israel, whether
a past historical king or the future Messiah, is subordinate to that of
God, the only true king.[64]

That being the case, the maximal liberty that Jews have in any polity of their own is juridical liberty: the right to judge what is the true meaning of law, all of which is taken to be God's law, whether directly revealed in scripture and tradition or surmised by human reason—none of which could be called autonomy in the strict modern sense of the term.[65] A number of implications can be drawn from this.

First, since the polity is defined by its adherence to the law of God and the perpetuation of it, no matter how important territory is in the covenant between God and Israel, the polity cannot be limited to those who live within the land of Israel. At most, it is the optimal place for the life of the covenant to be led and centered, but it is not the only place.[66] It is only at the time when the Messiah will gather all of the ex-iled into the land of Israel that polity and territory will coincide. (That will be similar to the recoincidence of bodies and souls that is prom-ised to take place at the resurrection of the dead, an event that is closely linked, if not identical, with the messianic redemption.) And yet, even then, polity will transcend territory inasmuch as Zion is meant to be the capital of a united humankind living under the explicit kingship of God throughout the earth. Therefore, the notion of the "disappearance of the Diaspora (*shelilat ha-golah*)," which some Jews have entertained, is not only bad historical prognostication (in many ways the reestablishment of the state of Israel has strengthened Jewish life in the Diaspora), it is also bad theology. It goes back to the claim made by the Jews of the first Exile in Babylonia that because they were in exile from the land of Israel, "we will become like the nations, like the families of the [other] lands" (Ezekiel 20:32).

Second, there is an implication for the granting of sovereignty to non-Jewish communities living at present under Jewish rule. For if the greatest sovereignty that even the Jews themselves have is essentially juridical, it would seem that if they can recognize the juridical inde-pendence of a non-Jewish community presently living under Jewish rule, then they have recognized as much liberty in and for that commu-nity as they can recognize in and for their own. This would be based on the notion of a legally constituted state (*Rechtsstaat*), which is not only a state that recognizes the rule of law, but one that is itself the creature of a prior law.[67] At this stage, this point about the priority of the juridi-cal realm over the political realm needs much more specific thought to be coherent even in theory. However, that law itself is rooted in *the* covenant between God and Israel. And other covenants can be made between humans based on that prior covenant. Perhaps, then, the same covenantal thinking, which is the only cogent way I can see, both theo-logically and politically, for the return of Jewish law in and for a modern nation-state, can lead to a coherent modus vivendi with the other communities who now share life with the Jews within the borders of the greater land of Israel.

Notes

1. *Politics*, 1.1/1253a29.
2. See Isa. 2:1–4, 56:6–7; Mic. 4:1–4.
3. See Ezek. 37:1–14; *Babylonian Talmud* (hereafter "B."): Sanhedrin 92b.
4. See David Novak, *The Election of Israel* (Cambridge: Cambridge University Press, 1995), 26ff.
5. See *Second Treatise of Government*, chap. 5.
6. See Aristotle, *Nicomachean Ethics*, 5.5/1133a30.
7. That is why the Talmud rules that certain forms of commercial transfer must still take place "on the ground." See B. Kiddushin 27a.
8. See Rashi, *Commentary on the Torah* thereon; also, B. Kiddushin 30b and B. Niddah 31a.
9. See *Midrash Aggadah* thereon re Ps. 49:12, ed. S. Buber (Vienna: A. Panta, 1894), p. 13.
10. See B. Pesahim 68b.
11. See *Palestinian Talmud*: Berakhot 6:1/9d.
12. See Deut. 32:8–9; B. Berakhot 35a–b and B. Shabbat 119a re Ps. 24:1. The earth and any of its goods are only to be enjoyed *after* acknowledgment that they have all been given by God and, ultimately, remain God's sole property.
13. B. Sanhedrin 57a.
14. *Murder in the Cathedral*, pt. 1, *The Complete Poems and Plays 1909–1950* (New York: Harcourt, Brace, and World, 1971), 196.
15. *Israel and Palaestina* (Zurich: Artemis-Verlag, 1950), 8.
16. B. Arakhin 32b re Lev. 25:10.
17. For the exact status of the commandment to dwell in the land of Israel, see David Novak, *The Theology of Nahmanides Systematically Presented* (Atlanta, Ga.: Scholars Press, 1992), 95.
18. See B. Baba Batra 120a–121a.
19. See David Novak, *The Image of the Non-Jew in Judaism* (New York and Toronto: Edwin Mellen Press, 1983), 53ff.
20. B. Shabbat 31a.
21. Thus even the apparently unconditional scriptural commandment to wipe out the Canaanite inhabitants of the land of Israel (Deut. 20:16) was interpreted by the rabbis to be enforceable only upon the prior refusal of the Canaanites to abide by universal moral law; if they chose to abide by it, they were to be politically recognized by Israel and left unmolested. See David Novak, *Jewish Social Ethics* (New York: Oxford University Press, 1992), 189ff. re *Palestinian Talmud*: Sheviit 6:1/36c.
22. See B. Sanhedrin 20b.

23. See *Mishnah*: Sheviit 6:1, Yadayim 4:4 re Amos 9:14.

24. See B. Yevamot 86b re Ez. 8:15; B. Ketubot 26a; also, Josephus, *Antiquities*, 20.8.8.

25. See B. Sotah 48a; *Mishnah*: Demai 2:2–3.

26. See B. Megillah 3a.

27. See B. Sanhedrin 52b; *Mishnah*: Zevahim 12:4.

28. See B. Berakhot 8a re Ps. 87:2.

29. For the original meaning of *am ha'arets*, see Gen. 23:7; for the later meaning, see B. Berakhot 47b.

30. Hence the ancient Jewish custom to have the worshipers in all synagogues, both in the land of Israel and the Diaspora, face the site of the Temple in Jerusalem. See *Tosefta*: Megillah 3:22 re Num. 3:38; B. Berakhot 6a and Tos., s.v. "ahorei bet ha-keneset."

31. See *Mishnah*: Sheqalim 3:4.

32. See B. Gittin 88b.

33. See n. 21 above.

34. See Novak, *The Election of Israel*, 177ff.

35. See B. Avodah Zarah 36b re Deut. 7:3–4; B. Kiddushin 68b.

36. *Mishnah*: Yadayim 4:4.

37. See B. Shabbat 118b and B. Gittin 52a.

38. See *Tosefta*: Avodah Zarah 4:3.

39. B. Arakhin 29a.

40. B. Hagigah 3b.

41. See n. 34 above.

42. See *Palestinian Talmud*: Bikkurim 1:4/64a re Gen. 17:5.

43. See B. Ketubot 11a; also, B. Yevamot 47a.

44. See Josephus, *Antiquities*, 13.9.1.

45. *Tosefta*: Demai 2:4; B. Berakhot 30b.

46. B. Avodah Zarah 64b.

47. See *Religion of Reason out of the Sources of Judaism*, trans. S. Kaplan (New York: Frederick Ungar, 1972), 124ff.

48. See B. Sanhedrin 27a re Exod. 23:1.

49. B. Kiddushin 68b re Deut. 7:4.

50. See M. Silberg, *In Inner Harmony*, ed. Z. Terlo and M. Hovav (Jerusalem: Magnes Press, 1981), 404ff (in Hebrew).

51. See B. Berakhot 32a re Exod. 32:13; B. Sanhedrin 44a re Josh. 7:11.

52. B. Shabbat 88a re Exod. 19:17.

53. See I. England, "The Problem of Jewish Law in a Jewish State," in *Jewish Law in Ancient and Modern Israel*, ed. H. H. Cohn (New York: KTAV, 1971), 143ff.

54. B. Avodah Zarah 36a–b; also, B. Baba Batra 60b.

55. See Maimonides, *Mishneh Torah*: Rebellion, 2.2–7.

56. See David Novak, *Law and Theology in Judaism* 2 (New York: KTAV, 1976), 87ff.

57. See Novak, *The Image of the Non-Jew in Judaism*, 3ff.

58. See B. Avodah Zarah 64b.

59. *Mishneh Torah*: Kingship, 10.11.

60. Ibid., note of Radbaz thereon. Cf. Nahmanides, *Commentary on the Torah*: Gen. 34:13.

61. *Bet ha-Behirah*: Baba Kama 38a, ed. K. Schlesinger (Jerusalem: Mosad ha-Rav Kook, 1967), p. 122. See David Novak, *Natural Law in Judaism* (Cambridge: Cambridge University Press, 1998), 77ff.

62. *Bemidbar Rabbah* 19:20.

63. See Aristotle, *Politics*, 3.11/1287a25–30.

64. See Maimonides, *Mishneh Torah*: Kingship, 12.1.

65. See Novak, *Natural Law in Judaism*, 82ff.

66. See B. Ketubot 110b–111a.

67. See Oliver O'Donovan, *The Desire of the Nations* (Cambridge: Cambridge University Press, 1996), 234.

6

Contested Boundaries: Visions of a Shared World

NOAM J. ZOHAR

THE TASK of producing, from within the Jewish tradition, significant responses to a specific set of questions regarding territorial boundaries calls for extensive reexamination—and sometimes, imaginative extension—of traditional sources. Because of the character of Judaism as a religious tradition focused on one particular people, the analysis often appears to deal exclusively with Jewish or Israeli experience. But my intent, paralleling that of David Novak in the preceding chapter, is to draw insights from this experience that may be applied to a more general context. My remarks below—even where they take issue with Novak's position—are deeply indebted to his original analyses and insights.

Broadly speaking, I endorse the view expressed by Novak, which accords priority to the definition of communal boundaries over the definition of territorial boundaries. In terms of the Jewish tradition, however, I wish to emphasize the contrasting vision of a world shared by all humanity together, contesting the rigidity of political boundaries, territorial and communal alike.

Territorial Boundaries and World Community

Novak begins by positing that "human life is inconceivable outside of a *finite* community"; then in the next sentence, he speaks of a *"defined* community" (emphases added). But "defined" need not be "finite," at least not in Novak's sense of a community which is one of many into which the human race is divided. Why not a world community? This question is raised in the next paragraph, which cites a "version of the Jewish messianic vision that sees one world polity as the goal of all human history." But I find Novak's answer to this insufficient, for he only stresses that even the future world polity is seen as "oriented around Zion as the *axis mundi.*"

What is the nature of this "orientation"? It might be spiritual, akin to the Catholic Church's orientation around Rome; this does not require maintaining territorial boundaries between communities worldwide.

But suppose it is meant in a more strongly political sense, as in the famous prophetic vision of world peace (Isaiah 2:1–4) which Novak cites. In that vision, Zion's spiritual centrality facilitates resolution of disputes by the messianic king: "Thus he will judge among the nations and arbitrate for the many peoples; and they shall beat their swords into plowshares," and so on. On a minimalist reading, Jerusalem is depicted here simply as the site of the world court. But it is hard to imagine effective adjudication of international disputes without some form of world polity. Indeed, the language of the biblical vision—and certainly its elaboration in post-biblical Judaism—points clearly to Jerusalem as the capital of a world state.[1]

It is true that in traditional messianic visions, the world's peoples are normally seen as retaining their distinct identities. But within the framework of a worldwide polity, this does not imply that the nations will continue to be divided by firm political boundaries. The suggestion seems rather to be one of a federation under which peoples maintain their ethnic and cultural diversity.

Moreover, according to the biblical account, even the division of humanity into separate communities is not part of the original scene. In the Bible, human history begins without inter-communal boundaries, and some versions of the messianic vision include elimination of even linguistic boundaries between the world's nations.

Throughout the first ten chapters of Genesis, humanity is one family. The rabbis stressed the anti-racist significance of this common origin: "That is why Adam was created only one—so that none should say to his fellow, 'My forefather was greater than your forefather'" (*Mishnah* San. 4:5). Only at the Tower of Babel does God decide to frustrate human unity and inflict on humans a division of languages (Gen. 11:1–9). The nature of the human trespass which supposedly called for this punishment is far from clear. In any case, latter-day prophetic visions clearly express the hope of a reunited humanity (cf., e.g., Zeph. 3:9).

In actual history, however, humanity is divided into disparate communities. Novak's analysis rightly stresses the primacy of communities over territorial states. It is not that the world is first divided by territorial boundaries and then the human aggregate within each area forms a community; rather, humanity is divided into communities who then in fact maintain territorial boundaries between their distinct living spaces. It is worth adding that this too is illustrated nicely in the Tower of Babel story: it was mutual incomprehension that reduced humanity to many different tongues, causing them to scatter "over the face of the whole earth" (Gen. 11:7–9).

The primacy of communities leaves room for wondering whether they must necessarily be coextensive with particular territories. Here the Jewish people seems to furnish a classic counterexample: a community that has maintained its identity over millennia without territorial integrity or continuity. Against this, Novak points to the Jewish aspiration to return to Zion. But toward the end of his chapter (under "Autonomy"), he seems to relegate this return to a point beyond history, connecting it to the resurrection of the dead, and asserts that denying the significance of Jewish existence in the Diaspora is "bad theology," as it suggests that access to God is restricted to one land. Similarly, at the end of the section on "Ownership," he writes that "the people could survive with her identity intact even when exiled from the land."

Thus the Jewish people do seem to illustrate that a community *can* exist in dispersion. And Novak apparently holds that there is no inherent deficiency in such existence, as long as Jews preserve a utopian dream of return to their land. Against this, it is worth citing the Zionist counterclaim that such existence was always more or less precarious and, in the era of the modern nation-state, was destined to produce catastrophe, as it did most infamously in the Holocaust.

On another level, we might ask whether the community's existence in dispersion and without sovereignty was in fact viewed as satisfactory in terms of the Jewish religious tradition itself. If we look to rabbinic records from the years following the fall of the Second Commonwealth (70 C.E.), it is possible to reconstruct a debate on whether there was any sense at all in continued observance of the Torah's commandments in exile.[2]

The upshot of rabbinic discussions on this point was that outside the land of Israel, an entire class of commandments do not, in fact, apply. These include, first and foremost, the laws relating to agriculture and to the earth's yield—the very same laws that embody most of the Torah's instruction pertaining to social justice. The concern for social justice continued to find partial expression in the communal institutions of *tzedakah* (welfare); but as a minority in foreign lands, Jews could not aspire to mold the shape of economic life around them.

It is perhaps possible that in modern democracies, Jewish communities will be able to flourish and even to extend their commitments to impact society at large, while respecting the traditions and commitments of other communities. If this proves viable, then the long Jewish experience of diaspora life will have yielded a striking example of full communal existence without a territory. Against this, some religious Zionists have argued that the vitality of Judaism in the modern world can be sustained only through life in a Jewish land.[3]

Ownership, Exclusionary Rights, and Violence

Even if people must exist in distinct communities, and even if each community has to exist in some specific place, it does not follow that any local community has a "right to be in a certain place" in the exclusionary sense intended by Novak. The "territorial imperative" on the collective level (Novak's usage—to my mind a dubious extension of the term) is grounded in the fact that control over land is indispensable for producing and maintaining property, to be passed on from one generation to the next. Novak compellingly connects this with ancient agricultural society and its urban centers, pointing to humanity's first child (Cain), who calls the first city by the name of his own child, linking "The perpetuity of the city and the perpetuity of the family/clan."

There is, however, a "missing link" in this narrative, namely, pre-agricultural society. There were—and, indeed, still are—human groups who do not settle down in one place, from the prehistoric hunters and gatherers to various nomadic tribes. The Bible posits the selfsame Cain as the first "tiller of the soil," in juxtaposition to his brother Abel—whom he murdered—the first "keeper of sheep" (Gen. 4:2).

In their classical midrashic commentary, the rabbis describe the altercation which led to the first murder (fratricide): "The one [i.e., Cain] said, 'The land upon which you are standing is mine!' while the other [i.e., Abel] said, 'The garment you are wearing is mine!' "[4] From the perspective of Novak's analysis we might add that the landowner may be able to survive without the wool garment, while no place at all is left for the nomad if title to the entire land is claimed by others. This reveals the inherent connection between agricultural communities, exclusive ownership, and lethal violence. Thus, besides recognizing the territorial forms of social organization covered in Novak's discussion, the Judaic tradition also echoes the moral rebuke implicit in the conception of a nomadic mode of communal existence.

This moral rebuke may be extended to form a critique of certain contemporary theories of political obligation. Specifically, it seems to apply to Locke's grounding of commitment to local laws in "tacit consent," given through one's continued residence within a polity—and particularly one's possession of land therein.[5] After all, Locke was a primary exponent—in modern political philosophy—of the biblical teaching (emphasized by Novak) regarding divine ownership of the world and all its resources. God had given over these resources to humanity collectively, and individuals are permitted to assert ownership only if sufficient similar resources remain for others to take. This seems to imply a significant qualification of Locke's "tacit consent" argument. Locke posits, in effect, that the initial members of the commonwealth make acceptance of its laws a condition for possessing land therein. Now, they can rightly require such a condition only if they may legitimately bar a prospective dweller from taking possession of land in their midst. Their own initial right of (exclusive) possession, however, holds only insofar as the supply of free land is not exhausted. Hence the "tacit consent" grounding of political obligation is valid only if there is land elsewhere, free for the taking—or at least if persons are permitted to reside in a land without incurring the full duties of citizens.[6]

The emphasis on divine ownership of the land—indeed, of the entire world—is certainly a central motif in both biblical and rabbinic Judaism. Minimally, this implies—as Novak notes—that human "domicile is conditional"; God may expel a people from His land because of their "abominations." But (pace Novak) in the Hebrew Bible these "abominations" seem *not* to include idolatry: the Canaanites are expelled because of various forms of incest, or particularly heinous modes of idolatrous worship, such as child sacrifices.[7]

While the Israelites too might be expelled for similar iniquities, their tenancy is dependent on living up to various additional demands. Regarding the nature of these crucial demands, the several books of the Bible do not speak in one voice. While some focus on idolatry,[8] others emphasize social injustice as the prime cause of the downfall of Israel and Judea.[9] This latter emphasis is perhaps closer to the strictures of Leviticus 25, where divine ownership of both land and persons is invoked as a principle of freedom.

The laws of Leviticus 25 forbid the full alienation through sale of either an individual's personal freedom or his inherited portion of the ancestral land. As a piece of "utopian legislation," this probably expressed a revolutionary voice against the supremacy of a landed gentry—corresponding to the prophetic critique: "Ah, those who add house to house and join field to field, till there is room for none but you to dwell in the land!" (Isaiah 5:8).[10] Nevertheless, this notion of unalterable, male-inherited ownership can also become a conservative or even reactionary force.

Similarly, on the collective level, the notion of a holy land allotted by God is liable to produce opposition to pragmatic compromises over internationally disputed boundaries. Such opposition is by no means a necessary implication of the idea of a holy land itself;[11] still, it is voiced by more than a few speakers in contemporary Israeli politics.

Distribution: Boundaries and Commons

Novak, focusing on the internal boundaries between the holdings of tribes, clans, and individuals in ancient Israel, shows how the ownership of land first gave access to status and to (an ancient form of) "citizenship," and then was eventually superseded by the valuation of Torah. This is, then, a story of gradual erosion in the importance of territorial boundaries. Insofar as status came to depend on Torah learning and observance, its attainment became independent of holding land or even of living within the boundaries of the Holy Land.

This does not address, however, the question of what territorial boundaries *do* serve to distribute. Specifically, do they—or should they—function in distributing (1) living space and (2) access to natural resources? The first of these questions will be discussed below, in connection with the issue of diversity. Here I shall touch on the second question, that of natural resources.

It is hard to find anything in traditional Jewish sources about (re)distribution of natural resources across international boundaries. The common assumption in these sources seems to be that inhabitants of each land rightly control whatever it yields: for example, there is mention of international trade, or of Hiram, King of Tyre, offering to supply cedars from Lebanon (1 Kings 5:15–25). I, too, will seek, therefore, to extrapolate from discussions concerning the boundaries established *within* the land of Israel, between the territories of the several tribes, or even between individuals.

The Talmud (B. Bava Kama 80b–81a) cites a list of ten stipulations attributed to Joshua, the leader who divided the land among the tribes. The idea seems to be that the initial title to discrete tribal territories was qualified by these stipulations. They include, for example, fishing rights in the Sea of Galilee (whose shores touch more that one tribal territory); collective rights to a water source that emerges in private land; rights of pasture in untilled open spaces (although they are privately owned); certain rights to free passage; and use of another's land for particular emergencies.

Thus, even though the tribal boundaries distribute living space and main title to the land as agricultural means of production, they are not taken to distribute rights to *all* uses of the territory or of the resources therein. Particular areas (like the Sea of Galilee) or scarce resources (like water) are retained for common access.

Now the Talmud (B. Bava Kama 81b) also appears to hold that these stipulations apply not only in the land of Israel, but also in other locations. This implies that they are seen not as idiosyncratic rules fashioned by a particular ruler, but rather as universal limitations upon land ownership by both individuals and tribes. There thus seems little reason not to extend a similar approach to international boundaries.

The particular details of these "ten stipulations," contained in a text composed roughly two thousand years ago, cannot conceivably serve, of course, as a recipe for industrial (or post-industrial) societies. But they can yield meaningful insights into a Jewish traditional stance favoring "universal commons" as qualifying—both spatially and functionally—the effects of territorial boundaries.

It is worth adding that another rabbinic tradition affirms that Jerusalem "was not included in the distribution to the tribes" (B. Yoma 12a), that is to say, it remained the holding of all in common. This may imply a conception that, insofar as a holy place is deemed crucial for access to spiritual fulfillment, it must not be owned by any particular group.[12]

Diversity: From Community to Nation

With the demise of the First Commonwealth and the exile to Babylon, the territorial boundaries of the Israelite people were dissolved. This eventually produced two opposite responses. Novak mentions one response, that of Ezra the scribe, who fiercely struggled against the assimilation of "the holy stock with the people of the lands." But this view, which may well be characterized as racist, was not universally shared. The post-exilic Isaiah prophesied: "Let not the foreigner say, who has attached himself to the Lord, 'The Lord will keep me apart from his people.' . . . For My House shall be called a house of prayer for all peoples" (Isa. 56:3, 7).[13]

Eventually, the Jews established what we might call a *social boundary*, in lieu of a spatial boundary, to retain their identity as a distinct people. As Novak indicates, this was the setting in which the institution of *giyyur* (Novak: *gerut*) was born: a formal procedure deemed both necessary and sufficient for a non-Jew to become a Jew. To the extent that non-sovereign Jewish communities were political units, the *giyyur* procedure—conferring membership in the community—can be seen as akin to naturalization. But given the political and geographic conditions of Jewish existence, attaining such membership did not often carry significant material advantages.[14] Thus the "social boundary" that defined the Jewish community, permitting scarce internal diversity, excluded outsiders from little other than membership in the community itself.

All of the above cannot be applied in any straightforward way to a sovereign state. Novak rightly notes the extreme novelty of contemporary Israeli concerns over diversity and pluralism; but I believe he is wrong in attributing the novelty solely to the emergence of a *secular* Jewish state.[15]

The significant transformation in Jews' self-understanding with regard to the nature of their collectivity preceded the founding of the Jewish state and even the rise of the Zionist movement. The political emancipation of Jews in the various European countries, which proceeded throughout the nineteenth century—combined with the cultural effects of "enlightenment" and secularization—greatly undermined the definition of the Jewish collectivity in exclusively religious terms[16] (indeed, it was mostly secular Jews who opted for Zionism, essentially a modern national movement).

Hence, the Jewish internal problems of accommodating diversity derive from the contrast between the narrowness of the traditional social-cultural boundaries on the one hand, and the actual diversity amongst modern Jews on the other hand. In the late nineteenth century, (Jewish) Orthodoxy defined itself by splitting away from the wider Jewish society, founding separate communities. All this has yielded a duality in contemporary conceptions of the Jewish collective: Is it a religious community or a nation?

At a crucial point in Novak's discussion, these two conceptions are insufficiently distinguished. He states that

> if the state of Israel is a secular, democratic polity, then there should be no ethnic or religious distinctions made between one group of *Israelis* or another. However, were this to be, the essentially *Jewish* character of the state . . . would no doubt be lost. . . . On the other hand, if the state of Israel is to be a state for Jews governed by traditional Jewish law, then the only full citizens should be those Jews willing to live under the rule of this law. As for secular Jews, or liberal religious Jews, let alone non-Jews, their obviously second-class status would have to be determined by the rabbinical interpreters of that law.[17]

This assumes that "Jewish" must imply adherence to the Jewish religion and to its rabbinic laws. Those who would "like to see Israel as a state for Israelis in the same way, let us say, that Canada is a state for Canadians" are accordingly described as "radically secularist."

What this leaves out is the possibility of Israel as a Jewish state in the same way, let us say, that France is a French state: a national home to the Jewish people. Surely for most Israelis, and for many Jews worldwide, Jewish identity is a matter of *national identity* rather than religious faith or praxis. I will turn shortly to the implications of such nationalism for non-Jewish minorities in Israel; at this point, I wish to emphasize that secular Israelis do not see themselves as less Jewish—and certainly not as enjoying a diminished citizenship in the "Jewish state"—on account of their rejection of religious traditions.[18] This has implications for both the question of joining the Jewish people and the status of non-Jewish citizens in Israel. Let us briefly address each in turn.

The struggle (which has recently received some notoriety) over the procedure for joining the Jewish collective is also not best understood in terms of the difficulties that Israel, as a Jewish-hence-religious state, has with democratic egalitarian ideals. Rather, this struggle reflects the same opposition noted above between two rival conceptions of the Jewish collective.

Those Orthodox Jews who adhere to a narrow definition of Judaism as a religious community have struggled to define the procedure of *giyyur* as the formal expression of a religious conversion. Novak's discussion appears to echo this understanding of *giyyur* in terms of a "prior commitment" to adopt "the full regimen of Jewish law." But others have argued that this understanding of *giyyur* is a modern innovation; classically, it was primarily a mode of joining the Jewish people. True, as long as the Jewish people as a whole adhered to religious faith and praxis, choosing to join them involved a willingness to share their religion. But the primary character of the procedure lies in being symbolically "reborn" into the people, joining an ethnic collective rather than a religious community.[19]

I believe that it is such an understanding of *giyyur* that has facilitated its retention as the only mode of joining the Jewish people recognized by Israeli law. Yet coalition politics leaves the control of the procedure in the hands of rabbinic courts whose members commonly subscribe to the Orthodox, narrow conception of the Jewish collective, and therefore prevent the "conversion" of the great number of persons who would want to do so without making a deep commitment to the Jewish religion.

This gap between popular sentiment and institutional behavior has resulted in a change in the Law of Return, which now grants the right of immigration to Israel, and of immediate conferral of Israeli citizenship, to (so-called) "non-Jewish" relatives of (legally recognized) "Jews." In effect, this gives legal expression to widespread support for an ethnic-national conception of Jewish identity.

That non-Orthodox Israelis have failed, to date, to remold *giyyur* in light of their own intuitive self-understanding is a fact that may have more general significance for theories of nationalism, beyond this specifically Jewish quandary. Insofar as a national state may adopt selective immigration laws, it gives preference to the repatriation of members of the nation living abroad. Such immigration rights would require formal criteria, and the question might easily arise: Who is a (legitimate) member of the nation? Can anyone join (and thereby gain a right to "repatriation")—and if so, how?

In the foregoing discussion I have assumed that if a nation-state, with regard to repatriation, distinguishes between would-be immigrants on the basis of their national affiliation, this does not constitute illicit discrimination. This does not apply, of course, to the treatment of the state's own residents. If "Jewish state" is understood, as I suggested above, as a political home to the Jewish nation, then the status of non-Jewish citizens should be addressed in terms of the normal discourse on the rights of ethnic and national minorities in a democratic nation-state.[20]

The particularly Jewish character of this nation is of concern here mainly to the extent that Jewish national culture, including the strong influence of biblical and post-biblical traditions, produces special obstacles (or, conversely, enhancements) to the toleration of some forms of diversity. Among such obstacles, surely the most serious is the strong Jewish tradition of uncompromising battle against "idolatry."

Novak properly cites here the teaching of ha-Me'iri, who excludes adherents of other monotheistic religions from the strictures against idolaters. Ha-Meiri taught that, unlike the barbarian pagans of old, these are civilized people and must be treated with full respect. It is worth emphasizing that, with regard to such people, ha-Me'iri stipulates that they are "[to be treated] exactly like Jews . . . without any distinction."[21] This is not, however, because they adhere to "religiously acceptable" law (Novak's translation, imprecise in my view), but rather because they are subject to the civilizing force of religion. It is not that social norms require religious scrutiny; quite the contrary, the quality of particular religions may be known by their (civilizing) fruits. The problem with the ancient idolaters was not, according to ha-Me'iri, in their religion per se, but in its barbaric moral import.

This difference in translation has great importance for contemporary issues. Ha-Me'iri certainly did not imagine that people could be civilized without *any* religion, and he would perhaps be greatly perplexed by the phenomenon of, say, civilized (and polytheistic) Hindu society. But since the importance he accords to religion in this context is *only* as (what he took to be) an indispensable force for inculcating civilized norms, his position paves the way for adherents of the Jewish religion to abandon traditions which allow (or even invite) discrimination against heretics or "idolaters."[22]

Mobility

Here I have little to add, except one consideration pertaining to resource allocation. Redistributive taxation is an integral part of the Jewish tradition: this is called *tzedakah,* sometimes imprecisely translated as "charity." Now the scope of *tzedakah* collection and distribution alike includes first of all the residents of a particular polity. Thus the funds collected in the communal *tzedakah* chest are meant primarily for meeting the needs of local indigent persons. The needs of persons in transit are to be met to a far lesser degree.[23]

Hence the halakic tradition may well endorse making it known that the right to move within a group's territorial boundaries does not entail claim-rights (above a certain minimum) to services offered to indigent residents.

Autonomy: The Jewish Traditions of Rabbinic and Political Authority

Novak's emphasis on subordination to God is valid insofar as its intent is a moral-spiritual constraint on politics. But those voices within the Judaic tradition that give greater weight to human autonomy are underrepresented in his exposition in two important senses.

First, it is true that the Torah's underlying premise is a commitment to live by God's law. But this does not confine rabbinic interpretation and implementation of that law to a mode of "discovery" as opposed to "creation" of norms. On the contrary, rabbinic *midrash* is markedly bold in its (re)interpretations of God's "written Torah."[24]

A second point has greater direct bearing upon Novak's proposal of how to deal with aspirations for autonomy by non-Jewish communities within the boundaries of a Jewish polity. Novak claims that if non-Jewish communities are able to have their own autonomous courts of law, they will suffer no political deprivation. This is because, from a traditional point of view, the Jews themselves wield no more than "essentially juridical" sovereignty.

This seems to me a vast understatement of the role of politics and of the autonomy of political authority in Jewish law. True, when the people turned to Samuel seeking a king, God perceived this as a rejection of divine kingship (1 Sam. 8, 12). But much has transpired since then in the Jewish political tradition. Eventually, Nissim Gerondi (fourteenth century, Spain) formulated a doctrine of parallel authority, virtually secularizing politics. Torah law reflects ideal justice, but the requirements of social order call for something else, which the king provides, guided not by Torah but by prudential considerations. And this was not mere speculation about a kingdom long lost, but a reflection of the autonomous powers of the *berurim* (selectmen) who acted as legislators and judges in medieval Jewish communities.[25]

There are many who view the ultimate grounds for such nonrab-binic authority as residing in the consent of the governed, and there-fore extend the same recognition to democratically elected legislatures and governments.[26] Non-Jewish citizens of a Jewish state are subject to the authority of such bodies insofar as they too consent and partici-pate in electing them (as well as being elected to them). And if they in-sist instead on a significant degree of self-government, their claim has prima facie merit—subject, of course, to whatever valid constraints there are on a right to full or partial secession; but that is for another essay.

Notes

1. Novak himself, toward the end of his chapter (in the section on "Auton-omy"), writes that "Zion is meant to be the capital of a united humankind liv-ing under the explicit kingship of God."

2. See *Sifre: A Tannaitic Commentary on the Book of Deuteronomy*, trans. R. Hammer (New Haven: Yale University Press, 1986), secs. 43–44.

3. For example, David Hartman has at one point argued that "The circum-stances of Diaspora existence prevent the development of Judaism as a total way of life," suggesting that even the viability of diaspora communities may depend on the Israeli reality. See David Hartman, "Israel and the Rebirth of Ju-daism," in his *Joy and Responsibility* (Jerusalem: Ben-Zvi–Posner, 1978), 276–86 (quote from p. 285).

4. *Genesis Rabbah* 22:7 (the text here is in my own translation).

5. John Locke, *Two Treatises on Government*, 2nd ed., ed. Peter Laslett (Lon-don: Cambridge University Press, 1967), Second Treatise, secs. 116–19.

6. See the discussion by Harry Beran, *The Consent Theory of Political Obliga-tion* (London: Croom Helm, 1987).

7. This is clear from the specific sins enumerated in Lev. 18 and from nu-merous other biblical passages.

8. Notably the books of Deuteronomy (e.g., 11:17) and Kings (e.g., 2 Kings 17:7–23).

9. Notably the so-called classical prophets, e.g., Micah 3:1–12. On all this, see Yehezkel Kaufmann, *The Religion of Israel, from Its Beginnings to the Babylon-ian Exile* (Chicago: University of Chicago Press, 1960).

10. Or also as protection against usurpation by a monarch; cf. the story of Navot in 1 Kings 22.

11. See Yeshayahu Leibowitz, *Judaism, Human Values, and the Jewish State*, ed. and trans. Eliezer Goldman et al. (Cambridge: Harvard University Press, 1992), 223–28.

12. See the discussion in S. Lieberman, *Tosefta Ki-Fshuta: A Comprehensive Commentary on the Tosefta*, 2nd ed. (Jerusalem: JTS, 1992), Order Zera'im, pt. II, pp. 722–23 (in Hebrew).

13. See M. Weinfeld, "The Universalistic Trend and the Isolationist Trend in the Period of the Return to Zion," *Tarbitz* 33 (1964): 228–42 (in Hebrew), and Noam Zohar, "From Lineage to Sexual Mores: Examining Jewish Eugenics," *Science in Context* 11 (3–4), 1998, 575–85.

14. On the contrary; the traditional response to persons seeking to join the Jewish fold was the warning: "Do you not know that Israel at the present time are persecuted and oppressed?" (B. Yevamot 47a).

15. Indeed, the very conception of a state as both "Jewish" and "secular" appears, in Novak's account, to be a definite oxymoron. Against this, we should recognize a distinction between the realm of Torah and the realm of politics, a point to which I shall return below.

16. See, e.g., Jacob Katz, *Tradition and Crisis: Jewish Society at the End of the Middle Ages*, trans. and with an afterword and bibliography by Bernard Dov Cooperman (New York: New York University Press, 1993).

17. See Novak in the preceeding chapter, under "Diversity."

18. As noted by Novak, instances in which state mechanisms are harnessed to enforce religiously inspired norms are experienced by such persons as unjust intrusions, extracted by an Orthodox minority through a lamentable process of coalition politics—*not* as proper expressions of the state's "Jewish" character.

19. See A. Sagi and Z. Zohar, "The Halakhic Ritual of Giyyur and Its Symbolic Meaning," *Journal of Ritual Studies* 9:1 (1995): 1–13; and more fully in their *Conversion to Judaism and the Meaning of Jewish Identity* (Jerusalem: Bialik Institute and Shalom Hartman Institute, 1994) (in Hebrew).

20. On the notion of a democratic—and liberal—nation-state, see Yael Tamir, *Liberal Nationalism* (Princeton: Princeton University Press, 1993); and David Miller, *On Nationality* (Oxford: Clarendon Press, 1995).

21. Meiri's novellae to tractate *Bava Kama* 113b; for a discussion, see Jacob Katz, *Exclusiveness and Tolerance: Studies in Jewish-Gentile Relations in Medieval and Modern Times* (London: Oxford University Press, 1961), 114–28.

22. Should anything at all be retained from the old war against idolatry? Is there any creed today which should be opposed with the zeal of the biblical prophets? For an illuminating discussion, see Avishai Margalit and Moshe Halbertal, *Idolatry*, trans. Naomi Goldblum (Cambridge: Harvard University Press, 1992).

23. See *The Code of Maimonides (Mishneh Torah)*, trans. Isaac Klein (New Haven: Yale University Press, 1979), bk. 7 (Agriculture), pt. X, "Laws of Gifts to the Poor," chap. 7.

24. See David Hartman, *A Living Covenant: The Innovative Spirit in Traditional Judaism* (New York: Free Press, 1985), 21–108; and Noam Zohar, "Midrash: Amendment through the Molding of Meaning," in *Responding to Imperfection: New Approaches to the Problem of Constitutional Amendment*, ed. Sanford Levinson (Princeton: Princeton University Press, 1995), 307–18.

25. For a discussion and analysis of Gerondi's views, see Menachem Lorberbaum, *Politics and the Limits of Law: Secularizing the Political in Medieval Jewish Thought* (Stanford, Calif.: Stanford University Press, 2001).

26. For detailed sources (in translation) and commentaries, see Michael Walzer et al., eds., *The Jewish Political Tradition, Vol. I: Authority* (New Haven: Yale University Press, 2000), esp. chaps. 8–10.

7

Diversity, Tolerance, and Sovereignty

MENACHEM FISCH

LIKE ALL RELIGIONS of long standing, Judaism does not speak in one voice, and perhaps never did—certainly not on the issues under consideration. It is customary to distinguish three major streams or movements within contemporary Judaism in the West—Orthodox, Conservative, and Reform—each standing for a cascade of further divisions. The three movements differ primarily in their attitude to halakah, the code of Jewish law. Whereas Orthodox Jews accept halakah as the first place of reference and sole arbiter of authority, Conservative Judaism sees halakah as a crucial source of value holding "a vote, but not a veto" in determining personal behavior. Reform Judaism, by contrast, insists upon the primacy and ultimacy of personal autonomy in grounding religious norm and individual conscience. Although all three are, sociologically speaking, relatively recent developments, Orthodox communities alone boast full allegiance to a code they consider dating back to at least the talmudic era of late antiquity. This essay is written from an Orthodox point of view, from that of halakah as it is understood and practiced today by the majority of Orthodox Jews. I do so for three reasons. First, in being an Orthodox Jew myself I prefer to "report" from a perspective I feel I can speak for, and to deliberate questions that are real for me. Second, and more significant, bound by deep religious conviction to a strict and richly detailed system of ritual and social norms, Orthodox Jews are challenged far more seriously by problems of ethical diversity than their more liberally motivated Conservative and Reform coreligionists. Third, and for me most important, is the extremely potent reality of these problems for the state of Israel. Israel is unique in being the only modern society in which many observant, halakically committed Jews not only serve as municipal and parliamentary representatives of their communities but partake actively in executive extracommunal governmental roles. It is here that traditional Orthodox Judaism is swiftly and uneasily awakening to problems akin to those discussed in other communities. I say "akin to" because they are not identical. Problems of ethical diversity loom large in this context but do not always manifest themselves in questions of citizenship,

physician-assisted suicide, or even same-sex unions as acutely as they
do from the perspectives of other ethical systems. I shall try in what follows to characterize the problem and a possible solution to it from the
viewpoint of halakic Judaism without straying too far from the guidelines we have been asked to follow.

Ideal Societies

In one sense Orthodox Judaism's choice of ideal society is obvious.
Owing to its built-in sensitivity to the right of all citizens to the culture,
lifestyle, and religion of their choice, modern multicultural democracy
is by far the form of host government most favored by Orthodox Jewish communities. The communal autonomy granted by such a state
provides and protects the cultural, educational, and religious space
needed for them to run their lives as they see fit. The price to pay,
though, is as obvious as the choice, for by the same token, in such a
state many whose cultural and religious choices promote or enable
forms of conduct deemed sinful and heretical in the eyes of halakah
will be equally provided for and protected. Preference for such a political setting requires (protest, civil action, and lobbying permitted by the
law notwithstanding) undertaking in advance to live and let live
within it. Ethical diversity is a necessary consequence of multiculturalism. To desire such an environment requires, at the very least, accepting as ethical a diversity that is sanctioned by the law of the land.
Needless to say, the more decided and rigid one's own ethical system
is, the greater the chance of finding within that permitted diversity systems diametrically opposed to one's own.

Setting aside the much-discussed question of how liberal a liberal
government should be toward violations of liberalism among its autonomous communities, let us look at the same tension from the opposite direction. To what extent, let us first ask, can observant Jews, participating in a larger liberal society, silently put up with what they strongly
consider to be sinful and heretic practices of neighboring communities?
How far does halakah permit one to go in tolerating others for the sake
of maintaining one's own autonomy? The question is one of ethical
plurality—not at the managerial level, but of ethical plurality nonetheless.

Of course, the question of tolerance only arises when *in*tolerance is a
viable option. If a community is powerless to raise its voice and take
action against the sinners and heretics outside its boundaries, its putting up with them means nothing. On the other hand, one does not actually have to be *in* power to take such action. The levels of protest,
civil action, access to the media, and boycotting permitted in most

modern democracies provide sufficient means for one community to make the life of another quite unpleasant. Today Orthodox Jewish communities in the Western world enjoy such power like any other and are fully capable of loudly voicing their views for and against the various ethical systems they encounter. For them, as never before, the decision to put up with sinful conduct outside the community has ceased to be a matter of necessity and become a matter of choice.

Let us be clear about the question we are asking: what is required of observant Jews in liberal democracies is not to rethink their notions of sin and heresy but to reconsider the appropriate *attitude* toward the sinful and the heretical required of them by their religion. Needless to say, the question does not arise with respect to all forms of conduct frowned upon by Jewish law but only with respect to those considered desirable by some, and at least permissible by state law. What is minimally required is not for Judaism to change, or even to relativize its ethics, only to be able, in meaningful religious ways, to justify passively turning a blind eye to the forms of sin and heresy legally practiced outside its own communities. On this, I argue, halakic Judaism comes relatively well equipped.

But is the culturally autonomous community, keeping politely to itself within a wider liberal state run by others, all that contemporary halakic Judaism aspires to politically? For many Orthodox Jews the answer is still a firm yes. Prior to the messianic era, they argue insistently, such an exilic existence is all God-fearing Jewish communities are allowed actively to pursue. On these grounds the vast majority of Orthodox rabbis vehemently opposed the newly formed Zionist movement at the turn of the century.[1] Since then things have changed, however. For the last hundred years, and especially since the establishment of the state of Israel in 1948, the comparatively small group of halakically committed pro-Zionists[2] has grown steadily to the extent that today the vast majority of observant Jews living in Israel participate actively in state and municipal politics. They are organized in a number of religious parties—ranging from the religiously pro-Zionist to the religiously a-Zionist (i.e., politically indifferent), and excluding the relatively small group of religiously anti-Zionists—whose representatives occupy key positions at the municipal, parliamentary, and governmental levels. For them, I submit, the question of the ideal society for halakic Judaism becomes exceedingly more difficult.

The reason is simple: at the managerial level turning a blind eye to the halakically objectionable is no longer enough. To partake actively in running (as opposed merely to living in) a liberal democracy requires more than to tolerate passively those with whom one disagrees. Observant members of the Israeli government—the ministers of education, the treasury, or the interior, for instance—cannot get away with merely ignoring those they consider sinful and heretic. As managerial level executives of a multicultural society they are required to take active responsibility for the well-being and welfare of all communities— including those whose lifestyles they consider blatantly objectionable. Jewish law distinguishes between passive toleration and active enabling. There is a clear halakic line to be drawn between employing passive judicial restraint and abstaining from taking action against the halakically objectionable, and going out of one's way to assist them. For halakic Judaism the question of the ideal society is hence an extremely tricky one depending on the nature of the halakic warrant sought.

Halakah as it stands permits Jewish rulers to grant considerably less freedom to their subjects than they would have liked their rulers to grant them as subjects. The discrepancy between looking at questions of ethical diversity from above and from below, as it were, becomes especially problematic in Israel where Orthodox Jewish communities find themselves for the first time in the modern era having to tackle the problem from both perspectives simultaneously.[3] In what follows I do my best to discuss the general question of ethical plurality, as well as a number of specific problems from each of the two halakic perspectives, with a view to highlighting the difference between the diaspora and Israeli case. I then conclude by suggesting a way of reconciling the two approaches within the world of halakic discourse.

One last word of introduction: rather than discuss ideal, theoretical models of statehood that have been suggested from time to time in premodern halakic writings, I concentrate in what follows on the two real latter-day contexts in which halakically committed Jews now freely confront ethical diversity—namely, latter-day Israel and the other Western democracies. With the establishment of the state of Israel Jews regained full political sovereignty for the very first time since long before the first formative halakic texts came into existence. For the best of two millennia self-rule was envisaged in halakic writings, if at all, only in the most remote and idyllic terms, never as a realistic possibility. The few texts in which a more detailed conception of Jewish statehood is attempted were written long before the emergence of the modern nation-state.[4] Modern Israel is not of Orthodox Jewish making. It preserves an ethical diversity far wider than halakah is capable of accommodating prima facie. It poses a real, rather than a theoretical challenge to traditional modes of thought—perhaps the greatest challenge to halakah of the modern era, certainly the most urgent one. But first to the problem of ethical plurality outside of Israel.

Ethical Diversity from Below

Halakic Judaism's capacity for passively tolerating objectionable ethical systems adhered to beyond the confines of the community is almost unlimited. In this respect, the question of ethical pluralism can be answered by halakic Jews, by means of a healthy, pragmatic, halakically motivated tolerance. "Ethical pluralism," in the normative sense of the word, is the wrong term to use in this context, however, and, I am tempted to say, so is "tolerance." Pluralists attach value to other systems of thought and welcome their existence. Halakic Judaism, as it is currently understood by its practitioners, does not.

Toleration is different. To merely tolerate a person, an idea, or a form of conduct does not imply attaching intrinsic value to its existence. To tolerate per se is minimally to agree to put up with the objectionable, to suffer in silence its unwelcome presence. To merely tolerate a person, idea, or form of conduct implies not looking upon it favorably in any way, or being curious to find out more about it, but only a willingness silently and passively to accept its existence. Most existing ideas of tolerance come grounded in liberal assumptions on the nature of humankind. We tolerate other people's beliefs because one's beliefs are regarded one's private business, or because individual autonomy is held sacred. As it stands, Jewish law contains nothing comparable with the sanctioning of an individual's right to cultural freedom or of individual autonomy in modern liberal thought. Halakic Judaism tolerates the objectionable not in respect of someone else's rights but in order to avoid unnecessary trouble. The halakic principles employed to justify slackening halakic standards (when applicable) out of a concern for social or political tension are *mipnei darkei shalom* and *mipnei darkei eiva*—that is to say, for the sake of peace or for the sake of avoiding hostility. In theory this boils down to a rather crude, ad hoc, and wholly practical version of Kant's categorical imperative—not: do not do to others that which you would not like others to do to you, but rather avoid doing to others what the law would have otherwise required you to do to them for fear of them not appreciating your noble intentions and retaliating by doing the same or worse to you. Such reasoning is morally coarse to say the least, pragmatic in the bad sense of the term, but it is genuine, and, most important, it works admirably well.

Like most religions, Judaism discriminates in two different and largely independent ways. Halakah discriminates, on the one hand, between prohibited and permitted conduct and, on the other, between people: between members of the faith and those who are not. (I am ignoring here discrimination within the community—for example, between male and female members—on which something more is said later.) In a variety of situations, Jewish law discriminates against gentiles qua gentiles—sinful or not. (These situations range from the purely ritual [e.g., exclusion from certain ceremonies] to the worryingly ethical [e.g., a status lower than Jews in certain life-saving situations].) One may speak therefore of two separate forms of religious toleration: a willingness to put up with objectionable conduct, and a willingness to include the other where the other would otherwise be excluded. Both are easily accommodated by the pragmatism of arguing "for the sake of peace." "In a city populated by Jews and gentiles, Jewish and gentile administrators are appointed," states the Talmud of Palestine, "taxes are collected [equally] from Jew and gentile, [from which] the needs of the Jewish and gentile poor are [jointly] supplied." One does not discriminate between the Jewish and gentile sick, the Talmud goes on to rule, one attends equally to the dead of each community (although strictly speaking Jews and gentiles should be allocated different cemeteries), and pays equal respect to their respective mourners—all in the interest of peace.[5] According to this fundamental ruling, halakah actually encourages forming shared, representative administrations for "multicultural" societies, to risk an anachronism, rather than insist on Jewish control. But that is a different issue.

In principle at least, observant Jewish communities encounter no problem refraining from taking the offensive action required of them by halakah whenever there is the slightest chance of retaliation. Though the metaphysics that back them may not always be to everyone's taste (e.g., when looking for ways around the halakic prohibition against desecrating the Sabbath to save the life of a non-Jew), overriding halakic prohibition with principles like "for the sake of peace" is about all that is needed for halakic Judaism to live peacefully amid the sinful, the heretical, and the non-Jewish.

An interesting point to notice is that while concern "for the sake of peace" provides halakically meaningful justification for not doing what one would otherwise be required to do, it provides no justification for remaining silent about it. Excluding situations where one prefers to keep a low profile for the sake of peace, one would expect communities with firm positions on controversial issues to at least participate in the public debate where such debate is allowed. To agree to tolerate other positions does not mean giving up your own. It is not as if Orthodox Judaism's views on the moral issues currently debated in the United States are uncomfortably extreme. Halakah may not always accord with the most liberal approach, but it hardly ever coincides with the other extreme. And yet, outside Israel, one hardly ever encounters serious Orthodox Jewish involvement in any of the public ethical debates. Such questions are frequently raised in sermons and in the lively responsa literature, and are firmly, and to a great extent unanimously, ruled upon by Orthodox halakists *without*, however, any visible proselytizing intention of causing anyone else to improve their ways. Orthodox Jews have quite thoroughly absented themselves from the public moral debate everywhere but in Israel—so much so that it seems inappropriate to describe their attitude to the moral diversity that they encounter outside Israel as one of toleration. Sheer indifference seems more like it. Orthodox communities in the West, though perfectly welcome as bona fide members of society, tend to keep to themselves politically, and appear to show extremely little if any interest in influencing the public sphere—other, of course, than to lobby for their own communal needs. It is not as if they would have liked to make a stand but refrain from doing so for the sake of peace. It is more as if they simply couldn't care less.

Paradoxically, the level of indifference exhibited by Jewish communities to the moral space facilitated by state law, and to the moral choices made by others, changes as if it were a direct function of their degree of halakic seriousness. The stricter one is, the more seriously one takes one's religious duties, the less, it seems in the Jewish case, is one concerned with how other individuals and communities live their lives. In place of the religiously meaningful mechanisms of judicial restraint and considered toleration made available by halakah (that serve in themselves to elevate the value of peaceful coexistence) diaspora Orthodox Jews largely display an attitude of unconsidered apathy toward the moral choices and lifestyles of all but their very own. Apathy and moral indifference are not uncommon Western maladies. Latter-day philosophical relativism doesn't help on this count either. Although of a kind, the Orthodox Jewish case is different, however, and hardly a modern or postmodern phenomenon. An understandable result of centuries of oppression and persecution, it is the defense mechanism of the less emancipated exhibiting an instinctive, disengaging, almost austere, ethnocentric dismissal of the outside world. Typical of very many Orthodox communities throughout the Western world is a deeply entrenched sense of not belonging, of having no responsibility, and of having no desire to be responsible for anything or anyone outside the enclave of their own community.

The upshot for the problem of ethical diversity is clear enough. Whether for the sake of the peace, or out of sheer indifference, as long as state law does not require Jews to violate halakah, the fact that it permits others to do so, or even sanctions such violations, poses Orthodox Judaism no problem at all. Observant Jews are by no means ethical pluralists, let alone ethical relativists. Their views on the problems under consideration (though not always identical) are firm and determined.

Still, halakically autonomous Jewish communities are ideal (if silent and inactive) partners to as widely diverse an ethical plurality as liberals would have. As long as they are allowed to keep to themselves, and their rabbis granted the authority to make their own decisions and issue their own rulings on such issues as abortion, physician-assisted suicide, and one-sex unions, ethical pluralism is not a problem for diaspora Judaism.

The situation in Israel, however, is another matter entirely.

Managing Ethical Diversity: The Problem of Sovereignty

As noted at the outset, there remains a minority of ultra-Orthodox Jews living in Israel who continue to view themselves "exiled by the hand of Israel."[6] Their hostility toward Israelis, Israeli society, and the Israeli government and legal system ranges from a furious tight-lipped scorn to passive disobedience. They refuse to engage. In particular, they exhibit no desire to form an opposition within Israeli society or in any other way influence anyone or anything beyond the locked gates of their own community. If one ignores their ideological hostility to the very idea of a (nonmessianic, secular) Jewish state, their attitude toward the ethical diversity existing outside the community is, in practice, much the same as that of their Orthodox brethren abroad—they too couldn't care less. In the past Jews were powerless to react. Today, in Israel as in other Western democracies, this is no longer the case, as Orthodox Jews know very well. And yet, as noted, many orthodox communities speak and act as if it were. They seem to prefer to be viewed and to view themselves as incapable of making a stand, than as having chosen not to. If diaspora Orthodox Jews can still be described as having not yet fully comprehended the fact that they are ruled by a genuinely benign and welcoming alien state, the same cannot be said of the Israeli ultra-Orthodox. Their insular exilic existence is consciously self-fashioned—far less a failure to adjust than a considered and largely self-constructed preference. They seem truly to prefer living inwardly devoid of civil or social responsibilities at the mercy of an oppressive alien state—not unlike ancient Israel's desire to return to Egyptian captivity rather than accept the responsibilities of freedom. Due to its self-imposed, exilic mind-set, the anti-Zionist, Israeli, ultra-Orthodox minority remains austerely indifferent to the ethical diversity of Israeli society, and hence unproblematic in terms of the issues under consideration. For the vast majority of observant Israeli Jews, however, the problems are real, and by no means as easily avoided.

By assuming municipal and governmental responsibilities, Orthodox Jews in Israel cannot remain indifferent to the moral choices of
other Israeli communities, especially those supported by Israeli law.
Nor are the halakic justifications for passively tolerating the sinful for
the sake of maintaining the peace of much avail. For it is one thing for
an Orthodox community to turn a blind eye to idolatry or to systematic
transgressions of the dietary laws or the Sabbath restrictions by neighboring communities "for the sake of the peace," but quite another for
an Orthodox Jew to take it to be his job to assist actively and systematically such sinful conduct.

The role of government and municipal executives in multicultural
democracies differs decisively from that of communal leadership.
Whereas the job of the latter, even when acting as representatives of
their home communities or cultures, is primarily to look out for their
own, the former, regardless of personal conviction, assume responsibility for the security and welfare of all. The Israeli ministers of education, religious affairs, the interior, tourism, and the like cannot perform
their governmental duties by merely turning a tolerating, peace-
maintaining blind eye to what their religion considers sinful. It is their
job, in their designated areas of responsibility, to actively ensure the security, the welfare, and the capacity of each and every community to
flourish according to its custom and conviction (insofar as, in doing so,
nothing is done to harm other communities, or to prevent them from
exercising their own, identical rights, of course). If halakah firmly forbids Jewish travel agents to assist actively or profit from Muslim and
Christian pilgrims, for instance,[7] it similarly forbids Jewish governmental officials to do so. But to volunteer such active assistance is the very
job of the Ministry of Religious Affairs, of Finance, and of Education to
name but three. Not only is the Ministry of Education, for instance, expected to assist Muslim and Christian communities in planning and
funding their annual school trips to the holy places of their respective
faiths but also, as a matter of course, is constantly engaged in improv-
ing the system—that is to say, in rendering their halakically objectionable activity all the more efficient and worthwhile. And the same goes
for the gravely sinful behavior of un-Orthodox Jews. The very same
ministry is responsible for the ongoing activities of the various Israeli
schools and youth movements—some of which are decidedly and, in
the latter case, even ideologically irreligious. Most of their out-of-town
activity—field trips, camping outings, hikes—are scheduled for the
days held most holy by halakah. And, again, personal convictions
notwithstanding, it is the ministry's job not only to assist and fund
such blatant and public desecration of the Sabbath and the High Holi-
days, but to study them year by year, learn from past mistakes, and

render them all the more enjoyable, efficient, and effective! This is a far cry from grudgingly turning a blind eye to sin for the sake of peace.

Although it is obviously the most desirable form of government when viewed from below, as things now stand halakically, the liberal, multicultural democracy is at the same time the form of government most awkward for observant Jews to manage from above. The discrepancy is not paradoxical, but it certainly premises a moral double standard that requires urgent attention. From the point of view of the current state of Jewish law, the discrepancy is unavoidable, and the problem of ethical pluralism acute. If they are to abide by their halakic convictions, Orthodox Jewish legislators and members of government are powerless to do for others what they would have expected others to do for them. The social- turned liberal-democratic vision of statehood on which modern Israel has modeled itself is one that halakah, as it is currently conceived, is incapable of accommodating. From the administrative viewpoint of the sovereign, liberal democracy and Jewish law are to a large extent diametrically opposed.

In principle, Orthodox Israelis have three options, none of them easy. One is to relinquish all Jewish pretension for sovereignty at the metacommunal level. According to this view, dreams of Jewish independence should be limited to self-rule in the narrowest sense of the term. Judaism should be considered a purely communal affair, harboring no desire to rule or to manage the lives of members of other cultural or religious groups.[8] Needless to say, such a position is untenable for those who regard national independence and political sovereignty as possessing religious significance. Orthodox Zionists reject it completely. Those for whom modern statehood is a religiously viable option—not to say a religious duty—have two further options: they can remain faithful to halakah as they find it and reject Western democracy as a halakically inappropriate model for Jewish statehood. Or they can attempt to make room, from the point of view of the state, for a religiously meaningful approval of ethical pluralism by rethinking halakah along lines akin to latter-day developments in political philosophy. There is no other option. As we have seen, in the role of sovereign, one cannot, in principle, remain loyal both to halakah and to the ideas of liberal democracy as each of them stands at present. One of them needs to be significantly modified.

The last option—that of refashioning halakah in ways capable of assigning religious value to actively assisting halakically objectionable forms of conduct—is both the most desirable and prima facie the most unthinkable. I believe, however, that the formative texts of halakic Judaism contain important resources for the meaningful construction of such a position—a thesis I briefly outline in the concluding section. The other two positions do not solve the halakic problem but merely lower the ante: either by abandoning political sovereignty or by abandoning the most advanced (and highly desired from below) model of statehood. I pursue them in the present context no further.

Social Regulation

Bearing in mind the fundamental ethical double standard I have pointed to between the two ideal social frameworks—that by which to be governed as opposed to that by which to govern others—let us turn to the first problem we have been set. The problem of social regulation arises, of course, for both. The issue here steers closer to the latter, however, in no longer being that of living in an ethical diversity, but that of stating normatively and in advance whether and, if so, when the power of the state should be invoked in order to determine the limits of ethical diversity. The difference between the situation inside and outside of Israel is still striking in this respect, despite the fact that the question is a normative one.

Questions of social regulation are relevant to both the upper and lower limits of ethical pluralism: how much and how little should be permitted? From a given ethical point of view the law can be found wanting either for enabling forms of conduct considered objectionable by the system in question, or for ruling objectionable forms of conduct that are held by the system to be one's duty, or are at least considered perfectly benign. Concern for problems of the first kind—those to do with the law permitting too much—often reflects consideration for others, a concern for the moral standards of those with whom one disagrees. Taking a stand on such issues often bespeaks a sense of responsibility that extends beyond the boundaries of the community. Questions of the second kind, by contrast, normally premise a concern for one's own.

Not surprisingly perhaps, the only questions of social regulation that have exercised Orthodox Jewish communities outside Israel have been those to do with the Jewish community directly. Despite the fact that Jewish law contains several categories of prohibitions addressed explicitly to non-Jews[9] (and, of course, many, many more addressed to Jews qua Jews), I know of no Orthodox Jewish action taken with a view to impelling Western legislators to "emend the world" by setting the permissible limits of ethical diversity in accord with these norms. Whatever Orthodox Jewish protest exists in this respect is motivated, as far as one can see, solely by self-interest. Although all Western systems of

law are excessively liberal by any halakic standard, its promiscuity is
challenged by Orthodox Jews only when they themselves are directly
effected—as when certain forms of anti-Semitic rallying, art, and literature are permitted in the name of freedom of speech. Other than that,
diaspora Orthodox Jews remain largely indifferent to the upper permissible limits of the ethical plurality in which they live.

Challenges to the lower limits are more common, yet equally, if naturally self-centered. Ritual slaughter, *shehita*, is a good example. One of
the basic Jewish dietary laws has to do with the way an animal is put
down. Halakah requires that it be done by means of a swift and deft
slitting of the throat performed by a specially trained *shohet*. Eating the
flesh of an otherwise kosher animal or bird killed any differently is
strictly prohibited. Swedish law, for example, requires that animals be
put down by certain, painless methods only, and prohibits Jewish *shehita* on moral grounds. Requests for separating men from women on
public transport in and out of ultra-Orthodox neighborhoods in New
York City are systematically turned down as unconstitutional, and the
building of Succoth during the feast of tabernacles is known to violate
municipal regulations in some cities. By the same token, although I
know of none, one can imagine societies legislating against ritual circumcision for similar reasons (customarily performed publicly without
an anesthetic). In cases such as these, Jewish attempts to impel legislators to allow the state to regulate cultural diversity more generously are
not uncommon.

The paradox I pointed to at the outset is thus intensified. Despite the
seriousness in which halakah is studied and followed by its practitioners, Orthodox Jewish communities remain generally unmoved by
society's promiscuity toward forms of conduct they regard ethically
or halakically offensive (except when they themselves are affected).
The law is, therefore, hardly ever criticized for being too liberal, but
only for not being liberal enough. There seems to be no general
(meta)ethical principle at work here beyond sheer ethnocentricity. If
there was, one would expect Orthodox Jews to speak up in defense of
other ethnic groups similarly constrained and on behalf of the morally
depraved, for whom, in their opinion, the law is not strict enough.
There is no sign of either. As long as exilic Orthodox Jews are allowed
to practice their religion freely and to make their own ethical choices,
they remain, it seems, all but indifferent to the limits of state involvement in setting the levels and regulating the boundaries of ethical
diversity.

The situation in Israel is very different. In fact it is almost wholly re-
versed. There exists a small measure of state-imposed banning of custom for ethical reasons, though not against Jews, and never of actual

religious law. (The state, for instance, prohibits marriages between minors although they are customary [but not religiously required] among certain Muslim communities.) No authentic Jewish custom or ritual is banned by Israeli law. With regard to community life proper, observant Jews do not find themselves in conflict with Israeli law. Orthodox Israeli Jews, in other words, have no reason to complain about the law being too restrictive. Orthodox complaint, and there is much of it in Israel, concentrates exclusively on the law being overly permissive.

Unlike anywhere else in the world, Orthodox Israelis campaign vigorously, and not unsuccessfully, for limiting what they take to be public violations of halakah proper and of what they take to be halakic sensibilities and sensitivities. For the most part, the issues in question are more ritual than ethical, although the involuntary imposition of ritual constraints certainly constitutes an ethical problem. Paradoxically, this is not altogether a bad thing. The bright side is that here one encounters, for the first time, at least in the modern era, real, if perspectival, Orthodox concern for the moral and religious character of the other. When Israeli television was first introduced, there was a huge fight about whether broadcasting should be allowed by law on the Jewish Sabbath. The question had nothing to do with the integrity of religious life among the Orthodox—many of whom continue to avoid television altogether. To this day, by the sheer force of Orthodox parliamentary bargaining power, public transport is discontinued by law on Saturdays and during the Jewish festivals in almost all Israeli townships, and food in state-owned institutions and modes of transport is kept strictly kosher. And one could cite many more examples of this kind. Unlike diaspora Orthodoxy, and unlike the militant anti-Zionist ultra-Orthodox minority, Israeli Orthodox involvement regarding questions of ethical plurality is motivated by more than narrow self-interest. Theirs is a deep concern for the moral and religious character of the wider society and the nature of the public sphere. Like their coreligionists abroad, Orthodox Israelis would prefer the ethical diversity in which they live severely limited; here, however, they are willing to do something about it.

And yet, energetic as the campaigning may become, at the metacommunal level the accepted rules of the game remain democratic. Once the majority has made its ruling, and the issue is settled legally, a grudging tight-lipped toleration kicks in naturally. There is bound to be some huffing and puffing, but by and large the rallying, lobbying, boycotting, and public protest remain well contained within the boundaries of perfectly acceptable civil action. As noted earlier, Jewish law comes well equipped when passive toleration is the order of the day. The problem for Israeli Orthodox Jews, I repeat, is far less that of living with parliamentary or municipal rulings they consider halakically objectionable than that of taking active responsibility as governmental executives for their implementation, once they're accepted. Abiding by majority rule, even when in violation of the spirit or letter of halakah, is for halakic Judaism the kind of *force majeure* they are fully capable of silently (if sullenly) living with, as long as it does not entail active violation of halaka on their part. Taking responsibility for implementing such rulings does—and it is here, I have argued, that the most pressing problems lie.

Still, Israeli orthodoxy has come a long way in taking civic responsibility for society at large and, allowing for the full range of legitimate protest and civil action, in accepting the democratic processes of decision making as the final arbiter. What it yet lacks is the capacity to view such diversity as religiously desirable, as something worthy of an enabling framework.

Citizenship

Although Jews have a long history of being denied the full rights of citizenship, it was normally not done on ethical grounds. Delineating the boundaries of nationhood and with them those of full-blooded citizenship is a problem the Western world has grappled with painfully until quite recently. The grounds for the debate, however, were hardly ever ethical. Israel too has its share of ethnic chauvinist extremists who, from time to time, question the right of non-Jewish Israelis to fully fledged citizenship and to determine the fate and national identity of the Jewish state. They demand that major national issues, ranging from questions of church and state to the sealing of peace treaties, require by law a "Jewish" or "Zionist" parliamentary majority. But, again, although the outcome is of major ethical consequence, the motivation of such groups is usually not.

Halakah has nothing to say on how civil society should handle ethically based disagreements about civil status, but from time to time halakists have been exercised by certain questions of civil status and of the proper deployment of civil rights and duties. Let me briefly discuss one such issue by way of an example.

The question of the right of women to vote and to run for office was raised and debated in Palestine around 1920. The context was halakic, but some of the main lines of argument utilized by both parties were ethical.[10] Rabbi Avraham Isaac ha-Kohen Kook, Ashkenazic chief rabbi at the time, ruled firmly against women's suffrage. He organized his reasoning under three headings as answers to three separate questions:

(a) Regarding the law: is it permitted or prohibited by halakah? (b) Regarding the common good: which of the options better promotes the common good for Israel? (c) Regarding the ideal: which is better supported by our moral consciousness? He goes on to explain: "The exposition must take all these values into account, for I must relate to all ranks [of the public]: the completely faithful of Israel for whom the halakhic ruling is central, those for whom the nation's is decisive, and those whose main view is to the moral ideal in itself." Rabbi Kook's consideration of all three aspects clearly bespeaks, even at that early date, a real sense of social responsibility extending far beyond the world of discourse of the community of his immediate followers.

Regarding halakah proper, he keeps his reasoning brief and simple: in all our canonical writings, he asserts, "we hear one voice; namely, that the duty of fixed public service falls upon men, for 'It is Man's manner to dominate and not Woman's manner to dominate.' Roles of authority, judgment, and testimony are not her domain, as all her honor is within [the confines of the home]."[11] The pragmatic and moral arguments he offers follow suit. It is also in the common good not to allow women's suffrage, because the "best of the gentiles generally and the best of the British people particularly" in whose hands lies the fate of the Jewish people's claim to the land of Israel, expect of us to realize the values of the Bible, which they too hold sacred but lack the ability to live up to, and in which "the special feeling of respect towards Woman . . . is based and centered on domestic life." The moral reasons offered by Rabbi Kook focus on the holiness of the Jewish household and the centrality of domestic peace and tranquillity for the quality of national life. "The psychological cause of the call for women's right to participate in public elections in [other] nations," he states, "comes fundamentally from the unhappy position of the masses of women in these nations. Had their family's situation been as peaceful and dignified as it is generally in Israel, women themselves . . . would not demand what they term 'rights' of election for women in a manner that might ruin domestic peace." He concludes that "We dare not obliterate the splendor of our sisters' lives, and embitter them through the din of opinions and disputations of elections and political questions." For the sake of family harmony, politics—the business of men—should be banned from the private domain and duly confined to its proper place: the public sphere.

Despite Rabbi Kook's considerable standing among the Orthodox community during those years, and the fact that he was joined in his ruling against women's suffrage by several other rabbinic authorities, his ruling went wholly unheeded. One reason for this was the sephardic Rabbi Ben-Zion Hai Uziel's very different ruling issued in response to Kook's. His conclusions were stated as firmly and as un-equivocally as Kook's: "A woman has the perfect right of participation in elections . . . [and a] woman may also be elected by the consent and ordinance on the community." He offers an ethical argument in favor of his position, and an ethical rejoinder to Kook's ethical argument against it. "It is inconceivable" that women be denied the right to vote. "For in these elections we raise leaders upon us, and empower our rep-resentatives to speak in our name, to organize the matters of our *Yishuv*, and to levy taxes on our property. . . . How then can one simul-taneously . . . lay upon [women] the duty to obey those elected by the people, yet deny them the right to vote in the elections?" His rejection of Kook's argument for domestic tranquillity is equally decisive: if women's suffrage is to be prohibited

> for the sake of preserving the peace at home . . . we must also deny the right of voting to adult sons and daughters still living in their father's home. For in all cases where our rabbis concerned themselves with preserving tran-quillity, they gave equal treatment to the wife and to adult sons living at home (see Bavli, *Bava Metzia* 12a–b). . . . But the truth is, that differences of opinion will surface in some form or other, for no one can suppress com-pletely his opinions and attitudes. Rather familial love based on mutual la-bor is strong enough to withstand such differences of opinion.

He proves that, in addition, women may be elected by showing that the prohibition against appointing a queen stems not from halaka deeming women ineligible in principle for the job but from a concern for the "dignity of the community." Public opinion is incapable of overriding considerations of the former kind, he argues, but has every-thing to do with the latter. If a majority of the community votes for a woman, it would be a violation of its dignity *not* to appoint her!

Rabbi Uziel won the day. Participation in the Israeli elections is still debated among the ultra-Orthodox, but even they make no halakic distinction between men and women in this respect. For Orthodox Judaism, women's suffrage is no longer a problem. Furthermore, in two of Israel's five Orthodox parties women also run for office.

However, the question under consideration is not that of Orthodox Judaism's position on the issue of citizenship but that of its position on the way ethically based disagreements about citizenship should be handled. Let us imagine, then, that Rabbi Kook had won the day and ask what would have been his and his followers' reaction to the state allowing women who felt differently to vote anyway. Although the question was never raised, had it been, it would have brought us back to the point I have been making all along. Orthodox women, even in Israel, would have followed the rabbi's ruling and piously refrained from voting while grudgingly accepting the fact that other women do. They would have no problem whatsoever with the fact that others might think differently, and be allowed to do so, as long as they themselves were able to live their lives as they see fit. Problems would only arise when an Orthodox Jew was put in charge of actively implementing the women's vote law. It would be halakically problematic even if all his job amounted to was to inform women of their rights. As I have stated repeatedly, ignoring violations of Torah is one thing, actively promoting them is another.

Life-and-Death Decisions, Human Sexuality, and Beyond: Valuing Ethical Diversity—Religious Possibilities

I think it has now become clear that the case studies selected for discussion add little to clarifying the main issue for halakic Judaism: namely that of accommodating ethical pluralism from a managerial position. The current halakic debates on physician-assisted suicide and same-sex unions are as fascinating as they are pressing, but bear little on the main issue in question. Those interested will find engaging and accessible introductions to the two issues in Noam J. Zohar's "Jewish Deliberation on Suicide"[12] and Bradley Shavit Artson's "Enfranchising the Monogamous Homosexual" respectively.[13] Here too, the halakic tradition and the current debate have nothing to say about the proper way to manage second-order regulation and accommodation of contrasting systems. On both issues, Orthodox communities outside of Israel, though firmly committed to the teachings of their rabbinic leaders, remain largely indifferent to the moral choices of other communities, as to the levels of legitimacy granted them by the law. The situation in Israel is quite different. Prior to voting, Orthodox Knesset members will do everything in their power to secure a majority in their favor. Protest may be loud and the rhetoric heated but only until the vote is taken. Once it is, the situation will closely resemble other Western countries, but with the one exception I have stressed repeatedly: in Israel there will inevitably be Orthodox government officials with the impossible task of actively enabling and vouching for the successful violation of norms they hold sacred.

The problem, to repeat, is not that of having to share political and social space with communities who knowingly conduct their lives in violation of halakah, nor is it the problem of determining the cultural-religious character of the public domain; it is that of taking responsibility for implementing and managing the very sharing. What is needed for halakically committed members of such a government is not tolerance, but some form of religiously justified pluralism (in the normative rather than in the descriptive sense of the word). But how is it possible to square pluralism with a system of thought and action that claims access to the ultimate Good based on transcendental truths? On what grounds can halakically committed Jews possibly view forms of conduct that are decidedly rejected *within* their religious communities as worthy of active promotion beyond their gates?[14]

Such grounds exist, I believe, along lines similar to those proposed, say, in Karl Popper's *The Open Society and Its Enemies*. According to such an approach, the grounds for ethical diversity are primarily *not* to do with a moral duty to defend individual autonomy, or with a moral obligation to keep out of one's neighbor's hair. Popper's position *entails* such liberal visions of individual autonomy but ultimately *rests* upon epistemological rather than moral or metaphysical arguments. Ethical systems diametrically opposed to one's own are valued by members of the open society, not merely on moral or legal grounds, but out of a realization that the environment of a plurality of engaging, especially conflicting voices, is the setting in which one's own system is best and most effectively articulated and developed.

The obvious advantage of grounding ideas in pluralism in this way is that it sidesteps the entire issue of fundamental rights, an idea halakic Judaism for one has great difficulty accommodating as an a priori given. The acknowledgment of humankind's profound fallibility especially in the public sphere, of the fundamental time-boundedness and context-dependence of ethical judgments, coupled to the almost built-in instability of those very contexts, premises little more than that life, especially social life, is exceedingly complex and unpredictable, and that the chances of us making a mess of things are enormous— with this few would disagree. The upshot is an epistemic hesitance, modesty, and openness and an awareness that we are poor critics of our own ethical choices, that things are best done piecemeal, and that other viewpoints are not merely to be tolerated but to be highly valued, not for their own intrinsic worth so much as for their capacity to challenge our own by highlighting its flaws and shortcomings.

Of course, the Popperian option need not *deny* the idea that people have fundamental rights to whatever belief system or inoffensive form of conduct they see fit. The liberal and Popperian options are independent of one another but are not mutually exclusive. Liberalism alone, however, provides little incentive for building and maintaining a society transcending the boundaries of one's own community. Acknowledging the other's right to the belief system of his or her choice offers, in and of itself, little reason for establishing frameworks for living with others. Liberal rights provide sufficient grounds for tolerating others once they are around, but not for *wanting* to have them around. Acknowledging a person's right to his beliefs entails an obligation to tolerate him holding to them but, of itself, attaches to them no intrinsic value. The Popperian option does. One wants to surround oneself with people who think and live differently in order to enrich one's own beliefs and lifestyle. On this inherently pluralistic model the other is not merely tolerated but is valued for his otherness. The beauty of it is that although the Popperian option is capable of delivering more than the traditional liberal options, it need not premise fundamental rights at all (although it need not deny them). If only for that, the Popperian option is an attractive alternative for religious systems whose capacity for accommodating a rights-based liberalism is severely limited. The argument from epistemic modesty is an argument for more than toleration. It is an argument for pluralism. Arguments from rights compel us to take seriously a person's ethical choices but, of themselves, attach no intrinsic value to what he or she chooses; arguing from epistemic modesty, by contrast, attaches great intrinsic value to the outcome of their choosing but, in itself, cares little about their liberty to do so.

Furthermore, and perhaps most important, by allowing one to sidestep the entire rights issue, the Popperian argument from epistemic modesty provides grounds for the type of two-tier thinking mentioned earlier. In fact, it justifies and encourages it. To recall, the problem of religious sovereignty is that of justifying religiously working at governmental level actively to ensure the security and thriving of forms of conduct held to be sinful in the eyes of one's own religion. It is that of viewing forms of conduct that are actively condemned within one's own community, as worthy of active support outside it. Now, the ideal Open Society comprises epistemically humble learners, rather than systematic agnostics. In a deep sense, the dynamic of Popperian enrichment is the more effective the greater the contrast between the various viewpoints, and the firmer they are initially held. Criticism—and subsequently the learning process that may come in its wake—is more effective the more there is at stake: the more serious the problems, the more cherished the solutions at hand. Ideally, a person or community prudently motivated by Popperian considerations of epistemic humility will seek partners to debate whose views are as seriously held as they are significantly different from their own. And when such considerations are applied to state politics, one, it seems, should regard as ideal a multicultural society comprising a plurality of relatively decided communities fairly confident in their views.

But is such an option available for halakic Judaism? Elsewhere, I have argued at length for the existence, within the formative texts of halakic Judaism, of a major school of thought whose self-conscious epistemic presuppositions closely resemble those of the Popperian school.[15] The approach to which I am referring is aptly described in the words of Rabbi Naftali Tzvi Yehuda Berlin, writing in 1865 or so, in the introduction, section 5, to his monumental commentary on the Pentateuch: *Ha'amek Davar*.

> Just as it is not possible for the wise student of nature ever to boast knowledge of all of nature's secrets . . . and just as there is no guarantee that what he has accomplished in his investigations will not be invalidated by colleagues in this generation or the next who elect to study the same things differently, so *it is not possible for the student of the Torah to claim that he has attended to each and every point that claims attention, and even that which he does explain— there is never proof that he has ascertained the truth of the Torah* [emphasis added].

However, Rabbi Berlin did not intend his surprisingly Popperian analogy of Torah study to science to apply to halakah. The model he attributes to the development of halakah is cumulative rather than revolutionary (resembling mathematical, rather than scientific, development).[16] Unlike the interpreter of scripture, the halakist, he urged, does not seek to invalidate and improve upon the efforts of his forebears, as does the exegete, but to build upon their rulings by concentrating exclusively on halakic lacunae.

Berlin's two models of development differ in the treatment of their legacies. Halakists, according to Berlin, are wholly bound and obligated by the body of law they inherit and are, therefore, limited in their legislative efforts to questions on which no ruling has yet been issued. Biblical exegetes, by contrast, motivated by a profound epistemic modesty, are encouraged to challenge and improve upon former interpretations. Owing to their different attitudes to tradition, I have dubbed the two approaches traditionalist and antitraditionalist respectively. Contrary to Rabbi Berlin's depiction—a view widely shared by halakically committed Jews—I believe there is strong evidence for the presence, within the talmudic literature, of a reflective and insistent antitraditionalist approach *to halakah*. As noted, I have made the case for this contention in a book-length study of the talmudic literature. It is a prevalent voice, which is detailed and valorized in a variety of talmudic texts and genres. One example will suffice in the present context.

The dispute between the Houses of Hillel and Shammai—schools of halakic thought that dominated the world of Jewish learning prior to the fall of Jerusalem in 70 c.e.—is regarded as the paradigm of halakic disagreement. The talmudic literature contains much legal and legendary material concerning the houses and the two sages to whom they owe their names. The dispute between them covers three hundred or so matters of halakah. In thirty-four cases, the texts record debates between them following the statement of their initial contrasting views. These allow the reader a glimpse of the different and the shared discursive practices attributed by the texts to the two houses. One such difference is highly significant. In seven of the fifteen dialogues in which the Shammaites are accorded the last word, the Hillelites are on record as having changed their initial view and "admitting" to that of their adversaries. In none of the eighteen cases in which the Hillelites are accorded the last word do the Shammaites change their mind. A willingness to retract and modify a bona fide halakic legacy in the face of counterargument is the hallmark of antitraditionalism. Nothing better attests to such a view than evidence of actual replacement of a former ruling. Unlike traditionalists, who are obligated absolutely by their traditions (and are, therefore, unable to abandon a ruling even in the face of a counterargument for which they have no answer), antitra-ditionalists, motivated by perpetual self-doubt, are constantly on the lookout for possible flaws and problems in the system. It is clear from this and a variety of other evidence[17] that the talmudic redactors re-sponsible for these texts envisaged the two houses—whose disputes are formative of the talmudic enterprise—as apt representatives of the two approaches I have been discussing. It is also evident that major tal-mudic texts that comment on the houses' controversy viewed it in the same terms. One such text asserts that the reason we follow the House of Hillel in matters of halakah is because it was humble and accommo-dating, and would not only give the Shammaite view a hearing, but went out of its way to hear it before stating its own.[18]

The talmudic antitraditionalist is what I have elsewhere termed a constructive skeptic, who translates his personal intellectual modesty into a powerful method of critical reasoning. The Hillelites' attitude to-ward the Shammaites is more than mere toleration. They accord their adversaries more than the right to an opinion and freedom of speech. No, they desperately need them around, for the keen challenge they af-ford their own hesitantly held views. They disagree with the Sham-maites bitterly, but value their presence not for the cozy security of agreement that they offer, but for the exciting, constructive effects of their criticism. They are valued for their profound otherness!

Of course, all of this is very much in-house, and there is much work to be done in order to be able to extrapolate from it to modern social multicultural environments. Still, the existence of a firm tradition of halakic antitraditionalism in the canonical halakic literature provides valuable resources for Orthodox Judaism to attend to the problems at hand. The most important of these resources are two: a legitimacy to re-think halakah on ethical grounds and, even more important for the present context, a healthy, religiously meaningful pluralism that allows one both to disagree keenly and to value deeply the existence of ethical systems opposed to one's own.

Notes

1. For a superb survey and analysis of the variety of Jewish religious reactions to the Zionist idea, see A. Ravitzky, *Messianism, Zionism and Jewish Religious Radicalism* (Chicago: University of Chicago Press, 1996). For the Orthodox opposition to early Zionism, see pp. 40–78; for their latter-day outgrowths in Israeli society, pp. 145–80.

2. These roughly speaking comprised two groups who differed in their disagreement with the majority. Some joined the Zionist movement claiming contrary to the majority that the messianic era should be actively ushered in. Others ruled that seeking a political solution for the Jewish people should have nothing to do with messianism and be pursued regardless of messianic aspiration. For further details, see ibid., pp. 10–39, 79–144.

3. The problem I am pointing to is, of course, a general one, that is by and large confined to Israel in fact, not in principle. The most notable example of a non-Israeli politician facing similar circumstances is, of course, U.S. Senator Joseph Lieberman of Connecticut. Nor is the problem, in principle, an exclusively Orthodox Jewish one. Any governmental executive firmly committed to a system of norms significantly less tolerant than the law of the land is bound to face similar dilemmas.

4. See, for instance, G. J. Blidstein, "The Monarchic Imperative in Rabbinic Perspective," *AJS Review* 78 (1982–83): 15–39; M. Lorberbaum, "Politics and the Limits of Law in Jewish Medieval Thought: Maimonides and Nissim Gerondi," (Ph.D. dissertation, Hebrew University, 1992); A. Ravitzky, *Religion and State in Jewish Philosophy: Models of Unity, Division, Collision and Subordination* (in Hebrew) (Jerusalem: Israel Democracy Institute, 1998); and M. Walzer, M. Lorberbaum, N. Zohar, and Y. Lorberbaum, eds., *The Jewish Political Tradition*, vol. 1: *Authority* (New Haven: Yale University Press, 2000), chap. 3, "Monarchy."

5. Yerushalmi, *Gittin*, v, 47c.

6. This was the official position of the vast majority of non-Zionist Jews even after the establishment of the state. Since then, however, most Orthodox communities have accepted the existence and political authority of the state (de facto at least), participate actively in the elections, and are keenly represented at the legislative and executive levels.

7. Some years ago Rabbi Eliyahu Bakshi-Doron, Sephardic chief rabbi of Israel, was approached by an observant Jewish travel agent inquiring whether halakah permitted him to serve non-Jewish pilgrims to the Holy Land. The chief rabbi's response is short and decisive. Although one is not required to hinder Muslim and Christian pilgrims actively, halakah clearly prohibits actively assisting them, let alone profiting from them in any way. ("Let the person

who raised the question be rewarded twice," the rabbi concludes, "once for his obviously genuine concern for peace, and again for concentrating hereafter on encouraging and assisting in bringing many, many Jews to The Holy Land.") With regard to private travel agencies Rabbi Bakshi-Doron's ruling poses no problem. It may sound awful, and terribly impolitically correct, but, in principle, can be lived with. Every religion has certain areas of seclusion from which nonmembers are barred. Such being the halakah (and as far as I can tell the chief rabbi's reasoning is halakically impeccable), one can easily imagine separate travel agencies serving Orthodox communities to the ritual exclusion of others just as special kosher restaurants, bakeries, and wineries cater to the Orthodox. A serious problem arises, however, when the person seeking the rabbi's advice is not a private entrepreneur but an Orthodox member of the Israeli cabinet.

8. Incredibly, despite their full participation in state politics, this remains the official ideology of one of the two Israeli *haredi* parties, who consistently pay it formal, ritual lip-service by insisting that their representatives receive full ministerial authority but without assuming the title of minister. By only becoming deputy ministers they avoid having to take the ministerial oath. Yet with no minister above them to answer to (the prime minister technically assumes the ministerial role himself), they are able to assume responsibility without actually accepting it. To the best of my knowledge this has always been the case since the state was established in 1948.

9. These are known as the Noahide Laws: laws supposed by the rabbis to have been binding upon all of mankind prior to Sinai, and upon non-Jews thereafter. There is considerable disagreement in the talmudic texts as to the precise list of Noahide laws. Basing their exegesis on Genesis 2:16 and 9:4 some sources list the following: (1) not to worship idols; (2) not to blaspheme the name of God; (3) to establish courts of justice; (4) not to kill; (5) not to commit adultery; (6) not to rob; (7) not to eat the flesh cut from a living animal (Genesis Rabba 16:9, 24:5). Elsewhere (Bavli, *Sanhedrin* 56b) blasphemy and the establishment of courts are dropped in favor of the emasculation of animals and the pairing of animals of different species. Elsewhere still (Bavli, *Hulin* 92a) the list is much extended.

10. The two parties to the debate were Rabbis Abraham ha-Kohen Kook and Ben Zion Hai Uziel, who were both approached by concerned members of the religious labor movement, Misrahi, around the same time. For the two responsa, see respectively A.I.H. Kook, *Ma'amre Ha-Re'ayah* (Jerusalem: Avner, 1984), pp. 189–94 and B. H. Uziel, *Piskei Uziel* (Jerusalem: Mossad Harav Kook, 1977), pp. 228–34. For excellent English-language renditions of the texts and commentary by David Novak, see M. Walzer, M. Lorberbaum, and N. Zohar, eds., *The Jewish Political Tradition*, vol. 2: *Membership* (New Haven: Yale University Press, forthcoming), chap. 13, "Gender Hierarchy."

11. Bavli, *Yevamot* 65b.

12. Dealing first with passive euthanasia and suicide, and finally with active euthanasia, Zohar skillfully traces the conflicting voices within halakic discourse. (More on the polyphonous nature of halakic discourse later.) Most agree that since God is piously regarded the sole bestower and taker of life,

death, when imminent, should be allowed to take its natural course. Some conclude that "we are, therefore, forbidden to do anything to hasten death" and prohibit any form of human intervention (e.g., Rabbi Eliezer Waldenberg, *Tsits Eliezer*, vol. 8, "Ramat Rachel," section 29, 1965), whereas others conclude to the contrary that it is, for the very same reason, our duty *not* to prolong a dying person's life "artificially" (e.g., Rabbi Haim David Ha'Levi, "Disconnecting a Terminal Patient from an Artificial Respirator," *Techumin* 2 [1981]: 304). Suicide, strictly prohibited for the same reason ("No creature in the world owns a person's soul, not even his own"), also has its exceptions—even biblical exceptions. Martyrdom is, of course, one. More important for the question at hand is Saul's apparently justified suicide. The nature of the legitimacy of Saul's act is disputed by the rabbis, however. The most widely accepted position is that of Nachmanides, who opines that to accept "God as sovereign does not imply He is a Master without compassion." In extreme situations, such as Saul's, suicide is permited. However, in such cases, argues Zohar, it hardly makes sense to prohibit helping one do so. Still this seems to be the position of all halakists (as it is the situation in many non-halakic jurisdictions). See, for instance, Rabbi P. Toledano of London's recent "A Responsum on Issues of Medical Halakha," in J. Sacks, ed., *Tradition and Transition* (London: Jews' College, 1986), pp. i–xv. For further details, see N. J. Zohar, "Jewish Deliberations on Suicide: Exceptions, Toleration, and Assistance," in M. P. Battin, R. Rhodes, and A. Silvers, eds., *Physician Assisted Suicide: Expanding the Debate* (New York: Routledge, 1998), pp. 362–72. See also by the same author *Alternatives in Jewish Bioethics* (Albany: State University of New York Press, 1997), chap. 2, "Death: Natural Process and Human Intervention."

13. Artson's intriguing paper is written with a view to break new halakic ground rather than summarize the halakic situation. Unlike euthanasia, there is very little, if any, halakic disagreement regarding homosexuality—which is flatly prohibited across the board. Artson sets out to meet the challenge, not by contesting former rulings, but by arguing that they were issued with a very different notion of homosexuality in mind than the type of relationship currently under discussion. Until recently, he argues, the very notion of a lasting, monogamous, sharing, single-sex union, of the type for which he seeks halakic recognition, was unheard of. All known ancient forms of homosexuality, he claims, were short-lasting, forced, abusive, and purely sexual. Single-sex marriage, he suggests, should therefore be treated as an halakic lacuna and dealt with irrespective of former rulings. For a keen and detailed discussion of this theme, see B. S. Artson, "Enfranchising the Monogamous Homosexual: A Legal Possibility, a Moral Imperative," *S'vara*, 3, 1 (1993): 15–26; J. Roth, "Homosexuality and Halakhic Decision-Making," ibid., pp. 27–34; B. S Artson, "Response to Rabbi Joel Roth," ibid., pp. 35–38.

14. This is a project very different from that of the halakic rethinking of specific forms of conduct. The innovative halakic moves suggested with respect to first-order problems such as women's suffrage or single-sex unions are of major importance in Judaism's ongoing confrontation with modernity. But they are of no significance to the problem of sovereignty, which asserts itself, I repeat, wherever the law supports violations of halakah. What is needed are

not ways of viewing such ethical choices as *un*sinful but of viewing their existence as religiously valuable *despite* them being sinful.

15. M. Fisch, *Rational Rabbis, Science and Talmudic Culture* (Bloomington: Indiana University Press, 1997).

16. See, for example, his commentaries to Exod. 34:1, 27, and Lev. 18:5, his preliminary remarks to Deuteronomy, and most importantly his introductory essay to *She'iltot de-Rav Ahai Gaon*, entitled "The Way of Torah" (Jerusalem: Mossad Harav Kook, 1986), esp. pp. 5–12.

17. For further details, see H. Shapira and M. Fisch "The Debates between the Houses of Shammai and Hillel: The Meta-Halakhic Issue" (Hebrew), *Iyyunei Mishpat* 22, 3 (1999).

18. Bavli, *Eruvin* 13b.

8

Responses to Modernity

ADAM B. SELIGMAN

As MENACHEM FISCH notes at the outset, Judaism does not speak with one voice. Indeed, it never has. In fact, as much as anyone, Fisch's own work has shown how a polyphony of voices constitutes the core moment of the Jewish legal tradition. Furthermore, and in terms of our interest here, it is well to remember that Jewish Orthodoxy, which Menachem has decided to take up in his essay, emerged in the nineteenth century as a reaction to modernizing and pluralistic tendencies within Judaism. With the spread of emancipation and its deepening within society, Jews began to accommodate themselves to modernity and sought ways to reshape tradition and its dictates. These moves were expressed in matters ranging from ritual slaughter, to the placement of the bridal canopy, to the length of time to wait before interring the dead, to the language of the rabbinic sermon, and to just about every imaginable regulation and custom in between.

The first Reform Rabbinic Assembly of 1844 (fifty-eight years after the death of Moses Mendelssohn) sought, in the words of the historian Jacob Katz, "to create harmony between public behavior and the injunctions of the halakah."[1] Less radical changes were instituted by the Neolog movement in Hungary, which, together with the Reform movement in Hungary and Germany, attempted to give institutional form to the growth of nontraditional forms of worship and behavior among both academically trained rabbis and their congregants. Orthodoxy arose in response, and virulent protest to these movements and their agendas—going so far as to prohibit not only attendance, but even entry into a Reform synagogue. (Jews, we should note, are permitted to pray in Muslim mosques.)

Of course, 150 years later the positions have somewhat changed, and movements such as Modern Orthodoxy have emerged which, under the banner of "Torah and science" betray an openness to aspects of modernity inconceivable only a few generations ago. This "openness" continues, however, to be mediated in matters of pluralistic behavior and the acceptance of any form of Jewish diversity. Thus we should recall the more contemporary version of the Hatam Sofer's prohibition on attendance in Reform synagogues in the twentieth century, the Orthodox Pesak Din (rabbinic court ruling) prohibiting membership in the (now defunct) Synagogue Council of America or the New York Board of Rabbis. Participation seemed to imply recognition, which remained an anathema.[2] On the other hand, the recent rulings of the Reform Rabbinic Assembly to return to broader forms of ritual observance (following what is essentially the lead of the congregants) indicate a new appreciation of aspects of Judaism not necessarily recognized in the famous (or infamous) 1885 Pittsburgh banquet of Reform rabbis where shrimp and lobster (but not pork, it should be noted) were served.

I remind us of the historical background then, not for its immediate relevance to current positions but because it highlights the two poles of Jewish response to modernity: acceptance and rejection. At the heart of both are the different Jewish responses to the modern value of individual autonomy and pluralistic values inherent in the political agenda of liberal regimes. Clearly traditional Judaism did not wish to remain disenfranchised and powerless. But it also did not wish to pay the cost that entry into the broader community brought with it. That cost, necessarily, was the acceptance of those pluralistic assumptions rooted in modern doctrines of individual rights and moral autonomy. As Menachem Fisch's essay makes clear, resources for individual autonomy are not abundant within traditional Judaism, which, to this day, puts Orthodoxy in a rather difficult situation vis-à-vis liberal political dicta, especially in conditions of political sovereignty.

While Fisch's essay makes these issues painstakingly clear—indeed, brings to our awareness issues that I believe will become of greater global concern in the next century—he does not address the overwhelming theoretical and philosophical set of problems that Judaism has with issues involving both ethics and pluralism. It is these issues that I wish, however briefly, to highlight here. I hope thereby to provide a brief theoretical postscript to Fisch's elegant argument.

My own contention would be that a position of ethical pluralism presupposes a commitment to individual rights, Kantian autonomy, and liberal ideas of the self as a self-regulating and autonomous moral agent subject to dicta of a transcendental reason rather than those of a transcendent heteronomy. Only from such a set of presuppositions with their inherent distinction between public and private realms, selves and desiderata, can a principled acceptance of ethical pluralism be advocated and advanced.

The universalism of reason, upon which the transcendental edicts of the French *Déclaration de la droits d'homme et citoyen* or the American Declaration of Independence are predicated, serve to anchor citizens' lives in a shared experience of reason. The very sameness of interest, posited by Hobbes, or later Hume, provide a new basis for that very modern, liberal society that Fisch discusses in his essay. Thus the social bonds existing between people were characterized by Hume in this now famous quote:

> Your corn is ripe today; mine will be so to-morrow. 'Tis profitable for us both, that I shou'd labour with you today, and that you shou'd aid me to-morrow. I have no kindness for you, and know you have as little for me. . . . Hence I learn to do a service to another, without bearing him any real kindness; because I foresee, that he will return my service, in expectation of another of the same kind, and in order to maintain the same correspondence of good offices with me or with others.[3]

And the adjudication of disputes between such self-regulating and autonomous agents was, in Adam Smith's words, achieved through appeal "to the eyes of the third party, that impartial spectator, the great inmate of the breast who judges impartially between conflicting interests." In Smith's terms:

> We endeavor to examine our own conduct as we imagine any other fair and impartial spectator would examine it. If, upon placing ourselves in his situation, we thoroughly enter into all the passions and motives which influenced it, we approve of it, by sympathy with the approbation of this supposed equitable judge. If otherwise, we enter into his disapprobation and condemn it.[4]

Before we can make any proper comparison of opposing interests, we must change our position. We must view them from neither our own place nor yet from his, neither with our own eyes nor yet with his, but from the place and with the eyes of a third person, who has no particular connection with either, and who judges impartially between us.[5] In both Hume and Smith we find that orientation based on the autonomous, contracting individual engaged in exchange with other such individuals that constitute modern politics and society.

The practical problems that Fisch parses out in terms of contemporary Orthodoxy in Israel and elsewhere, all turn, in the end, on the only mediate (at best) acceptance of these philosophical positions within traditional Jewish thought. Note that even the Catholic Church, in the second Vatican Council, came to accept not the rights of error but the rights of those who erred. This was in marked reversal of the Church's prior position that "Error has no rights." As indicated earlier, Judaism—which recognizes individual responsibility and agency—does not privilege the type of modern, post-Hobbesian vision of the individual upon which a politics of rights may rest. Nor does it share, for obvious historical reasons, the Christian privileging of intentionality and *Innerlichkeit*, which provided important foundations for the modern doctrine of rights.[6] Again, then, the presuppositions of individual rights as a precondition of a principled position of pluralism is a difficult position to sustain from within a traditional Jewish conception.

The philosophical problem of pluralism, however, rests on the analytically prior problem of ethics, that is, on the acceptance of a realm of normatively desirable behavior that is independent from the realm of legal injunctions. The diremption of ethics from law, of conscience from obligation, is extremely problematic in Judaism, although it is central to Christian and most especially to Protestant consciousness. Not surprisingly, pluralism is a most American value, reflecting this society's roots in seventeenth-century sectarian Protestantism and the illuminism of the "inner light." From the apostle Paul's rejection of the law as the necessary vehicle of salvation for gentiles to Moses Mendelssohn's exposition on the centrality of the law to Judaism, it has always been recognized that what distinguished Jewish civilization from Christian civilization is precisely this small matter of the relation between legal obligations and ethical ones.

To be sure, Judaism has had its pietistic movements, such as the Musar movement of R. Israel Salanter in the mid-nineteenth century, but this was far from stressing any position of ethical pluralism or, indeed, of ethics separate from the law.

The philosophically intriguing question from the perspective of Jewish tradition is thus of the relevance and status of ethical dicta in relation to legal edicts. This issue has been explored more extensively in terms of the status of the dicta *lifnim mishurat hadin* (beyond the line of the law) upon which nearly all attempts to argue an ethical orientation autonomous of the law have rested. Just how extralegal or extrahalakic (the corpus of Jewish law) the injunctions of *lifnim mishurat hadin* are, however, has been a point of continuing controversy. Although this is not the place to enter into this controversy, we should note that, on the whole, Orthodox commentators have stressed the seamless web that binds the legal injunctions of the halakah with those of *lifnim mishurat hadin*, whereas liberal commentators have tried to use the concept in order to argue for an extrahalakic standard by which the halakah itself could be critiqued.

However much I would like to support the liberal reading, I am afraid that I am unconvinced. We must note, for example, that none of the (nine) examples given in the Babylonian Talmud for *lifnim mishurat hadin* involves breaking the law to follow the dictates of conscience. All, in fact, turn on acts of supererogation and the forgoing of legal rights and waiver of benefits usually by rabbis of extraordinary piety and virtue. The concept of *lifnim mishurat hadin* thus sanctions certain acts that the law does not require, but never acts that the law does not permit!

Indeed, for Maimonides *lifnim mishurat hadin* represents nothing more or less than the standards of saintly behavior that are neither required nor even desired for the majority of the populace.[7] For Maimonides, we recall, natural morality was both incorporated and superseded with the Sinaitic revelation. Indeed, so much has the unity of halakah and *lifnim mishurat hadin* been the majority view that even statements that would seem to point in other directions—such as R. Yohanan's lament that the Temple was destroyed because the populace only followed the law and did not "go beyond its limits"—have been interpreted to point to *a halakhically mandated* edict to "go beyond the law." Indeed, the writings of both Nachmanides and the Maggid Mishneh (commentator on Maimonides) have explained the presence of areas unspecified by law as existing only to permit casuistic interpretation of general principles, not autonomous or pluralistic directives.[8] The realm of independent ethics is, throughout, seriously circumscribed. As argued by one contemporary commentator: "The very character of halakah as both legal system and divine revelation . . . blurs the distinction between law and ethics. Ethical obligations, like all divine imperatives within the tradition will be understood as part and parcel of the halakah, that divinely revealed law that governs the ongoing life of Israel. Moreover, the close relationship in Judaism between ethics and piety, between doing the right thing and doing the holy or godlike thing, tends to blur the distinction between moral obligation and supererogation."[9] Again, heteronomous dictates as prescribing normatively binding action defines Judaism's attitude toward both the halakah and any behavior that may be adduced from *lifnim mishurat hadin*.

There are, however, other possible approaches to the issue of ethical pluralism in Judaism. One of these is noted at the end of Fisch's essay and turns on a certain humility or what he terms epistemological modesty toward our own truth-claims. Not possessing the means to ascertain ultimate truths, we must entertain the possibility that our own understanding is faulty. A road from here to a more principled pluralism can well be imagined and that is one that Fisch more than others has argued for. Interestingly this resonates with the argument put forward by Jean Bodin in his famous *Colloquium heptaplomeres de rerum sublimium arcanis abditis* (Colloquium of the seven about secrets of the sublime), written in the later third of the sixteenth century.[10] This dialogue between a Catholic, a Lutheran, a Calvinist, a Jew, a Muslim, an advocate of natural religion, and a skeptic refuses to reconcile all differences of religion, in one single and unitary truth-claim. Bodin's *Colloquium* seems to value dialogue for dialogue's sake. Valued is not the art of discourse for the sake of achieving a single and unitary truth but, as it were, for itself. The exchange of diverse views is for itself valuable. Not the negation of difference but its very upholding is the point of dialogue. None converts. None is bested in the sense of having lost his argument. Nor do they agree that their differences are only in matters inconsequential, marginal, or inessential. Nor, yet again, do they adopt an argument of skepticism toward religious truths, or lack of faith or relativism (which would, of course, be the modern version of such a dialogue). All keep their faith or their belief in both the existence of truth and in their own version thereof. Yet, they *tolerate* difference and argument, even revel in it. In this Bodin's work is perhaps analogous to the Jewish notion of *torah l'shma* and very close to the polyvalence of Talmudic discourse found in the Babylonian Talmud that Fisch and others have emphasized as containing seeds of pluralist perspective.[11]

A rather different notion of epistemological modesty as sustaining not pluralism but at least a degree of tolerance can be culled from the writings of certain ultra-Orthodox thinkers. One such scholar, the Hazon Ish (R. Avraham Yeshiya Karelitz, d. 1958)—the main ideologue of ultra-Orthodoxy in contemporary Israel—argued that since we live in a time when the sources of revelation are occluded, there is no authority for implementing divine commandments. As explained by Shlomo Fischer, because the epistemological condition of exile sustains unbelief, adherents thereof cannot be held culpable.[12] Although such a position does not perhaps support a positively privileged pluralism, it does maintain a position of principled tolerance and restraint, which is a critical component of religious traditions not inculcated with Christian and most especially Protestant notions of individual moral autonomy.

Yet another possibility of gaining some pluralistic ground (assuming that such is a good thing, though I have my doubts) is through the idea of *dina d'malchuta dina*. This very important dictum states that the law of the land is the law and must, as such, be obeyed. Now the traditional intepretations of this dictum have understood it as a concession to political expediency and nothing more. Yet some recent work by R. Bleich and by Suzanne Last Stone on Rashi's (eleventh-century commentator on Bible and Talmud) understanding of *dina d'malchuta dina* stress his interpretation of its roots in the Noahide commandments as a non-halakic yet substantive component of the Jewish legal system. In Stone's terms, "the Noahide command of *dinin* is a residual source of law for Jews."[13] This fascinating argument opens up the possibility of a legal pluralism based on a common human morality, akin to natural law, as foundational of all social order, including presumably that of Jewish collectivites.

Note, however, that here too the terms are of a *legal* pluralism, not necessarily an *ethical* one (regardless of which we may hold as a stricter standard). For, once again, the case for an ethics independent of law is a difficult one to make in Judaism. Having said this and assuming that ethical pluralism (or even talk of ethical pluralism) is a desirable "good," I should perhaps reframe that "good" in broader terms, relevant to those cultures and traditions that did not participate in the Pauline revolution.

Notes

1. Jacob Katz, *A House Divided: Orthodoxy and Schism in Nineteenth Century Central European Jewry* (Hanover, N.H.: Brandeis University Press, 1998), p. 45.

2. Schubert Spero, "Orthodoxy vis-à-vis the General Community: Does Participation Imply Recognition?" *Tradition: A Journal of Orthodox Jewish Thought* 8, 4 (Winter 1966): 56–64.

3. David Hume, *A Treatise of Human Nature* (Oxford: Clarendon Press, 1960), p. 520.

4. Adam Smith, *The Theory of Moral Sentiments* (Indianapolis, Ind.: Liberty Press, 1982), p. 110.

5. Ibid., p. 135.

6. On this see Benjamin Nelson, *On the Roads to Modernity* (Totowa, N.J.: Rowman and Littlefield, 1981); George Jellinek, *The Declaration of the Rights of Man and Citizens: A Contribution to Modern Constitutional History* (London: Nicholson, 1863).

7. Mishne Torah, Faith, 1:5.

8. Aharon Lichtenstein, "Does Jewish Tradition Recognize an Ethic Independent of Halakha?" in Marvin Fox, ed., *Modern Jewish Ethics, Theory and Practice* (Ohio State University Press, 1975), pp. 62–87.

9. Louis Newman, *Past Imperatives: Studies in the History and Theory of Jewish Ethics* (Albany: State University of New York Press, 1998), p. 43.

10. Jean Bodin, *Colloquium of the Seven about Secrets of the Sublime.* trans. and ed. Marion Leathers Daniels Kuntz (Princeton: Princeton University Press, 1975).

11. The theoretical basis of such argumentation can be found in Menachem Fisch, *Rational Rabbis, Science and Talmudic Culture* (Bloomington: Indiana University Press, 1997); Avi Sagi, *"Elu va-Elu": A Study on the Meaning of Halakhic Discourse* (Hebrew) (Tel Aviv: Hakibbutz Hameuchad, 1996).

12. Shlomo Fischer, "Intolerance and Tolerance in the Jewish Tradition and Contemporary Israel," paper presented at the ISEC Conference on Religious Toleration, Institute for Human Science, Vienna, April 1999.

13. Suzanne Last Stone, "Sinaitic and Noahide Law: Legal Pluralism in Jewish Law," *Cardozo Law Review* 12, 3–4 (Feb.–Mar. 1991): 1211.

9

Judaism and Cosmopolitanism

DAVID NOVAK

Theology and Contemporary Political Discourse

Before one can intelligently present a theological perspective on any matter of contemporary political discourse, he or she must first indicate how any theology, which stems from the perspective of a singularly constituted faith community, can possibly contribute to discussing any normative issue defined largely by those who do not share this faith or any faith. I think the answer to this question depends on how one views the role of religious tradition or traditions (the distinction will soon become evident) in post-Enlightenment secular societies. Here there seem to be four possibilities.

One, any religious tradition could be regarded as a historically limited, hopelessly particularistic, point of view, based on the irrational acceptance of an authority. In terms of the topic of this essay dealing as it does with "international" society, it would seem that reason and not revelation is what we should be seeking since the universalism of reason is more appropriate to what pertains *between* particular nations. We can assume a universal operation of reason, whereas such an assumption about any revelation cannot be made. That would mean that discussion here of teachings from any of these traditions is at best superfluous and at worst dangerously distracting. This is the most predominant "secularist" view at work in secular societies. It is a common enough view among many intellectuals today to warrant mentioning it at the outset since it is one that any religious public intellectual, that is, any public intellectual whose religious commitments are integral to his or her intellectual opinions, must be prepared to counter.

Two, it can be maintained that the division between universal reason and particular traditions, which fundamentally becomes the division between reason and revelation, is one of degree rather than one of kind. In other words, religious traditions can be seen as cultural matrices out of which reason slowly develops. If this is the case, then these traditions can be taken as historical sources that cannot be ignored because all rational attempts, in the case at hand the rational attempt to constitute an international society, are themselves historically located and do not, therefore, spring up de novo. In this recognition of the cultural factor in reason itself, the religious character of traditional cultures (the very word "culture" comes from *cultus*) cannot be ignored.[1] This could be seen as a "conservative" Enlightenment position, "secular" but not strictly "secularist" like the more radical position mentioned previously. The question is, however, whether the religious themselves should be contributing to this secondary, supporting role for their own traditions. After all, adherents of living religious traditions are, by definition, living in the present not the past. Their respective traditions must be more than footnotes.

Three, one could reject the Enlightenment altogether, opting for the medievals over the moderns, and return to a position that regards *a* (one's own, of course) theology to be once again "queen of the sciences." Adherents of this view could show that the preference for reason over revelation has been that reason seemed to unify people whereas revelation divided them. That is, there are always *many* revelations without there being a universally valid transcendental criterion by which to judge critically which is true and which is false. During the seventeenth century, with its interminable "wars of religion" that seemed perpetually to threaten peace, such an aversion to all revelations seemed to be politically wise. However, our historical experience since that time has shown us that secular points of view, ideologies claiming to be rational not revealed, present just as many incommensurable political options, and that they have been every bit as divisive and bellicose as those of the religious traditions. Furthermore, as Alasdair MacIntyre more than anyone else has brilliantly shown of late, even the viewpoints of "universal" reason themselves come out of quite particularistic traditions.[2] With the historical evidence now being at least equal, so to speak, the adherent of a theology can now claim that he or she has the advantage of providing the certitude of a faith that cannot be matched by mere human knowledge.

Nevertheless, just *which* faith perspective is to be adopted as authoritative cannot be established by simply arguing that a *general* faith perspective is preferable to secularist alternatives. For authority is always the function of a *particular* authority; and just as there is no rationality in general but only rationalities, so is there no faith in general (what the French would call "la religion même") but only faiths. Adherence to any faith perspective seems necessarily to presuppose some sort of actual conversion or personal confirmation. To assume that one is argued into faith as one is argued into an intellectual opinion is to confuse faith with philosophy, which does a great injustice to both.

Finally, a theologian can present what he or she thinks is the most coherent view of international society coming from his or her religious tradition, and then see which aspects of various secular political philosophies are compatible with that vision and which are not. This hopefully has the effect of showing that traditions based on revelation can and should take seriously philosophical points of view dealing with issues facing all people who live in the world. Religious traditions—like Judaism, Christianity, and Islam—themselves have constituted more general horizons of concern and are thus not only concerned with their own singular communities. In other words, although not *of* the world, they are still *in* it and *for* it.[3]

This is different from the previous approach, which could be termed "triumphalist," because it does not attempt to convince anybody who is not already convinced of its superiority. It is more an attempt to interact *with* someone else than to act *upon* someone else. If the various philosophical viewpoints can do the same thing with the teachings of religious traditions—each accepting the fact that the others will not and should not be dismissed or conquered—then a volume like this can be an occasion for true dialogue, a model of mutuality that itself is appropriate in seeking some sort of international society. In other words, just as the religious can and should acknowledge the rightful presence of the secular in public discourse, so the secular should be able to do likewise as regards the religious. Without that, however, we are only left with subservience on one side and dominance on the other. Transcending this impasse is itself a necessary precondition for any international society that is not based on force exerted by any one group over all the others. For, after all, any attempt to reorder international society must counter the claim that the most powerful efforts in this direction, especially in this century, have been made by totalitarian regimes.

Where to Locate the Jewish Vision of International Society

It has been the opinion of many modern Jewish thinkers that the place to locate a Jewish vision of international society is in Jewish eschatology, particularly in the messianic doctrine of Judaism. This is a result of the Jewish entrance into a larger political world that has come about because of the emancipation of the Jews from the medieval ghetto. For although so much of the actual teaching of Judaism, past and present, seems to be specifically constituted for the Jews alone, the messianic doctrine about the future clearly involves all humankind, whose members are minimally the subjects of any international society. A number of modern Jewish thinkers have been quite proud to point out that Judaism seems to have introduced the notion of genuine futurity into the world. This Hebraic idea is seen as having a vision of the ultimate union of all humankind that is unlike any comparable idea from any other culture about humankind and its ultimate unity.[4]

The link between the Jewish past and present and the universal future, in this modern Jewish view anyway, seems to be the idea of progress. Greatly encouraged by what appear to be secular acknowledgments of this Hebraic idea, most prominently by Hegel and Marx, it is assumed that the ongoing upward development of Judaism, especially its social ethics, sets a trajectory that can be followed by all humankind in its quest for a universal order of justice and peace.[5] Although many Jews who have been involved with progressivist, let alone utopian, social and political movements have simultaneously divorced themselves from their Jewish backgrounds, regarding their old Judaism as an impediment to their universalist dreams, other Jews have assumed that these new involvements themselves are an authentic part of Judaism.

Although it is not to be denied that there are aspects of Jewish messianic doctrine that do lend themselves to this type of modernist appropriation, a very good case can be made that the preponderance of Jewish teaching of this doctrine is in truth antiprogressivist.[6] For what most of the modern Jewish progressives seem to miss altogether is that most of Jewish eschatology is decidedly apocalyptic. The progressivist constitution of the relation of the past, present, and future is fundamentally different from the way Jewish apocalypticism constitutes that relation. As such, the question of the constitution of international society coming out of these two competing visions is as fundamentally different as they themselves are.

In the progressivist view, the past contributes to the present, which in turn contributes to the future. Thus the present can judge the past as to how much it has contributed to the present that is valuable for it, and then the present determines where its activities are to be directed for their final and valuable consummation. The present determines both its background and its foreground. The future is the directed extension of the present; it is its project.

Jewish apocalypticism, conversely, can be seen as rejecting this progressivist view for two reasons. One, progressivist messianism seems to overlook the mysterious role of divine judgment, assuming that once the world has been created it is totally turned over to the authority of humans. Two, it seems to overlook the tentativeness of all human judgments, and how so much of what humans project into the future is evil and destructive precisely because of its totalizing arrogance.[7] Certainly, the events of the twentieth century alone have convinced many thoughtful persons of the pretentious dangers of progressivist messianism, even if few of them have been able to embrace the positive alternative of apocalypticism itself and the faith it presupposes.

Whereas for the progressivist faith, the present determines both the past behind it and the future before it, for apocalypticism, the future is not an extension or project of the present. Instead, the future invades the present precisely because it is the judgment on all that has transpired and is still transpiring, and it is a judgment, a final judgment, coming from a totally transcendent perspective. The faith that this messianic culmination of history stands over all of human efforts in the past and the present means that these efforts must regard themselves as partial, tentative efforts to comply with God's ultimate plan for the world he has created.

This apocalyptic messianism in turn requires a more major emphasis of the present necessity of revelation for those who are waiting for God's kingdom to finally come. For if humans cannot by their own efforts predict, much less realize, the universal realm of justice and peace for which they long, then they need direction from God in the present to teach them how to live so that their lives will be consistent with that kingdom, and how they can live with hope for it. Indeed, the very human effort to constitute a sufficient human society here and now and by progressive projection into the future is essentially at loggerheads with the notion that the present needs revealed direction here and now and a hidden horizon of future redemption in order to be worthy of the kingship of God. For this reason, then, Jewish eschatology, even in its most political aspect, which is its messianism, cannot be invoked to equate any human effort at international society with its intended redemption. It can only function as a negative limit on the suggestion that the establishment of any such international society can itself be the solution to the human predicament in this world. That predicament seems to me to be that humans are still not fully at home in this world as evidenced by their essential restlessness, however much at ease they might be in certain specific areas of their existence.

Nevertheless, this does not mean that the Jewish tradition has nothing to say about international society. The only provision seems to be that this society recognize the present pluralism of the human condition, especially in its political manifestations, and that it be recognized as both necessary and tentatively desirable short of the true culmination of this world by the apocalyptic act of God and God alone.

Because of this, it seems that the best place to look for Jewish sources to contribute to this vision is in the Jewish doctrine of creation, especially as it intersects with the Jewish doctrine of revelation. For Jewish tradition has been quite adamant that although the Torah is the word of God, its function in the world is determined by human criteria of judgment.[8] Now human criteria of judgment are both singular and general. The singular criteria of judgment are those concerns in the interpretation of the Torah that come from the unique history of the Jewish people. However, there are other criteria of judgment that are more general because they are concerned with the situation of the Jewish people in relation to other human communities. These criteria are taken to be more natural than historical in the sense that they are seen as dealing with aspects of the human condition itself that are permanent and ubiquitous in any humanly significant situation. This is the realm of what the ancient rabbis called *sidrei bere'sheet*, "the orders of creation," that is, the nature of the world created by God.[9] In the traditional Jewish discussion of this order, one can find material of interest to those concerned with international society, which does not attempt to usurp the essential mystery of the final and complete redemption of humankind and the world. This should lead one to distinguish between the desirability of a more closely interrelated world society and the undesirability of an overarching and all-powerful world state. There is certainly an essential difference between an *inter*national society and a *super*national state. The latter would seem necessarily to entail the sin of the builders of the Tower of Babel, who according to rabbinic interpretation, subordinated the rights of all humans to their end of universal power, and attempted to wage war against God himself.[10]

It is now appropriate to begin to examine some of the issues raised by the various philosophical positions that are usually invoked when there is discursive speculation about the international order. Unlike the religious doctrines of revelation and redemption, which are the domain of religious tradition per se and thus whose questions must be originally theological, the doctrine of creation is about the world in general. As such, its questions must be originally philosophical. That is, it is concerned with the realm of ordinary human experience and wisdom which, even for many religious believers, is something that is constituted prior to revelation in and for the present and redemption in and for the future. Creation is the past inasmuch as it represents that which is *already there* for all humans to understand and appropriate as best they can. And regarding essential questions of human polity, among which the question of international society is certainly paramount, even theologians can assume with full integrity that the various options are best presented by political philosophy. That is, when one understands the word "philosophy" to designate the most profound and systematic effort to understand the most basic structures of the world in which humans are now consigned to live and work.

The Primacy of Law

The first point that anyone committed to the Jewish tradition would
have to make in terms of suggestions for the proper ordering of world
society is the primacy of law in any ordering of human life, either lo-
cally, nationally, or internationally. Indeed, the worst thing that can be
said about anyone, according to the rabbis, is that he or she assumes
"there is no law (*leyt din*) and there is no judge."[11]

Because of the primacy of law in the Jewish tradition, many Jewish
scholars are partial to what might loosely be called legal positivism.[12]
This is because so much of Judaism developed without a state of its
own, but always with a law of its own. Therefore for Judaism especially, the rare discussions of anything resembling what we today
might mean by international society must often take place in a decidedly legal context.

In an essay on this subject, Terry Nardin explicitly mentions the Jewish concept of Noahide law, which contains those norms that Judaism
sees as binding on all human beings and which are to be enforced by
all human societies.[13] For many this is the opening for Jews to speak to
the normative issues facing the world outside its own particular community, that is, from a formal definition of law per se.

The "Seven Commandments of the Noahides" is a term that appears
regularly in rabbinic literature.[14] It designates seven basic laws (actually, seven groupings of laws) that the rabbis assumed are binding on
all human beings (who, after the Flood, are the descendants of Noah).
These laws pertain to three areas of human relationships: those with
other humans, those with God, and those with other sentient beings.
They are: (1) the requirement to appoint judges, that is, establish a regular system of adjudication; (2) the prohibition of blasphemy; (3) the
prohibition of idolatry; (4) the prohibition of incest, homosexuality,
adultery, and bestiality; (5) the prohibition of murder (including abortion[15]); (6) the prohibition of robbery; (7) the prohibition of tearing a
limb from a living animal for food (apparently a common practice in
the ancient Near East).

This body of law, however theoretical its origins might have been,
has become the standard in the Jewish tradition for dealing with non-
Jewish individuals and societies. By extension, it is the only cogent
standard for dealing with the question of international society. This is
important at a point in history when we Jews now have a state of our
own, Israel, and when we are equal and active participants in states
that have international interests and involvements.

Without a universally accepted literary source as the permanent
promulgation of these laws, one comparable in function to the Bible

and the Talmud for the Jews and their laws, the question arises as to how the gentiles are supposed to know what God requires of them. Three answers have been provided by Jewish thinkers. The first answer points to common normative experience (akin to the later meaning of *ius gentium* in Roman jurisprudence), namely the very generality of the Noahide laws suggests that they denote some international normative commonalities.[16] The second answer points to a political institution, namely that the Jews are to teach and, if they have the power, even enforce these laws among the gentiles they reach (akin to the original meaning of *ius gentium* in Roman jurisprudence).[17] The last answer points to human reason, namely these are norms that humans as rational-social beings should affirm and practice as minimal conditions for their allegiance to any society worthy of it.

This last answer is the most attractive, especially when arguing for the validity of these norms to and for the present world.[18] Surely, the notion of any common normative tradition among all the nations is less and less valid as the world becomes more and more pluralistic and multicultural. And the notion of instruction, let alone the enforcement of morality basically validated by political power, should make anyone committed to contemporary democracy in the world very nervous, especially considering our overall experience with the tyrannies and totalitarianisms in the now concluded twentieth century.

For the legal positivism described by Terry Nardin, law is justified, not by the command of someone with political power, but by its own internal coherence. As is the case with other legal positivists, like H.L.A. Hart, this criterion of internal coherence is offered as sufficient to answer the charge leveled against legal positivism by such critics as Leo Strauss (specifically against Hans Kelsen) that it could ultimately be used to justify any totalitarian regime that was not erratic in its commands.[19] But as Lon Fuller argued, legal incoherence, as one inevitably sees it in the commands of any tyrant, just as inevitably leads to political collapse.[20] In other words, tyranny and a coherent system of law are, ultimately, mutually exclusive. Thus it is the concept of law itself (to borrow the title of Hart's most important book), embedded in normative experience that can be seen as international as well as just national. As such, a world society would have to be primarily a legally constituted order.

There is support for this view of the self-sufficiency of law itself in the usual order of the Noahide laws, where the requirement of adjudication seems to be foundational. The first Noahide law is the requirement that adjudication (*dinim*) be institutionalized in permanent courts of law. This seems to base the authority of the law on the concept of law itself, not on any of the other three alternative foundations just noted above. In this notion, there is precedent, especially in the treatment of the concept of Noahide law as a Jewish expression of the concept of law per se by the Neo-Kantian Jewish philosopher and theologian Hermann Cohen (d. 1918). Cohen saw Noahide law as a prototype for the modern secular state where citizens function as part of a legal order (*Rechtstaat*) irrespective of their religious beliefs or practices. Cohen also saw this concept of the state entailing the concept of a world state.[21] Indeed, he saw a world state as being in essence the realization of the classical Jewish hope for the Messianic Age (a problematic point as we have already seen above).

As for the two religious requirements (the prohibitions of blasphemy and idolatry), Cohen noted that they are both negative and, therefore, not requirements of any positive affirmation of religious belief or practice. Moreover, they can be seen at most as requirements to respect the religious-cultural climate of monotheism in which the concept of law has received its most consistent and powerful encouragement.[22]

However, there is another ordering of the Noahide laws that reflects a different view of their essential meaning. In this ordering, the prohibition of idolatry, not the prescription of adjudication, is the first and thereby foundational law.[23] Just as Hermann Cohen's more secular notion of Noahide law relies on one textual presentation of these commandments, so does the more religious notion of Noahide law, whose foremost advocate was Maimonides, rely on another textual presentation of them. But what is the difference in principle?

This latter version emphasizes the assumption that all law, whether for Jews or for humankind at large, is in essence divine law. All law is thus divine command in one form or another. The prohibition of idolatry is the first manifestation of God's command because it outlaws anyone or anything else from in any way competing with the absolute authority of God and hence confusing the humans who are to give their primal allegiance to God's will alone.[24] For this reason, idolatry consists of either substituting any creature for the Creator, or even giving any creature parity with the Creator. The acknowledgment of that fundamental truth is prior to the moral judgment of what is good and the legal judgment of what is lawful. Its acknowledgment is negative, I think, because one has to know what the word God *does not mean* before one can identify God if and when God reveals himself. Minimally, God is *not* identifiable with any finite entity in the world. To make any such erroneous identification is idolatry.[25]

If all law is divine law, and if the difference between the Mosaic law for Israel and the Noahide law for humankind is one of degree rather than one of kind, then one cannot speak of any system of law as being conceptually self-sufficient as legal positivism seems to assert. The fact

is that the strength of the system of Jewish law for those Jews who
have always been faithful to it (often despite tremendous threats or
temptations) has not been because of its systematic legality. It has been
because we observant Jews believe this is what God requires of us and
that we are doomed if we disobey God. Furthermore, the doctrine of
Noahide law has taught that Jews cannot claim to be the sole recipients
of God's law in the world. Thus Jewish law is quite different from the
other two types of "decentralized legal orders" Nardin mentions, common law and international law. To miss this difference is to lose sight
of the very evident theological foundations of Jewish law, an error into
which secularist interpretations of Jewish law inevitably fall.[26]

Despite this, though, once one does not posit a foundational role to
legal positivism, there is much of what its adherents say about it that
those of us in the Jewish tradition can find resonance with, and even
resonance with its application to the question of international society.
For Jewish legal literature, beginning with the Talmud itself, recognizes that the Jewish legal order, as a real legal order operating in the
world, does not function alone in the world. Thus there are numerous
occasions where legal overlappings and even more essential commonalities are affirmed and built upon. In this area, there has often been a
recognition of a secondary role for the realm of the secular. Let me give
one good example of this recognition of the secondary function of the
secular realm.

In the Mishnah (which is the core text on and around which the discussions of the Talmud are arranged) we read: "All documents de-
posited in the courts of the gentiles (arka'ot shel goyyim) are Jewishly
valid (kesherin) except for bills of divorcement for women and bills of
manumission for slaves."[27] What is the difference between these two
types of documents, and why are the latter type seen as requiring a different validation? The answer to these correlated questions that comes
closest to legal positivism comes from the most important of the medieval exegetes of both the Bible and the Talmud, Rashi of Troyes. His
answer is that when it comes to ordinary documents (shtarot) such as
commercial documents, any system of law that on its own terms requires integrity in these matters of common concern can be trusted.[28] In
other words, one can recognize here a basis for a certain international
jurisdiction even without formal political commonality. (It is important
to remember that when Rashi wrote this interpretation, Jews were not
citizens of Christian France. They were, rather, a tolerated alien community in France but not of it.) But in the case of bills of divorcement
and bills of manumission, we are now dealing with matters of specifically religious significance. Both marriage and divorce are matters of
religious covenant, not secular contract; and the manumission of slaves,

that is gentile slaves owned by Jews, makes them full Jews with all the religious privileges and responsibilities this status entails.[29]

The ultimate question a Jewish thinker must pose to legal positivism is whether it requires the acceptance of the *philosophical* premises of positivism in order to operate cogently? That is, must one take it to be the primary political-legal order? Or can one take it on a secondary level only? If the latter, then legal positivism has much to say to and hear from the Jewish tradition, because we can both assume that most law is *positive*, that is, it is posited by those having legal authority most evidently derived from the law itself as a system. (This is true about Jewish law as well, because even though its foundation is divine law, most of the specific rulings are made by rabbis, who are authorized both by a general warrant in the divine law and popular acceptance of their authority.)[30]

Natural Law

Unlike legal positivists, advocates of the idea of natural law see law as having a translegal foundation apprehended by human reason. Natural law theory in our day is usually contrasted with legal positivism, although these two points of view about law are not the only two options for jurisprudence, hence they are not the only two options for ordering international society.

Positive law itself does not answer the fundamental question of obedience. In other words, it does not answer the question: Why should I obey what the law commands? If the legal positivist answers that I should obey what the law commands because I will be punished by the legal-political-penal authorities, then it is conceivable that my legal obligation could be in direct opposition to my moral obligation. For such an answer could justify obedience to the commands of the most evil authorities possible. How can I protest if these legal authorities derive their authority from Hitler, and construct a legal order based on that authority as the Nazis indeed did in Germany from 1933 until their military defeat in 1945? It is this fundamental question more than any other that has enabled a revival of natural law theory in the years since 1945 (a *terminus ad quem* in world history and even more so in Jewish history). Only the extreme type of legal positivism that denies the separate existence of morality at all could avoid this question. The old question *quid sit juris?* ("what is the law to be?") is ultimately a moral question presupposed by the law itself.

And if one answers that obedience to the commands of a legal system is useful, what if that legal system commands me to do things that are contrary to my experienced benefit? For example, what if it commands me to pay in taxes the only money I have to save my business from bankruptcy? In other words, the utilitarian version of legal positivism does seem to operate from a moral base in the sense of being translegal and noncoercive. But being based in experienced human selfishness, it is hardly one that can make any unqualified demands, which seems to be a sine qua non for any such system. For these reasons, the challenge to legal positivism must come from morality, and the type of morality that coherently transcends merely procedural questions. For the question "why be legally obedient" cannot be satisfactorily answered by saying, circularly, "because the legal system requires obedient adherents." For those who acknowledge it in the Jewish tradition (as opposed to those who vehemently deny it), natural law theory is constituted in the following way. God is seen as commanding both through nature and in history. God's commands in history are seen as being direct and specific, and these commands are seen as being addressed to the people of Israel singularly in the Torah. *Torah* means both the Bible and the ongoing tradition of the Jewish people, whose chief literary record lies in the Talmud. But God is also seen commanding more generally and less directly through nature, especially human nature as a rational-social permanent structure, coeval with all human existence in the world.[31] This more general revelation is seen as being available to practical reason. Its affirmation seems to me to be most succinctly and cogently expressed in the rabbinic doctrine of Noahide law that we examined in the preceding section of this chapter. The distinction between this general Torah and the more specific and complete one of Israel is that Israel *receives* her Torah by a definite act of historical revelation whereas other humans have to *discover* their Torah from experience of their natural, created limits and by their rational reflection on what this means in terms of human action.

Natural law theory lies at the juncture between the doctrines of creation and revelation. So, even if some of the precepts of natural law are not deduced from creation theology, nonetheless they cannot be seen as intelligible without it. Any theological proponent of the idea of natural law must reject the famous statement of Hugo Grotius, considered to be the founder of modern natural law theory, namely, that one could constitute natural law "even if we say there is no God" (*etiamsi daremus non esse deum*).[32] If Jews are to engage in natural law theory with authenticity, then it is going to have to be considered as a type of divine law. On this point, one could find a surprising amount of agreement between Maimonides, Aquinas, and Calvin.[33] For all of them, all law comes from God, but not all law is specifically revealed to their respective faith communities in history.

Social Contract

The notion of a social contract, so attractive to Hobbes, Locke, Rousseau, Kant, and most recently John Rawls, poses serious difficulties for any adherent of Judaism. For it seems to be based on the primacy of human will to autonomously constitute local society and even international society.[34]

Just as for legal positivism, law itself is self-sufficient, so for advocates of the social contract it seems to affirm the fundamental self-sufficiency of humans to contract the basic norms that are to govern their lives. Social contract theory has immediate implications for an international society precisely because it is always imagined as if contract is or should be the basis of every form of human association. So, my question to advocates of this position is similar in its logic to my earlier question addressed to the legal positivists: Must one accept contractarianism as primary, or can one be more eclectic and accept some of its points on a secondary basis? If the latter, I can show how there is a contractarian strain in the Jewish tradition, which can be employed with religious integrity by Jews concerned with international society.

Let me return to the example from the Talmud that I used in dealing with legal positivism, namely, the one about the acceptance by Jewish authorities of civil documents that have been validated in non-Jewish courts. The commentator Rashi gave what seemed to me to be an explanation for this rule that is consistent with legal positivism, namely, one can respect a legal system that functions coherently with definite, systemic procedures. However, another reason is given by the Talmud itself: that "the law of the state is also the law for the Jews therein" (*dina de-malkhuta dina*). And Rashi's grandson, the great exegete Rashbam, argued that the non-Jewish state enjoys secular authority because the state (particularly, the king as the head of state) has contracted with all its citizens, giving its protection in return for obedience to its laws (an argument as old as Plato's *Crito*).[35]

Although the Jews were not citizens of the state (the kingdom of France) in which Rashbam lived, as a community they did have a contractual relationship with the state: that it would tolerate their presence in its midst and give that tolerance legal expression. Of course, Jews regard their primary moral and legal obligations as based on their covenant with God. The covenant is not a contract because although it involves mutual consent, it is not based on such consent but, rather, on God's election of the community. The consent of the community is a *con*firmation of what has already been presented by God.[36] Thus any contract they make with the secular state has to be viewed as secondary. It has to be first authorized at the primary level, even though the specifics of the contract need not (most often cannot) be deduced from that primary level. Minimally, these secondary secular contracts must not be inconsistent with what is viewed as the primary and indispensable covenantal reality.[37]

It has been this ability to engage in contracts on the secondary level that has historically enabled Jews to engage in international relations without having to subordinate ourselves ultimately to the rule of anyone but God. In this sense, we have the basis in our tradition for a partial pluralism, which by virtue of its being partial seems to have more realistic value in the international world in which we are increasingly finding ourselves. As the Talmud puts it: "One who grasps too much grasps nothing; one who grasps less grasps something."[38]

Cosmopolitanism

Cosmopolitanism begins with an assumption bequeathed by the religious traditions of the West: the fundamental equality of all humans' souls. In this view, elementary human equality seems to be essential to any international society having true moral claims on its members.

My question here is: Does the Jewish-Christian-Muslim doctrine of the equality of souls before God simply translate into the secularist version of the equality of rational human selves before each other, or is something essential lost in this translation, something that can speak to our present political reality and the ideals that are projected from it? The fundamental question is: *Before whom* are we claimed and do we make our claims in the world? Here is where the great difference between a religious view (in this case, the common religious view of Judaism, Christianity, and Islam) and a secular view is most essentially manifest. There is a fundamental difference between saying that one is primarily claimed by God and claiming of God, and saying that one is primarily claimed by other humans and claiming of them.

In the secular position, the claims made by and to humans are those of rational moral agents. However, what about those who are incapable of making a choice? Such a group would include the irreversibly comatose, the mentally retarded, the senile, the unborn.[39] And what about those whose choices we might not consider to be rational? Such a group would include members of cultures who make their decisions based on such supernatural phenomena as revelations. In other words, the range of persons who can make moral claims is largely dependent on whether or not they are the kind of people those in power can and want to communicate with. The principle of exclusion at work here is often as powerful as the principle of inclusion. The very fact that human freedom in this worldview is inevitably constituted along economic lines of property suggests a criterion governed by those already possessing power in a bourgeois society and culture. How does that augur for the construction of some sort of world society in which mostly nonreligious Westerners will no longer be dominant?

It is, therefore, quite different to say that all humans have essentially equal claims on all other humans because both the claimants and those being claimed are claimed by the God in whose image they are all created and whom they can make a claim upon for justice in the world.[40] Thus the first question posed to a human in the first case of human conflict in the Bible is the question God addresses to Cain: "Where is Abel your brother?"[41] And the first claim made upon God by a human is made by a human whose voice is no longer audible to other humans, that of the murdered Abel. "The voice of your brother's blood cries to Me from the ground."[42] That is why the pursuit of mercy and justice in the world is seen as being an act of imitation of the creating-revealing God, "to keep the way of the Lord, to do mercy and justice."[43] Indeed, it is this vision of the way of the Lord that envisions a world society to be brought about in which "they will not do evil or harm in all my holy mountain for the knowledge of the Lord shall cover the earth as the water covers the sea."[44]

Of course, secularists might well object to the introduction of biblical *myth* into a rational discussion of justice in the world. By "myth" I mean an assertion about the human condition that itself is not based on factors readily accessible to ubiquitous human experience, but one that locates itself in the transmission of a particular story. However, is not the position of those who advocate a hypothetical choosing situation (namely, contractarian adherents of cosmopolitanism) also not a matter of ubiquitous human experience (to which most natural law theorists refer)? It would seem to also be the presentation of a story.

It would seem that the value of either a hypothesis or an actual narrative in determining a moral course of action lies in its heuristic strengths. Furthermore, since those who believe a story to be true, even though they cannot demonstrate that truth by any neutral criterion, do have the advantage of seeing the political reality they are attempting to understand and direct to be part of a larger reality rather than what in essence is a fiction. And although every legal system does employ some sort of legal fiction from time to time, it stretches this privilege quite a bit to posit a generally fictitious situation, such as a "state of nature" or an "original position," as actually foundational.

This last point impinges on the philosophical debate over the question of whether thought is prior to language or language to thought.[45] If one follows the view that language is prior to thought, then a paradigmatic story like the biblical account of creation would seem to have normative priority over a mental construct like the social contract. For this story is the historical source for most of our Western notions of human equality. "For all souls are Mine."[46] Moreover, it is a story that still shapes the thought of many in the West and beyond. How can it not be included in speculation about a world society?

In conclusion, then, I reiterate a point I made at the beginning of this chapter about the need to include the perspectives of religious traditions in moral and political discourse without any special privileges or liabilities being placed on them at the outset. Only such an even playing field will enable both religious and secular voices to be heard in discussions like this one concerning international society. Indeed, such a society would hardly be *inter*national without simultaneously being *inter*cultural. Thus my initial methodological concern about the conditions for real communication is very much germane to the substantive issues of international society that are the subject of this essay. In a real sense, as the late Marshall McLuhan became famous a generation ago for asserting, *the medium is the message.*

Notes

1. See Ernst Cassirer, *An Essay on Man* (New Haven: Yale University Press, 1944), 79ff.

2. See his *Whose Justice? Which Rationality?* (Notre Dame: University of Notre Dame Press, 1988), esp. 389ff.

3. See David Novak, *Jewish-Christian Dialogue: A Jewish Justification* (New York: Oxford University Press, 1989), 114ff.

4. See Hermann Cohen, *Religion of Reason Out of the Sources of Judaism*, trans. S. Kaplan (New York: Frederick Ungar, 1972), 249ff.

5. The most interesting effort in this direction was made by the Jewish Marxist philosopher Ernst Bloch (d. 1977), especially in his three-volume *magnum opus*, which he entitled *Das Prinzip der Hoffnung*. Note: "Men can want to be brothers even without believing in the father, but they cannot become brothers without believing in the utterly un-banal contents and dimensions which in religious terms were conceived through the kingdom. What a faith which, in its knowledge, as this knowledge, has destroyed are the illusions of mythical religion. . . . And the religion which is itself believed, i.e., religion as content, is also valid here, though in a highly corrected form, namely as the religion of knowledge of what is germinating, of what is still unfinished in the world." *The Principle of Hope*, vol. 3, trans. N. Plaice, S. Plaice, and P. Knight (Cambridge, MA: MIT Press, 1986), 279f.

6. See David Novak, *The Election of Israel: The Idea of the Chosen People* (Cambridge: Cambridge University Press, 1995), 152ff.

7. See Reinhold Niebuhr, *The Nature and Destiny of Man*, vol. 1 (New York: Scribners, 1941), 186ff.

8. See, for example, *Babylonian Talmud* (hereafter B.): Baba Metsia 59b re Deut. 30:12; also David Novak, *Halakhah in a Theological Dimension* (Chico, CA: Scholars Press, 1985), chs. 1, 2, 9.

9. B. Shabbat 53b.

10. See Louis Ginzberg, *Legends of the Jews*, vol. 1 (Philadelphia: Jewish Publication Society of America, 1909), 179ff.

11. See Targum Jonathan ben Uziel: Gen. 4:8, where this phrase is put into the mouth of Cain, the first human criminal. See also *Vayiqra Rabbah* 28.1 re Ecclesiastes 11:9; B. Baba Batra 78b and Rashbam, s.v. "avad heshbono."

12. The best example of this can be seen in the most comprehensive modern work on Jewish law, which is especially concerned with those aspects of Jewish law that could be normative in a modern, secular, nation-state, viz., Menachem Elon, *Jewish Law: History, Sources, Principles*, 4 vols., trans. B. Auerbach and M. J. Sykes (Philadelphia and Jerusalem: Jewish Publication Society, 1994). See esp. 1:93ff.

13. See T. Nardin, *International Society* (Princeton N.J.: Princeton University Press, 1998), ch.1.

14. The rabbinic *loci classici* of this doctrine are *Tosefta*: Avodah Zarah 8.4 and B. Sanhedrin 56a. For the most complete study of this doctrine, see David Novak, *The Image of the Non-Jew in Judaism: An Historical and Constructive Study of the Noahide Laws* (New York and Toronto: Edwin Mellen Press, 1983).

15. See B. Sanhedrin 57b re Gen. 9:6.

16. See A. P. d'Entrèves, *Natural Law: An Historical Survey* (New York: Harper, 1965), 17ff.

17. See David Daube, "The Peregrine Praetor," *Journal of Roman Studies* 41 (1951): 66ff.

18. See David Novak, *Jewish Social Ethics* (New York: Oxford University Press, 1992), intro. and chs. 1–3.

19. See Strauss, *Natural Right and History* (Chicago: University of Chicago Press, 1953), 4, n. 2.

20. See Fuller, *The Morality of Law*, rev. ed. (New Haven: Yale University Press, 1969), 137ff.

21. See *Religion of Reason*, 236ff.

22. Ibid.

23. See Maimonides, *Mishneh Torah*: Melakhim, 9.1.

24. See B. Sanhedrin 56b re Gen. 2:16 (the opinion of R. Isaac).

25. See Maimonides, *Mishneh Torah*: Avodah Zarah, 1.1ff.

26. For the most cogent presentation of this a-theological view of Jewish law, see Haim H. Cohn, *Human Rights in Jewish Law* (New York: KTAV, 1984), intro.

27. *Mishnah*: Gittin 1.5.

28. B. Gittin 9b, s.v. "huts."

29. See B. Gittin 38b.

30. See B. Shabbat 23a and B. Avodah Zarah 36a.

31. See Nahmanides, *Commentary on the Torah*: Gen. 6:2, 13.

32. *De Jure Belli ac Pacis*, prol. 11. See also Anton-Hermann Chroust, "Hugo Grotius and the Scholastic Natural Law Tradition," *New Scholasticism* 17 (1943): 126ff.

33. See Maimonides, *Mishneh Torah*: Melakhim, 8.11; Thomas Aquinas, *Summa Theologiae* 2.1, q. 94, a. 4 ad 1; John Calvin, *Institutes of the Christian Religion*, 2.7.10 and 4.20.16.

34. Cf. Novak, *Jewish-Christian Dialogue*, 148ff., for a critique of the plausibility of any notion of primary autonomy for humans.

35. See B. Baba Batra 54b and Rashbam, s.v. "mi amar"; *Crito*, 50Aff. Also see *supra*, n. 27.

36. See Novak, *The Election of Israel*, 115ff.

37. See B. Kiddushin 19b.

38. See B. Rosh Hashanah 4b; also *Mishnah*: Avot 2.15–16.

39. See David Novak, *Law and Theology in Judaism*, vol. 2 (New York: KTAV, 1976), 108ff.

40. See Gen. 18:25

41. Gen. 4:9.

42. Gen. 4:10.

43. Gen. 18:19.

44. Isaiah 11:9.

45. See Ludwig Wittgenstein, *Philosophical Investigations*, 2nd ed., trans. G.E.M. Anscombe (New York: Macmillan, 1958), 1.18.

46. Ezekiel 18:4.

Part III

WAR AND PEACE

10

Commanded and Permitted Wars

MICHAEL WALZER

THERE IS NO JEWISH theory of war and peace, and until modern times, there were no theories produced by individual Jews. Discussions of war and peace indeed find a place, though a very limited one, within the Jewish tradition. One might even say that there is an ongoing argument, and I will try to describe its central features in this chapter. But the argument is at best tangential to, and often at cross-purposes with, standard just war theory and international law. Jewish writers argued almost entirely among themselves, in the peculiar circumstances of exile, without reference to any actually existing international society with its practices and codes.

It might be better to say that the only references are to the international society of the biblical period, but even these are highly indirect. For the text from which the arguments begin is Deuteronomy 20, written (so we are told by contemporary scholars) in the seventh century in a literary/religious genre that requires the pretense of Mosaic authorship. Hence the wars immediately referred to were fought, if they ever actually were fought, some five centuries earlier; the wars proposed, as it were, for the future had been fought some two or three centuries earlier; and it is impossible to say what impact King Josiah's wars, fought presumably in the lifetime of the Deuteronomist, had on the writing of his text. Present-mindedness is at no point a feature of Jewish writing about war. The crucial categories are rabbinic, but they are drawn from biblical experience and never adapted to the experience of the rabbis themselves. They are meant to explain the wars of Joshua and David. We have to guess at rabbinic attitudes toward, say, the Hasmonean wars or the wars fought by the Persians or the Romans.

In fact, Persian and Roman warfare does not figure in the tradition at all. That non-Jews fought wars, against the Jews and against one another, was a presupposition of the rabbis, the background but never the focus of their own arguments. Prophetic accounts of Assyrian or Babylonian imperialism are never picked up or developed in rabbinic legal discourse, and the crusading warfare of Muslims and Christians, despite its horrifying consequences for Jewish life in the Diaspora, is rarely made the subject of critical reflection (it figures in dirges and laments, not in treatises or responsa). The concerns of the rabbis are particularistic in the strong sense: they write about the wars that the Jews should or should not, can or cannot, will or will not fight and about the internal decision-making process and rules of conduct relevant to those wars.

But a Jewish war was, for almost two thousand years, a mythical beast. There are no examples; none of the rabbis after Akiba (who may have participated in the Bar Kochba revolt) had any experience of warmaking. This is one of the meanings of exile: Jews are the victims, not the agents, of war. And without a state or an army, they are also not the theorists of war. It might be worthwhile to try to imagine what a full-scale theory of war would look like written from the perspective of the victims, but nothing in Jewish literature comes near to this. What does exist is fragmentary and undeveloped, so much so that any account has to be a construction rather than an analysis. Since the establishment of the state of Israel, there have been a number of constructive efforts, but nothing on a large scale. This much has changed: whereas before 1948, the argument's typical form was that of the commentary (the Jewish version of an "academic" discussion) it now takes a form that resembles that of the legal response; that is, the argument now takes a practical form.

So the literature that I shall be reporting on and explaining is extremely limited in its "real life" references, highly particularistic, and theoretically undeveloped. It is an interesting outcome of their exile that Jewish writers, religious and secular, played an important part in working out the idea of oppression but virtually no part at all in working out the idea of aggression. Their attention was focused on justice in domestic society, where they had an uncertain and subordinate place, not on justice in international society, where they had no place at all.

Conceptions

The Hebrew word for "peace," *shalom*, derives from a root that indicates completion, wholeness, or perfection. As the derivation suggests, peace isn't the normal state of the world in this historical age. In its fullest sense, it describes the achievement of the messiah (who must fight wars for the sake of this ultimate peace). It is obviously, then, a desirable and much-desired condition. The paean to peace is a fairly common literary genre, though peace among individuals figures more largely in it than political peace; prophetic visions of an end to war among nations, swords beaten into plowshares, are cited in rabbinic writings but not elaborated. *Shalom* also has a more local and immediate meaning, "not-war," as in the biblical command to "proclaim peace," that is, to offer one's enemy the opportunity to surrender without fighting. Both surrender and victory bring peace, but this is a temporary condition, also associated with the idea of "rest," as in passages like, "and the land rested from war" (Josh. 11:23). One of the longer periods of rest was during the reign of Solomon, whose name means peace and who was responsible for the building of the Temple, called a "house of rest." David was not allowed to build the Temple because he was "a man of war and hast shed blood" (1 Chron. 28:3). But the Temple, once built, survived many years of unrest and war. Only the messiah, last of the Davidic line, can bring a permanent peace.

War, *milkhama*, seems always to have the local and immediate meaning, not-peace; it is a generalized term for "battles." There is no articulated conception of a state of war (like that described, say, by Thomas Hobbes and later political realists). But international society looks in most Jewish writing from the prophets onward very much like a state of war, where violence is the norm and fighting is continuous, or at least endemic. After the destruction of the Temple, when Israel no longer figures as a member of international society, the sense of danger, of living always under the threat of violence, colors most Jewish perceptions of the gentile world. The idea that all the nations are hostile to Israel even plays a certain justifying role in arguments (entirely academic) about the legitimacy of preventive attacks. But this experience of generalized and prevailing hostility conceptualized as *eivah*, enmity, and often given as a reason for prudential behaviour does not take on theoretical form, as in the contemporary idea of "cold war."

The Jewish account of types or categories of war deals only with Jewish wars. So far as the rabbis are concerned, it is a theoretical, and in no sense a practical, typology. It is also an incomplete typology, for it has only two categories where three seem necessary. The first category includes all wars commanded by God; the list is very short, drawn from the biblical accounts of the conquest of the land, though it is subject to some modest rabbinic expansion for the sake of the subsequent defence of the land. The second category includes all "permitted" wars, and seems to be a concession to Israel's kings, since the only examples are the expansionist wars of David. These are the wars that disqualified David from temple-building, but they're permitted to him as king. If he fights, he cannot build, but there is no religious ban on fighting.

The missing third category is the banned or forbidden war. It cannot be the case that all wars not required are permitted, for it is fairly clear that there were wars of which the rabbis disapproved. But the disapproval is usually explained with reference to conditions of various sorts imposed on the permitted wars, not with reference to wars that are never permitted. Two kinds of warfare seem indeed to be ruled out by at least some Jewish writers, though without any generalizing argument. The first of these is the war of religious conversion, against which Maimonides may well be writing when he says that "no coercion to accept the Torah and the Commandments is practiced on those who are unwilling to do so."[1] His immediate reference is probably to non-Jewish residents of a Jewish state, not to foreign nations, but the general rule would seem to cover both. What are his sources? I do not know of any explicit rabbinic rejection of the forced conversion of the Idumeans by the Hasmonean king John Hyrcanus—a useful test case.

The second possibly prohibited war is what we might call the war for civilization, or against barbarism—in Jewish writings, against idolatry, commonly understood to include all sorts of moral as well as spiritual "abominations." The biblical text on which the relevant discussion is centered is Genesis 34, which describes the campaign of the sons of Jacob against Shechem after the rape of Dinah. This campaign has much else to disrecommend it, but what is of interest here is whether the Shechemites were liable to attack by virtue of their idolatrous culture (even without regard to Dinah's rape). Nachmanides says flatly that "it was not the responsibility of Jacob and his sons to bring them to justice,"[2] and a number of major writers agree with him. There is probably a larger number of writers, including Maimonides (see the section on intention, below), who disagree. In any case, there is no theoretical follow-up to this discussion, and in no classical text are wars of conversion or wars against idolatry identified as forbidden wars.

So the rabbis work with only the two categories, commanded (*mitzvah*) and permitted (*reshut*, also translated as "optional" or "discretionary"). We might best think of these two with reference to monarchic politics, which is the assumed background of most rabbinic writing on military matters. In 1 Samuel 9:19–20, the elders of Israel ask Samuel for a king to "go out before us and fight our battles." The battles that need to be fought are against Midianite and Philistine invaders in defence of "the land of Israel," hence, in rabbinic terms, commanded wars. The "battles of the Lord" (to conquer the land) were the first commanded wars, and the elders' battles (to defend it) were the second. But the rabbis were tough-minded about politics: a king who fights "our battles" will also fight his own—in order, as Maimonides wrote, "to extend the borders of Israel and to enhance his greatness and prestige."[3] These battles are permitted: *his* battles, the price we pay for ours. The rabbis seem to believe that an Israelite king cannot be denied, as a matter either of principle or of prudence, the right to fight for reasons of state and dynasty. They attend instead to the legal conditions constraining the king's decision to go to war. Much of what they say is probably best read as an effort to make his battles, in practice, very difficult to begin or sustain.[4] But they do not prohibit them, or any set of them, and so the more standard dichotomy of just and unjust wars makes no appearance in their arguments.

Attitudes

The realism of the rabbis leads to an acceptance of the normality of war in these days, before the messianic age. But the acceptance is grim. There is no value attached to war or to warriors in rabbinic literature; biblical passages that seem to celebrate military prowess are systematically reinterpreted to prove that "the mighty (*giborim*, also heroes) are none other than [those who are] strong in Torah."[5] Until the appearance of Jewish Nietzscheans in the early years of this century, no one wrote in praise of war. It was probably regarded as a gentile activity "in these days." At the same time, there is no critique of war comparable to the critique of capital punishment, where some of the rabbis are clearly abolitionists. And, although medieval Jews practiced passive resistance, *faute de mieux*, there was no defense of pacifism or nonviolence. The standard view was summed up in the talmudic maxim: "If someone comes to kill you, kill him first" (Sanhedrin 72a). Most of the rabbis assume that this means: you are permitted/enjoined to kill him only if there is no other way to stop him from killing you. But there is little desire to require risk-taking from the innocent victims of attack. This argument about self-defense carries over, as in other traditions, to arguments about defensive (and preemptive and preventive) war and obviously works against any commitment to nonviolence.

   The tradition is abolitionist only with reference to the messianic age. It has to be said that the messiah himself is often described as a warrior-king (though in some versions of the messianic story, God does all the fighting). There really are evil kingdoms in the story, which have to be forcefully overcome. But the messianic war is the classic case of a "war to end all wars," and it is, of course, necessarily successful: if the messiah does not win, he is not the messiah. His victory brings a genuine peace, which is also the perfection of the social world.

Grounds

Here and now, there are indeed grounds for war, though discussion among the rabbis, as I have already said, is focused mostly on procedural issues—the conditions that must be met before the king can actually fight. The immediate ground of a commanded war is the divine command, recorded in the Bible, to conquer the land. The same command is understood early on to include wars to defend the land, and it seems to be extended as well to defensive wars generally (which only means that if a Jewish kingdom were to be established outside the land, its wars of self-defense would also be "commanded"). I do not know of any explicit attempt to include the Maccabean or the Bar Kochba revolt in the category of commanded wars, but they would seem to fall well within the reach of the extended command. It does not follow, however, that every (Jewish) war of national liberation is religiously sanctioned. For the tradition clearly recognizes that God can grant (and at specific times has granted) legitimate power over the land of Israel to foreign emperors. Wars of preemption and prevention are even more problematic: although they are in principle defensive, they seem to be subject to all the conditions attached to permitted wars.

In the absence of a developed conception of prohibited wars, there is no limit to the grounds of permissibility. So far as the king's wars are concerned, any ground will serve, including, as we have seen, the glory of the royal name. Some rabbinic commentators were obviously made uncomfortable by such possibilities, and tried to avoid them by a radical reduction of all permitted wars to a single type. Since the nations of the world were assumed to be permanently hostile to Israel and forever plotting acts of aggression, any war against them, whatever its reasons in the king's mind, served in fact the purposes of prevention: "to diminish the heathen so that they do not come up against them [the Israelites]."[6] This reductiveness is all-inclusive, justifying all imaginable wars. At the same time, it suggests that any writer who holds that there might be nations not forever preparing to attack Israel could criticize (some of) the king's wars. Without the reductiveness, however, Maimonides' wars of expansion and prestige regain their independent standing—legitimate if all the conditions are met.

The clearest statement on preventive and preemptive attacks, and the only one I have found that attempts to distinguish between them, comes from the fourteenth-century sage Menachem ha-Me'iri, who describes two kinds of permitted war: when the Israelites fight "against their enemies because they fear lest [their enemies] attack and when it is known by them that the enemies are preparing themselves [for an attack]."[7] The distinction does not seem to make a practical difference, but it follows from this account, as David Bleich has argued, that "absent clear aggressive design" (or, at least, a plausible fear that such a design exists), no military attack is permitted.[8] On the other hand, ha-Me'iri does not claim here to exhaust the category of permitted war. If the "enemy" cannot be attacked on the assumption that he is preparing an attack of his own, he can be attacked for simpler and grosser reasons, "to extend the borders," and so on.

Ruling out these latter wars requires a more drastic move, giving up not only the assumption of universal hostility and the idea of "diminishing the heathens" but also the acceptance of monarchic ambition. The crucial text here comes from the hand of an eighteenth-century Italian rabbi, Samuel David Luzzatto, in a commentary on Deuteronomy 20:10–11. Luzzatto is working his way out of the commanded/permitted dichotomy, toward something like just/unjust.

> The text does not specify the cause for a permitted war or [say] whether Israel may wage war without cause, merely to despoil and take booty, or to expand our domain. [But] it seems to me that in the beginning of this section [20:1], in saying "When thou goest forth to battle against thine enemy," Scripture is determining that we may make war only against our enemies. The term "enemy" refers only to one who wrongs us; hence Scripture is speaking only of an invader who enters our domain in order to take our land and despoil us. Then we are to wage war against him offering peace first.[9]

The repetition of the word "only" (three times) suggests that Luzzatto knows what he is doing, even if he seems to commit himself, imprudently, to fighting only against an invasion-in-progress. I cannot say, however, that he has had many followers within the halakic community. Secular Jews commonly assume that the "Jewish tradition" allows only defensive wars, but the evidence for this is scant.

The more common rabbinic strategy is to retain the broad category of permitted war but to make the wars that fall within this category very difficult to fight. Before they can be fought, the king must meet a set of legal requirements. First, he must get the approval of the Sanhedrin, and he must consult the *urim* and *thumim*—two conditions that are literally impossible to meet in these latter days (and that were already impossible in talmudic times) since the Sanhedrin can no longer be convened and the priestly breastplate through which or on which the urim and thumim delivered their oracles is long lost. (The function of these two is disputed. Presumably, the Sanhedrin debates the legal issues and the urim and thumim foretell success or failure.) Then the king's officers must proclaim the exemptions from military service listed in Deuteronomy 20:5–8, sending home soldiers who have recently built a house or planted a vineyard or betrothed a wife as well as all those who are "fearful and faint-hearted." By the time the early rabbinic commentators finished expanding on this list, the king could count only on his mercenaries: effectively, there can be no conscription for permitted wars.[10] Finally, these royal wars can be fought only after the commanded wars, conquering and securing the land, have been won (God's battles and our battles come before *his*). All in all, permitted wars are only barely permitted; they are not, however, positively ruled out—probably because the Deuteronomic text seems to countenance territorial expansion, that is, military campaigns against "cities which are very far off from thee" (20:15). Luzzatto deals with these cities by ignoring them, exercising the sovereign right of any commentator to choose his passages. But they seem to loom large in rabbinic consciousness.

Resistance

It is a commonplace of rabbinic thought that illegal commands of the king should be resisted—or at least disobeyed. "If the master's orders conflict with the servant's," says Maimonides, answering a rhetorical question in the Talmud, "the master's take precedence. And it goes without saying that if a king ordered [the] violation of God's commandments, he is not to be obeyed."[11] This is the minimalist position; the talmudic texts seem to require active "protest" against the king, though it is not clear exactly what this means, and there is, as usual, no explicit doctrinal elaboration of the duty involved. Interestingly, the cases, all of them biblical, are each connected to war or civil war: Saul's command to massacre the priests of Nob (in the course of his pursuit of David's rebel band), David's command to send Uriah to his death (in the campaign against Ammon), Joab's killing of Abner and Amasa (in different cases of civil war and rebellion).[12] Discussing the first two of these cases, the thirteenth-century commentator David Kimchi alludes also to what we now call the "superior orders defense" and seems to acknowledge its possible legal, though not its moral, force:

> Even though it is always the case that "there is no agency for wrong-doing," the case of Uriah is different: the text calls David the killer. Similarly with Saul, who ordered the massacre of the Nob priests—it is as though he killed them. Now it is true that in such a situation one should not execute the king's orders . . . but since not everyone is aware of this or knows how to construe [the relevant texts], punishment falls on the king.[13]

The Talmud also reports a philosophically (or theologically) more interesting discussion of disobedience of the immoral commands of God himself, once again in the context of a military campaign. The biblical starting point is Saul's war against the Amalekites, in which, say the

Rabbis, expanding on what is reported in 1 Samuel 15, the king refuses the divine command to slaughter the enemy, man, woman, and child (Yoma 22b). "If the adults have sinned," he asks God, "what is the sin of the children?" The rabbinic inventors of this story seem to have a clear sense of the rights of the innocent in war. But they must take God as they find him in the biblical text, even if, as the reply they put in God's mouth suggests, they take him with a touch of irony: "A heavenly voice came forth and said to him [Saul]: 'Do not be excessively righteous!'" There is no irony with kings, however, and no similar compromise. The story continues by reporting that when Saul ordered the killing of the priests of Nob, a heavenly voice came forth and said to him: "Do not be excessively wicked!" The servants of the king, who refused the order, are not charged with too much righteousness.

Challenging God may be excessive (unwise? imprudent? presumptuous? self-righteous?); challenging kings is not. No doubt, a certain aura of divinity attaches to the person of an anointed king, as David says when he lets pass an opportunity to kill Saul; the king's words, however, are human words, not divine commands. They can be refused. But the king himself, presumably because of his anointment, can only be challenged and overthrown with prophetic support. That seems to be the biblical doctrine, and the doctrine of the rabbis too, though they are not greatly interested in such matters. The gentile kings under whose rule they live must be disobeyed, exactly like Jewish kings, if they command violations of God's law (thus the stories in the book of Daniel), but there is no question of overthrowing them. Indeed, the focus of rabbinic literature, as of popular religious writing throughout the Middle Ages, is on martyrdom, not resistance or rebellion.

Modern Zionist writers have sought to reverse this order of interests, celebrating the Maccabean revolt, for example, as a legitimate and heroic military struggle against a foreign ruler.[14] The rabbis are surprisingly reluctant to offer a similar endorsement, even in their own terms: they would presumably describe the struggle as a commanded war (to defend the land and oppose idolatry within it). But they are more concerned to stress God's miraculous intervention (see, for example, the prayer *al ha'nisim*) than to describe the fight itself, more ready to celebrate Hannah and her seven martyred sons than the military heroes of the revolt.

Had the revolt been a "commanded" war, as Zionists would certainly argue (in their terms: just and necessary), everyone would have been obliged to fight: in commanded wars, the Talmud declares, "all go forth, even a bridegroom from his chamber and a bride from her canopy" (Sotah 44b). But none of the rabbis seems to have questioned the formal announcement of the biblical exemptions reported in 1 Maccabees 3:56 (did they know this text or have access to other historical accounts of the revolt?), even though rabbinic doctrine holds that individuals are to be sent home only in permitted (optional) wars.

It is important to recognize that those who return home from such a war are not protesting the war; they just have more important things to do (or they are cowards). What is involved here is nothing like the early modern Protestant idea of conscientious objection. Such an idea might have been developed out of the Deuteronomic exemptions had Jewish commentators been forced, over many years, to face the urgencies of military service. Instead, they merely expand upon the exemptions so as to make it very difficult, as we have seen, for the king to fight his "permitted" wars. Presumably, they would not have wanted to make difficulties for the Maccabees, but there is no engagement at all with such particular questions.

Two expansions of the list of individuals not bound to fight in permitted wars are of special interest. First, people engaged in religiously commanded activities are not required to give up those activities in order to join what will be, after all, a secular struggle. This is the source, or one of the sources, of the exemption of yeshiva students in Israel today (though this exemption can only be claimed by non-Zionists, who do not regard the defense of the present-day state as a "commanded" war). A more radical exemption is suggested by a singular, and until very recently unrepeated, interpretation of the biblical phrase "fearful and faint-hearted." It is a maxim of rabbinic interpretation that doublings of this sort must carry more than one message since no word in the Bible is superfluous. Hence Rabbi Akiba is quoted as saying that whereas "fearful" refers to the coward, "faint-hearted" must rather mean "soft-hearted" and refer to the compassionate. He goes on to argue that even a soldier who is a "hero among heroes, powerful among the most powerful, but who at the same time is merciful—let him return" (*Tosefta*, Sotah 7:14). This passage has been seized upon by modern commentators (particularly in the United States during the Vietnam War) as a possible foundation for a Jewish form of conscientious objection, though not, obviously, one focused on particular wars.[15] The effort suggests what might be done with the available texts, but does not connect with anything actually done in the past.

Since commanded/permitted does not translate into just/unjust, there is nothing in the Jewish tradition that requires, or even that provides a vocabulary for, a moral investigation of particular Jewish wars. And since for almost two thousand years there were no wars that demanded investigation, and no political arena within which the investigation would be a relevant activity, questions of protest, objection, and opposition arise only marginally and indirectly with reference to the conduct of war, and not at all with reference to its overall character. There is no parallel in Jewish thought to the extensive Catholic discussions about whether individual soldiers should participate in wars they take to be unjust. (Whether they should participate in gentile wars was a question more frequently discussed, but, given the conditions of exile, what the rabbis have to say is self-censored and highly sensitive to the political needs of the communities they represent—not useful for any sort of theory construction.)

Intention

Given the latitudinous ground on which permitted wars may be fought, one would not expect intention to be a central issue in Jewish discussions. It is certainly central to the tradition as a whole, playing its expected part in criminal and civil law, and figuring in what are, from a philosophical standpoint, very interesting discussions of prayer and the fulfillment of religious commands. But no one seems to have taken up the intentions of kings and warriors—except for Maimonides in one very strong, but also very odd, statement in his treatise on the book of Kings. The statement is odd because its parallels are more easily found, as Gerald Blidstein has argued, "in the literature of crusade and *jihad* than . . . in the Talmud."[16] Maimonides seems to allow only commanded wars (though he has an expansive sense of that category, apparently including within it the war against idolatry—and the immediately following section of his treatise contains the more traditional, also rather expansive, account of permitted wars that I have already quoted). Indeed, only in commanded wars can a singular moral or religious intention be required. The king's "sole aim and thought," says Maimonides, "should be to uplift the true religion, to fill the world with righteousness, to break the arm of the wicked and to fight the battles of the Lord." His warriors are similarly enjoined: they should know that they are "fighting for the oneness of God."[17]

Perhaps Maimonides' purpose here is to rule out wars fought by the king for personal or dynastic reasons (despite his apparent permissiveness later on) and to admonish warriors who think only of plunder and booty. The only legitimate reason for fighting is religious: the elimination of idolatry from the world. I suppose that this can plausibly be described as one of the reasons (in the biblical text, the justifying reason) for the original conquest of the land: were it not for their "abominations," the

Canaanites would never have been dispossessed. But the later wars to defend the land, what the elders of Israel called "our battles"—clearly had another reason: they were in no sense religious crusades, and there would have been no need and, presumably, no desire to fight them had Midianites and Philistines remained at home, worshiping their gods as they pleased. Nor were David's wars of expansion crusades: his subject peoples in the north and east were not, so far as we know, denied their idols. So Maimonides can hardly be describing these latter wars. His most likely purpose is to describe the intentions of the future king-messiah and the soldiers who join him. No contemporary wars would come under his purview. Even if he is borrowing from Muslim writers here, it would never have occurred to him that the jihad was a commanded war (but did he secretly admire the spirit with which it was fought?). In any case, by stressing the religious motives of the messiah, he is arguing against any kind of Jewish (national) triumphalism. The messiah will not fight so "that Israel might exercise dominion over the world, or rule over the heathens."[18] Intentions that may (or may not) be acceptable in the permitted wars of premessianic kings are clearly unacceptable in the days to come.

This is probably the best place to say a word about non-Jewish wars, like the jihad to which I have just referred. These are obviously not commanded wars; whether any of them are permitted is a matter of dispute among the rabbis. According to the Talmud (Sanhedrin 59a and Rashi's comment), wars of conquest against Jews and non-Jews alike are simply lawless, fought without authority or right—though these wars may nonetheless play a part in God's world-historical design. Even when they do, however, Jewish writers have nothing good to say about them. The rabbis acknowledge God's sovereignty but criticize the intentions of his gentile agents. The argument begins in the work of the prophet Isaiah, who recognizes God's hand in the wars of the Assyrians. The Assyrian king is "the rod of [God's] anger," sent into battle and charged to administer divine punishment.

> Howbeit he meaneth not so;
> Neither does his heart think so;
> But it is in his heart to destroy
> And cut off nations not a few.
>
> (Isa. 10:7)

So God's purposes are achieved, but the Assyrian king gets no credit for what he does, since his reasons are his own, aggressive and brutal. A postbiblical version of the same argument can be found in the talmudic tractate *Avodah Zara* (1a and b), where Roman and Persian imperialists claim before the heavenly court that their conquests brought peace to the world and freed Israel for the study of Torah. God replies, "All that you have done, you have only done to satisfy your desires"—and goes on to list the economic and political benefits they derived from their wars. But these examples should not be taken to suggest that the rabbis held some doctrine according to which wars could never rightly be fought for the sake of such benefits. Israelite kings fought for similar reasons, without embarrassment or (explicit) condemnation.

Conduct

Perhaps the surest sign of good intentions in war is restraint in its conduct. In the Jewish tradition, the moral necessity of restraint seems to have been widely assumed, but it is not so easy to find clear arguments. The rabbis labor, of course, under the burden of the biblical command to exterminate the Amalekites and the seven Canaanite nations. They cannot explicitly repudiate the command (though King Saul is allowed, as we have seen, to challenge it), but they do succeed first in limiting it and then in permanently bracketing it, so that it has no present or future application. The limiting argument, drawing on biblical texts and midrashic elaborations, is that these peoples are to be killed only if they persist in their abominations, not as a punishment for past behavior. If they abandon idolatry, they must be allowed to live in the land alongside the Israelites (they cannot be forced to adopt the religion of Israel). Nachmanides says flatly that many Canaanites did abandon their idols, and that is why, as the Bible makes clear, they survived in the land—still there, in fact, in the time of Solomon.[19]

The bracketing argument is probably best understood as a precaution against the messianic future, when Israel would come again into the land. Would it be bound to slaughter the inhabitants? No, says Maimonides, drawing on a text from the Mishna (*Yada'im* 4:4) written, to be sure, with a different, though not unrelated, purpose: "Sennacherib came and put all the nations in confusion." Hence it is no longer possible to identify Amalekites or Canaanites, and so although in principle they are still subject to the ban (*herem*), in practice the ban is ineffective. I take this to mean that Maimonides and presumably many of his predecessors were not ready to countenance wars of extermination. But, again, he does not say that; nor do they.[20]

There is an alternative strategy to this uneasy engagement with the biblical text: to ignore entirely the commanded wars against the Amalekites and the seven nations of Canaan. And this may be the more direct path to a general argument for military restraint. The Alexandrian philosopher Philo, who is the first Jewish writer to make the general argument, addresses himself only to the biblical passages dealing with what the rabbis called permitted wars—though he writes without reference to, and presumably without knowledge of, the commanded/permitted dichotomy. Deuteronomy 20:13–14 holds that when a city has been conquered, "thou shalt smite every male thereof with the edge of the sword: But the women, and all the little ones, and the cattle, and all that is in the city, even all the spoil thereof, shalt thou take unto thyself." Philo's first interpretive move is to separate the women and children (all the commentators agree that "little ones" includes male children, up to arms-bearing age, despite the previous sentence) from the "spoil" or legitimate booty of war. He says simply that they must be spared. And then he gives the crucial reason: "When [the Jewish nation] takes up arms, it distinguishes between those whose life is one of hostility and the reverse. For to breathe slaughter against all, even those who have done very little or nothing amiss, shows what I should call a savage and brutal soul."[21]

I doubt that this argument played much of a part in the great anti-Roman revolts of 68 and 132 C.E. But when the Jewish nation next "took up arms," in the 1930s and 1940s, Philo's distinction was incorporated into the official doctrine of the armed forces. The Zionist political leaders and publicists who defended *tohar ha'neshek*, purity of arms, claimed to be drawing upon the ethical teachings of the Jewish tradition as a whole. But when they argued that the use of force was only "pure" if it was directed specifically and exclusively against armed enemies, it was Philo, too Hellenistic and too philosophical to play much of a part in the tradition, whose work they were echoing. The rabbis themselves have no such (explicit) doctrine. Why is it that we think them committed to humanitarian restraint? Why were the modern theorists of "purity of arms" so sure that theirs was the natural, with-the-grain reading of the tradition?

In fact, the tradition is rather thin, for the usual reason: there were no Jewish soldiers who needed to know what they could and could not do in battle. The law against murder would no doubt rule out direct attacks upon civilians, but the issue does not seem to have arisen (after the biblical period) until very recent times. Indirect attacks and unintended or incidental civilian deaths figure even less in the tradition. The only extended discussion by a major figure comes from the hand of Judah Loew of Prague, writing in the sixteenth century about the biblical encounter of Jacob and Esau (*Gur Aryeh* on Gen. 32:18).[22]

The argument begins from another rabbinic interpretation of a biblical doubling: " 'Then Jacob was greatly afraid and distressed.' R. Judah ben

R. Ilai said: Are not fear and distress identical? The meaning, however, is
that [Jacob] was afraid lest he should be slain and distressed lest he
should slay [others]."[23] Loew takes Jacob's concern to be with the men accompanying Esau, since Esau himself was assumed to be an enemy
whose obvious intention was to kill Jacob (so it would be lawful to "kill
him first"). But perhaps Esau's men had been coerced to join his forces;
perhaps they had no intention of participating in the attack. Loew concludes that Jacob would not be acting unlawfully to kill them in either
case since, by accompanying Esau, they had taken on the guilt of his enterprise. Nonetheless, he is respectful of Jacob's scruples, and the whole
passage suggests that it would indeed be a sin to kill innocent people,
even in the course of a legitimate military engagement. The suggestion
remains only that, however; it is not yet a developed argument, and it
stands in the literature more as the resolution of a biblical difficulty than
as a firm declaration of military policy. I am inclined, then, to accept with
only minor reservations Bleich's claim that "there exists no discussion in
classical rabbinic sources that takes cognizance of the likelihood of causing civilian casualties in the course of hostilities legitimately undertaken
as posing a halakhic or moral problem."[24]

And yet the rabbis did deal fairly extensively with the law of sieges,
in which this issue arises in paradigmatic form, and they seem to have
written, if not with an explicit recognition of "a halakhic or moral
problem," at least with the fate of the besieged civilians very much in
mind. They may have won their reputation here, for their argument,
picked up by Grotius, survived as the radical alternative to the standard version of international siege law.[25]

This is Maimonides' summary (based on a second-century teaching recorded in the *Sifre* to Numbers): "On besieging a city in order
to seize it, we must not surround it on all four sides but only on three
sides—thus leaving a path of escape for whomever wishes to flee to
save his life."[26] Of course, a city surrounded on only three sides is not
in fact surrounded. If people can leave, then the food supply inside
the city can be stretched out, perhaps indefinitely; or other people can
enter, bringing supplies and reinforcements. It is hard to see how the
city could ever be taken given this rule, which seems clearly designed
for the sake of the inhabitants, not of the army outside, though this is
ostensibly a Jewish army. Nachmanides, writing a century after Maimonides, strengthened the rule and added a reason: "We are to learn
to deal kindly with our enemy."[27] It is enemy civilians who are treated
kindly here, for the ordinary or four-sided siege is a war against civilians. The radicalism of the Jewish law is that it pretty much abolishes
siege warfare. But there is no acknowledgment of this, and other legal
discussions (see Nachmanides on Deut. 20:19–20) assume the legitimacy

of the siege and evince little concern with its impact on the civilian population.

Maimonides also proposes a general rule against the sorts of violence that commonly follow upon a successful siege: anyone "who smashes household goods, tears clothes, demolishes a building, stops up a spring, or destroys articles of food . . . transgresses the command *Thou shalt not destroy*."[28] This sort of thing the tradition is fairly clear about, and the clarity may help, again, to account for its reputation. What's missing are any analyses of underlying principles (such as Philo's distinction between individuals whose life is one of hostility and all others) and any casuistic applications. These discussions have no cases—even the biblical cases are largely unmentioned. What, for example, would Maimonides have said about the Prophet Elisha's call for an all-out war against Moab (2 Kings 3:19): "And ye shall smite every fenced city . . . and shall fell every good tree, and stop all wells of water, and mar every good piece of land with stones"? This sounds like an easy case, except that Elisha's advice could not easily be denounced. And how would besieged civilians fare when really hard choices had to be made, when the capture of the city was held to be militarily urgent or necessary?

Debate about such questions in contemporary Israel has not yet produced a major theoretical statement. A number of rabbis have criticized the official "purity of arms" doctrine, writing as if it were an alien ideology (secular, Kantian, absolutist) and demanding a relaxation of its ban on the killing of enemy civilians.[29] The critics do not argue that enemy lives are worth less than Jewish lives, for at least with regard to protection against murder, the tradition is basically egalitarian. Their argument seems to follow instead from a deep suspicion, learned in the centuries of exile and probably better remembered among religious than secular Jews, about the extent of the enmity of the others. Nor is the enmity—this is the concrete fear that goes with the generalized suspicion—reliably confined to soldiers; civilians, too, wait and plan to do us harm.

But if this argument has traditionalist roots, it is also very close to all the (secular, anti-Kantian, permissive) arguments that have been worked out in every contemporary nation whose soldiers have fought antiguerrilla or counterinsurgency wars. The guerrilla is hidden among the people, who thus become complicitous in his struggle; or he hides himself and is thus responsible for the civilian deaths we cause when we try to find and attack him. Anyway, war is hell: "For that is the nature of war," wrote Rabbi Shaul Yisraeli after the Kibiyeh incident in 1954, "that in it the innocent are destroyed with the wicked."[30] There exist both secular and religious responses to these arguments, but none of them seems to me specifically or in any strong sense Jewish.

The resources of the tradition have not yet been fully mobilized and brought to bear in this (highly politicized) debate.

Extremity

Jewish discussions about overriding the law or setting it aside in wartime emergencies have focused on religious rather than moral law—Sabbath observance above all. The first arguments took place during the Maccabean revolt when Jewish soldiers, attacked on the Sabbath and refusing to fight, were massacred by their enemies (1 Macc. 2:32–38). Subsequently, a general decision was made to pursue the military struggle without regard to the Sabbath laws. Josephus reports further debates and a similar decision some two centuries later during the Roman war. The rabbis endorsed these decisions, without any specific reference to them, on the grounds of "saving lives." The law was given, they argued, so that we might live by it, not die by it (Sanhedrin 74a). But to this general rule, they made three exceptions: Jews were to accept death rather than violate the laws against idolatry, murder, and incest. If noncombatant immunity rests on the second of these, then it would appear to be safe against emergency. Soldiers cannot deliberately take aim at and kill innocent people to save themselves or even to save the community as a whole. This would at least seem to be the Jewish position, though I do not think it has ever been stated with explicit reference to a military crisis.

All other prohibitions are probably subject to suspension in wartime emergencies: the rules against surrounding a city on four sides, for example, or cutting down fruit trees, or destroying property, can be overridden for the sake of "saving lives" (the Jewish version, perhaps, of military necessity). These prohibitions apply to both commanded and permitted wars, but they apply differently. Commanded wars must be fought even if it is known in advance that the prohibitions will have to be violated in their course, whereas permitted wars are permitted only if it is reasonable to assume that violations will not be necessary. The halakic principle here is that one should avoid deliberately putting oneself in a position where it will be necessary (and permissible) to break the law. This is the only link that I know of in the Jewish tradition between *jus ad bellum* and *jus in bello*: in the case of permitted wars, one must think about how the fighting will be conducted before one can rightly begin it. But once the fighting has actually begun, there is no link at all. The rule about "saving lives" operates whatever the grounds of the war, and murder (now that it has become impossible to identify Canaanites and Amalekites) is everywhere and always ruled out.

Concluding Note

The clearest need in the tradition that I have been examining is to find some way to a comprehensive and unambiguous account of legitimate and illegitimate, just and unjust, war making. Would a category of "prohibited" wars open the way? Such a category would be symmetrical with "commanded" and "permitted," but who, at this late date, could issue the prohibitions? Commanded wars are specifically commanded by God, at least in the original cases, but he is not known to have announced any specific (or general) prohibitions. Nor, however, is he known to have commanded defensive wars; there is no record of such a command in the biblical texts. So, in principle, there could be prohibited wars of aggression in the same style as the commanded wars of defense—derived through interpretation and *s'vara* (common sense, reasonableness). And commands and prohibitions of this sort might also plausibly be "given" to Jews and gentiles alike, in contrast to the original command, given to Israel alone. But would these divine commands and prohibitions be, in any sense, authentically *divine*? I cannot answer that question. Perhaps it is better to argue that after the original command, no longer operative, these matters are "not in heaven"—everything else is human work, though still carried on within a religious/legal tradition.

The category of "permitted" wars is well worth preserving, since it answers to certain difficulties in the just/unjust schema. Some just wars seem almost to be "commanded," that is, the goods at stake (the survival of the political community, say) seem urgently in need of defense. *They should be defended*, unless the defense is utterly hopeless, in which case the principle of "saving lives" might justify appeasement or submission. But some just wars are clearly "optional." They can rightly be fought, in response to some small-scale aggression, say, but political compromise, even if its terms are unjust, is also a permitted choice. Or, similarly, in the case of preemption: it is obviously permitted, though it may be imprudent, to wait for the enemy attack.

The hardest questions arise in the case of third parties in wars of aggression: they would be justified in coming to the rescue of the victim nation, but are they "commanded" to do that? International law recognizes a right of neutrality, a right that, for obvious reasons, makes many just-war theorists uneasy. The issue is not taken up in classical Jewish texts though individuals in analogous cases in domestic society are not permitted to "stand by the blood of [their] neighbour" (Lev. 19:16).[31] Might states have rights that individuals do not? A theory with three, rather than only two, possibilities at least facilitates the arguments that this question requires. So, once the category of prohibited wars is recognized and elaborated, it would be useful to divide the remaining wars into two kinds: those where the moral assumption is that they *should* be fought and those where such an assumption is either weak or nonexistent (they *can* be fought). (It also seems plausible to suggest that exemptions from combat make more sense in wars of the second kind than in wars of the first kind.) Permitted wars are the king's wars in the sense that they depend upon a political decision, and so we ought to take an interest, as the rabbis did, in the complexities of the decision-making process.

A similar argument can be made with regard to the conduct of war, where there exists an urgent need to elaborate a full account of non-combatant immunity—a concept frequently intimated in the tradition, but nowhere developed—and to repudiate the moral nihilism of "War is hell." And in both these cases, with reference to the conduct and the classification of war, it is time to work the argument through and refine it out of a much larger number of examples than the Bible offers. After all, the Jewish encounter with war, in one form or another reaches far across time and space: the Hasmonean wars, the Roman wars, the Crusades, the Christian conquest of Spain, the two world wars, and the Arab-Israeli wars. If the tradition is to serve contemporary uses, it must address itself to the full range of Jewish experience.[32]

Notes

1. Maimonides, *Mishneh Torah: Book of Judges*, trans. Abraham M. Hershman (New Haven, CT: Yale University Press, 1949), Kings 8:10.

2. Nachmanides, *Commentary on the Torah: Genesis*, trans. Charles B. Chavel (New York: Shilo, 1971), 419 (Gen. 34:13).

3. Maimonides, *Book of Judges*, Kings 5:1.

4. So argues Donniel Hartman, "The Morality of War in Judaism," *S'vara* 2, 1(1991), 20–24.

5. *The Fathers According to Rabbi Nathan*, trans. Judah Goldin (New York: Schocken, 1974), 101.

6. See the argument on Maimonides, Kings 5:1, in *Lehem Mishneh*, a commentary on Maimonides' *Mishneh Torah*, untranslated; it is quoted in David Bleich, "Pre-emptive War in Jewish Law," *Tradition* 21, 1 (Spring 1983), 8–9.

7. *Bet ha-Behirah*, Sotah 43a. *Bet ha-Behirah* is a commentary on the Talmud, quoted in Bleich, "Pre-emptive War," 11–12.

8. Bleich, "Pre-emptive War," 12.

9. Luzzatto's biblical commentaries are not translated; Menachem Lorberbaum brought this text to my attention.

10. For a theoretically sophisticated account of the exemptions, see Geoffrey B. Levey, "Judaism and the Obligation to Die for the State," in this volume.

11. Maimonides, *Book of Judges*, Kings 3:9.

12. I follow here the argument of Moshe Greenberg, "Rabbinic Reflections on Defying Illegal Orders: Amasa, Abner, and Joab," *Judaism* 19, 1 (Winter 1970), 30–37.

13. Kimchi, commentary on 2 Sam. 12:9, quoted in Greenberg, "Rabbinic Reflections," 35–36.

14. Anita Shapira, *Land and Power: The Zionist Resort to Force* 1881–1948 (New York: Oxford University Press, 1992), 14 and passim.

15. For example, Samuel Korff, "A Responsum on Questions of Conscience," Rabbinical Court of Justice, Boston, 1970 (mimeo).

16. Gerald Blidstein, "Holy War in Maimonidean Law," in Joel Kraemer, ed., *Perspectives on Maimonides* (Oxford: Oxford University Press, 1991), 209–20.

17. Maimonides, *Book of Judges*, Kings 3:10.

18. Maimonides, *Book of Judges*, Kings 12:4.

19. Nachmanides, *Commentary on the Torah: Deuteronomy*, trans. Charles B. Chavel (New York: Shilo, 1976), 238–41 (Deut. 20:10).

20. Maimonides, *The Commandments*, trans. Charles B. Chavel (London: Soncino, 1967), 200–201 (Positive Commandment 187).

21. *Philo*, Loeb Classical Library (London: Heinemann, 1940), vol. 8, "The Special Laws," 4.225.

22. This text was brought to my attention by Noam Zohar. The *Gur Aryeh* has never been translated into English.

23. Loew, *Midrash Rabah: Genesis*, trans. H. Freedman (London: Soncino,1983), 2: 702 (Gen. 76:2).

24. Bleich, "Pre-emptive War," 19.

25. Hugo Grotius, *The Law of War and Peace*, trans. Francis Kelsey (Indianapolis: Bobbs-Merrill, 1963), bk. 3, ch. 9, sec. 14 (pp. 739–40).

26. Maimonides, *Book of Judges*, Kings 6:7.

27. Quoted in Maimonides, *The Commandments*, app. 1 to the Positive Commandments, 263.

28. Maimonides, *Book of Judges*, Kings 6:10.

29. See, for example, the responsum of Shimon Weiser, "The Purity of Arms— An Exchange of Letters," in David Hardan, ed., *The Moral and Existential Dilemmas of the Israeli Soldier* (Jerusalem: World Zionist Organization, 1985), 84–88.

30. Shaul Yisraeli, "The Kibiyeh Incident in Halakhic Light," *Torah and State*, vols. 5–6 (Tel Aviv, 1954), in Hebrew. But see also "After Kibiyeh," in Yeshayahu Leibowitz, *Judaism, Human Values, and the Jewish State* (Cambridge, MA: Harvard University Press, 1992), 185–90.

31. See the symposium on the talmudic discussion of this passage (Sanhedrin 73a) in *S'vara* 1, 1 (1990), 51–73.

32. I wish to express my thanks to Noam Zohar, who provided advice and support at every stage in the writing of this chapter.

11

Prohibited Wars

AVIEZER RAVITZKY

MICHAEL WALZER'S CHAPTER presents a comprehensive picture of the status of war, its limitations, and its manner of conduct, as reflected in central trends of the Jewish tradition. The chapter clearly explains the implications of the unique situation that has generated most of the relevant rabbinic literature, namely, a situation of exile (*galut*), in the absence of a sovereign Jewish state, in which Jewish communities had no political or military impact on international society. But Walzer's discussion also reveals possibilities immanent in the classical religious sources, even if what these sources have to say on the subject is partial and fragmented, for developing a contemporary Jewish ethic of war.

The sources in question, however, are in the nature of things quite diverse. They have been composed by representatives of many schools, both of halakah and of Jewish thought, spanning the centuries from ancient times to the modern period and the contemporary state of Israel. Any generalization regarding these sources would therefore be open to criticism and unable to encompass all the manifold alternatives developed over the generations. This is all the more true when one is dealing with so crucial an issue as that posed in Walzer's discussion: just and unjust wars.

Types of Prohibited Wars

According to Walzer, Jewish religious tradition has not developed a concept of prohibited war. It distinguishes, indeed, between an "obligatory war" and an "optional war," imposing many restrictions upon the latter, but "it has only two categories [of war] where three seem necessary. . . . The missing third category is the banned or forbidden war." True, Walzer points out, Samuel David Luzzatto in the eighteenth century proposed such a view, but he did not have "many followers within the halakic community." Walzer concludes by suggesting the need to formulate a clear halakic distinction between permitted and prohibited wars, between legitimate and illegitimate warfare.

It seems to me, however, that one may point to several conceptions of forbidden war that have already been developed within the traditional halakic community. Most of these were explicitly formulated only in recent generations, but all are based upon earlier Jewish sources and accept the religious authority of these sources.

Against What Kind of an Enemy May One Wage War?

According to one important halakic approach, the permission to attack in war can only be applied against those nations that transgress the "seven Noahide commandments," those minimal religious-ethical demands that make man human (according to the Jewish religion). Civilized peoples, whose members refrain from bloodshed, incest, idolatry, robbery, and the like, are ab initio protected from any attack by a Jewish army.

Maimonides ruled: "One does not wage war against any human being, whether in an optional war or an obligatory war, until one calls for peace."[1] True, Maimonides' concept of "making peace" with an enemy includes political subjugation[2] as well as accepting the seven Noahide commandments. But what is the rule in the case of those nations that have long lived according to the universal religious-ethical code and have not accepted it only from fear of war? "According to Maimonides . . . one is not allowed to make war against those who had previously fulfilled the seven commandments."[3] Thus states the "Hazon Ish" (Rabbi Avraham Yeshayahu Karelitz), the leading rabbinic figure of ultra-Orthodox Jewry in prestate Palestine. Note that the traditional Jewish view conceives idolatry as directly connected with general ethical corruption. Maimonides excluded Muslims from the rubric of idolaters, and the thirteenth-century rabbi Menahem Hameiri likewise excluded Christians from this category.[4] Against whom then, according to the present view, would a Jewish army be allowed to wage an aggressive, discretionary war?

Furthermore, Rabbi Avraham Isaac Kook, the first chief rabbi of Palestine (d. 1935), believed that, already in ancient times, when the Sanhedrin was called upon to decide whether or not to allow the king to launch an optional war, a decisive criterion was the degree of ethical corruption of the potential enemy: "The matter was given over to the Court to examine the moral condition of those idolaters" against whom the king sought to declare war, "since not all [idolatrous] phenomena are alike."[5] That is to say, according to the former restriction (that of the Hazon Ish), a war against a civilized nation is forbidden a priori; whereas according to the latter restriction, that of Rabbi Kook, even a war against a pagan nation that is not utterly decadent, though not categorically prohibited, will also be ruled out by the Sanhedrin.

For What Ends Is It Permitted to Wage War?

Needless to say, Jewish law permits defensive wars, that is, wars "to deliver Israel from an enemy that attacks them."[6] Maimonides describes this kind of war as an obligatory one that does not need the approval of the Sanhedrin; all are called to participate in it, "even the bridegroom from his chamber and the bride from her canopy."[7] The same holds true regarding the biblical wars against the Canaanite and Amalekite peoples. But what of a war in order to conquer the land of Israel in the present historical time? And what of a war of expansion intended "to augment the greatness and reputation" of a Jewish king? Can one point to halakic writings that have developed a prohibited norm regarding such wars as well?

Nahmanides (writing in the thirteenth century) was the first to establish the commandment of conquering the land of Israel as a formal, independent commandment, binding subsequent generations.[8] But what is the nature of this obligation of "conquest"? Nahmanides presents it as a permanent commandment, applicable to every Jew even during the time of exile. Did he mean to demand of his contemporaries that they declare private holy wars against the rulers of the land? Did any of the many sages who endorsed this approach over the generations approve such an option? In point of fact, halakic language has always recognized a concept of "conquest" carried out, not by military means, but by collective settlement. Some authorities, among them Rabbi Shaul Yisraeli, a scholar of the highest authority among contemporary religious Zionists, have therefore claimed that in this case, too, one is not speaking of "a commandment of conquest through war, but of settling and inheriting the land." The commandment of military conquest was "of a singular nature. It referred to the time of Joshua only, where the master of the prophets [Moses] [had] himself expressed an explicit command." But no such command is applicable after that time.[9]

The question arises whether, if one is not in fact *commanded* to conquer the land in war, one is *permitted* to do so. Rabbi Nahum Rabinowitz, head of the Maaleh Adumim Yeshiva, is a leading spokesman for the prohibitory position. According to his interpretation of the tradition, there is no legitimate "conquest" of the land of Israel save by "permitted means, and warfare is *not permitted to us* unless enemies threaten to attack or do attack" (that is, unless it is a case of either a preventive or a defensive war). Indeed, Rabinowitz infers from Nahmanides' text that even the biblical command to Joshua to conquer the land of Israel by war reflected a deficient state of affairs, a temporary fate that befell the people of Israel as a punishment for their sins. One does not find in Nahmanides' writings, however, "any basis for concluding that war is permitted [in the present era] for the sake of conquest of the Land. What is worse, such a reading entails indifference towards bloodshed. Such indifference undermines the very foundations of society and endangers the entire enterprise of the beginning of our redemption."[10]

Of course, not everyone will accept this interpretation of Nahmanides' teaching, even though it is based upon a careful analysis of the source.[11] In any event, this reading of Nahmanides reveals an additional possible aspect of the idea of prohibited war in Jewish tradition. As mentioned, the biblical command to wage war against the inhabitants of the land is conceived here as being a consequence of sin. Similarly, Rav Kook in his day saw these biblical wars as a result of sin. Were it not for that, "the nations who dwell in the land would have reconciled with Israel. No war would have needed to have been conducted, and the [spiritual] influence of Israel would have emanated peacefully, as in the future Days of Messiah. It was sin which caused [the realization of] this hope to be postponed for thousands of years."[12] Already in the fourteenth century, Gersonides had argued that in the last days the people of Israel will inherit their land "in a manner that will not involve warfare."[13]

But what of the permitted wars of the kings of Israel? Did not Maimonides, as Walzer writes, permit an aggressive war of expansion by the king (at the advice of the Sanhedrin) only in order to augment the king's "greatness and reputation"? Not necessarily. "An optional war is not, God forbid, one which may be initiated arbitrarily or on the basis of purely pragmatic reasons," says Rabbi Aharon Lichtenstein, head of the yeshiva in Alon Shevut. "Launching an optional war requires deliberation, . . . ethical no less than political. . . . The decision should be guided by value considerations also, which even if not rooted in explicit *halakhot*, are obligatory as the law of conscience." The royal goal of the war may be political, but "the justification for the war" confronting the Sanhedrin cannot ignore the "ethical plane" (as we already found above in the remarks of Rav Kook).[14] As Yaakov Blidstein has remarked, the demand for an ethical justification of the optional war corresponds to the positive connotation of the term "optional" in Geonic literature.[15]

Moreover, Maimonides negates ab initio any secular activity on the part of a king—*any* king—that is not ultimately directed toward the religious and ethical perfection of the world ("to uplift the true religion, to fill the world with righteousness, to break the arm of the wicked, and to wage the battle of the Lord").[16] Here, according to many readings, an opening existed to introduce the demand for value considerations on the part of the king himself, considerations that restrict and overrule his practical goals.[17]

Is It Permissible to Conduct a War That Causes the Enemy Indefinite Losses?

According to one halakic tradition, one may not conduct an aggressive war in which one anticipates killing more than one-sixth of the enemy. The Babylonian Talmud states: "A kingdom that killed one in six is not punished."[18] Who are these casualties? According to the interpretation offered by R. Samuel Edels (Maharsha) in the seventeenth century, this refers to enemy casualties during an optional war![19] In other words, if the casualties among the enemy reach the ratio of "one out of six," the Jewish king "is not punished"—but if the war causes the death of more, he *is* punished. It is superfluous to note that such a proscription against warfare causing large-scale death is particularly significant in light of the modern development of weapons of mass destruction. In the words of R. Moses Sofer (the Hatam Sofer), writing in the nineteenth century, "The king does not have the right to destroy an entire human genus."[20] Rabbi Yehudah Gershuni, a distinguished contemporary halakic scholar, interprets this prohibition as applying not only to discretionary or "permitted" wars, but even to wars of self-defense. The prohibition is inapplicable only with regard to the biblical holy war launched against Amalek and the Canaanite nations.[21]

Prohibited War in Contemporary Rabbinic Discussion

The new Israeli reality brought in its wake a radical reinterpretation of the question of the limitations on wars. According to this new approach, the point of departure of the halakah is that war as such is forbidden in principle: "For in every war there are two apprehensions: that one will be killed and that one will kill. . . . Both are related to violations of Torah."[22] Consequently, a special religious sanction (*heter*) is required in order to conduct any war, and in present times such concrete permission cannot be warranted save in the case of a clearly defensive war. From this point of view, we may find an interesting answer to the question of why Jewish tradition has developed only two categories (that is, optional and obligatory war) when a third category (prohibited war) seems necessary. The prohibition is the starting point for any specific discussion; it is the given norm, and only against this general background was it possible to develop two particular concepts of commanded and permitted war.

"There are three kinds of war," writes Rabbi Yehudah Shaviv:

> *prohibited* war, optional war, and obligatory war. The *halakhah* details the lat-
> ter two cases only. It does not need to speak about the first, as any war
> which does not belong to the latter two is by definition prohibited: such a
> war involves the prohibition of bloodshed. For if an individual is prohibited
> by the Torah to spill the blood of another individual, how much more so for
> a people to spill the blood of another people![23]

Other rabbis have also made explicit statements about this question. For example: "Apart from the obligatory war, commanded to Moses by the Almighty, and the [optional] war conducted according to the counsel of the Great Sanhedrin, any war is prohibited"![24] These authoritative figures, like those mentioned above, are therefore likely to provide a direct answer to Walzer's question: "But who, at this late date, could issue the prohibitions [against 'prohibited war' . . . since God] is not known to have announced any specific (or general) prohibitions?"

Moreover, Rabbi Shaul Yisraeli makes the claim that the very halakic force of the concept of permitted war is drawn from the conventions of war accepted among the nations. "War is one of the means of solving disputes between one people and another. Only in our generations do they exert effort that war should be recognized as unlawful, but the generation is not yet ready and the nations are not prepared to enter into a mutual agreement of this sort."[25] This is indeed a problematic approach, for if one assumes that warfare would be prohibited were it not for the existence of an international consensus, how can a general agreement make it permitted? Does a universal consensus to violate a religious or ethical prohibition (such as bloodshed) cancel the prohibition? One could support this argument, however, by the principle of self-defense. That is, it is not the consensus itself that renders warfare permissible, but its destructive consequences, the universal violence and aggression expressed by or stemming from it. As Rabbi Kook writes: "Regarding the question of war: at a time when all of their neighbours were literally desert wolves, it was utterly impossible for Israel alone to refrain from fighting; for then their enemies would gather together and Heaven forbid destroy all of our remnant."[26] In any event, may one not conclude that, should international conventions and behavior alter, the halakic permissibility of engaging in voluntary wars will likewise change, without any need for new religious legislation?

Divine Authority and Human Response

Professor Walzer has drawn our attention to the problems involved in the need to obey an immoral divine command. He mentions the talmudic story about King Saul, who refused to carry out the command to destroy Amalek: "If the adults have sinned, what is the sin of the children?"[27] was Saul's question. As we know, the divine reply was, "Do not be excessively good." The human ethical protest receives no legitimization. But other midrashic sayings have exploited the scriptures precisely to defend the status of an ethical opposition to war, conferring full legitimation upon that opposition. I will cite two such examples.

Midrash Tanhuma (*Zav*, ch. 3) states:

> You find that the Holy One, blessed be He, negated His edict for the sake of peace. When? At the moment that the Holy One said to Moses: "When thou besieged a city a long time" [Deut. 20:19], the Holy One told him to destroy them. But Moses did not do so, but said, "Shall I now go and smite he that has sinned and he that has not sinned? Rather, I shall come to them in peace." [Only] when the enemy did not come in peace, he beat them. The Holy One blessed be He said: "I said, 'You shall utterly destroy them' [Deut. 20:17], and you [at first] did not do so. By your life, as you said, so shall I, as is said: 'When thou comest nigh unto a city to make war against it, then proclaim peace unto it.'" [Deut. 20:10]

That is to say, Moses, like Saul, lodged a moral protest against the command to smite innocent people. This time, however, the human protest not only received divine recognition, but was eventually given constitutional, legislative status, regulating the halakah for future generations. From now on, "When thou comest nigh unto a city to make war against it, then proclaim peace unto it."

A similar response is related of another ideal figure, that of the messiah (*Midrash Tehillim*, 120):

> "I am for peace, but when I speak they are for war" [Ps. 120:7]. What is the meaning of "I am for peace"? Thus said the Holy One blessed be He to the Messiah: "Smash them with a rod of iron" [Ps. 2:9]. He said to Him: "Master of the Universe, no! Rather, I shall begin to speak to the nations with peace." Therefore it is said: "I am for peace, etc."

In these texts, the human conscience is granted an autonomous status vis-à-vis the divine imperative. Perhaps this is the difference between

Moses and the messiah, on the one hand, and Saul, on the other: because God could not have answered the former, "Do not be overly wicked" (as in the talmudic story attributed to the latter), He could not have pushed them away with the ironical answer, "Do not be overly righteous."[28]

In any event, the tradition allows room for human ethical response even regarding obligatory war. It therefore should not be surprising that in the course of time, Rabbi Yitshak Aramah, a fifteenth-century Spanish sage, would come to argue that the commandment given by the Torah to proclaim peace does not simply refer to a formal call for the surrender of the enemy. Rather, it requires

> entreaties and supplications offered in the most conciliatory possible way, in order to turn their hearts. . . . *for this follows necessarily from the human wisdom of peace, and the Divine will consent.* . . . For if we find that He commanded "You shall not destroy its tree [that is, that found in the city of the enemy], to lift against it an axe" [Deut. 20:19], all the more so should we take care not to commit damage and destruction to human beings.[29]

God invited, so to speak, the human initiative against warfare, and it is this initiative that underlies the primal notion of the "prohibited war" in halakah—that is, any war in which one does not initially call for peace.

Spiritualization of War and Peace in the Jewish and Christian Traditions

Because of the historical situation of the Jews in their exile, Jewish sources tended to concentrate more on historical, theological, and anthropological reflections about war than on ethical guidelines for wartime. Jews speculated about the reasons leading mankind to take up the sword and asked whether war represents given human nature or a decline in that nature, but they were less concerned with the immediate political and practical questions concerning warfare.

Nevertheless, did Jews, the rabbis included, really have no experience of warfare throughout the period of exile, as Walzer suggests? In the nature of things, such a generalization also has several interesting exceptions. For instance, many Jews in Spain were active in assisting the Muslim conquerors and later served as a home guard. In later generations as well, some of them were in the habit of bearing arms, to be involved in wars and to protect their cities. The best-known example is that of Rabbi Samuel ha-Naggid, the commander of the army of the kingdom of Granada, a warrior and officer whose military experience is preserved in poetry. Some Ashkenazic sages likewise report the battles fought by persecuted Jews against the Crusaders. Rabbi Solomon b. Samson depicted in a colorful way the army of the community of Mayence, who "wore armour and girded their weapons, from old to young,"[30] and rose up against their enemies. Rabbi Eleazar ha-Rokeah told of "an occasion when many great armies laid siege to the city of Worms on the Sabbath, and we permitted all the Jews to take up their weapons."[31] He portrays the heroes of Israel as feudal lords girding iron weapons. Even if we may doubt the accuracy of some of these claims, weight must be given to the self-consciousness and self-image regarding the fighting Jew.

Hence, among both Sephardic and Ashkenazic medieval sages, one occasionally encounters admiration of the Hasmonean rulers and their military accomplishments; Rabbi Abraham ibn Ezra, for example, writes of "the king Judah son of the Hasmoneans who was a warrior, whose hand was strong against the Hellenists, [even though] at the beginning he had neither wealth nor horses."[32] Rabbi Abraham ibn Daoud[33] in Spain and Rabbi Eliezer of Beaugency[34] in Franco-Germany express similar sentiments.[35]

These were the exceptions, however. Throughout the course of Jewish history, the wars of the gentiles belonged to concrete historical reality, and that reality was the Jews' involuntary lot. The wars of Israel, in contrast, were a matter more for theology than for politics. They took place in scripture, either in the distant past or in the messianic era, in the distant future. The Jew waged concrete war against the evil inclination more than he did against any historical foe. Peace, too, was discussed primarily from a utopian perspective, in light of the biblical vision of the End of Days, and it, too, belonged mainly to the theological realm.

Thus, the course of history set the Jewish scholars an exegetical challenge that was the opposite of that faced by their Christian counterparts.[36] In the postbiblical Jewish sources, we find a distinct trend toward spiritualizing scriptural passages dealing with war, might, and the sword. The "sword and bow" mentioned in the Bible (Gen. 48:22; Ps. 44:7) are in fact "prayer and beseeching."[37] The "soldier and warrior" and "those who repel attacks at the gate" in the book of Isaiah (3:2; 28:6) are not warriors in the literal sense, but "those who know how to dispute in the battle of the Torah."[38] The sword of the mighty is the Torah.[39] The generals of the Bible were transformed into scholars and heads of the Sanhedrin,[40] and even "David's warriors" (2 Sam. 23:8) were none other than manifestations of the might of his spirit "as he took part in the session [of scholars]."[41] This tendency to spiritualize scriptural verses dealing with might and war is prevalent throughout the aggadic (as opposed to the halakic)[42] homiletical literature, and reappears in new and different guises in the philosophical and mystical literature of the Middle Ages: these verses are interpreted in the former as referring to the struggle between different faculties of the soul,[43] and in the latter as referring to divine attributes.[44]

There is a most illuminating converse parallel to the tendency we have described in the Christian exegesis of New Testament passages. Christianity started with a pacifist message. This message was expressed in several passages in the New Testament, particularly in the Sermon on the Mount, and it was as pacifists that the early Christians were depicted in their own time.[45] Later, however, when Christianity had become the religion of the Roman Empire, it developed the doctrine of the "just war." Augustine, the chief spokesman for this doctrine,[46] buttressed his arguments by citing sayings of the prophets in their literal, original sense; the pacifist verses in the New Testament, however, had to be given a new, nonliteral interpretation. Here, too, this was done by way of spiritualization—not, however, of texts that called to battle, but of those that rang with pacifism. The latter were interpreted as referring to man's inner state, to the depths of his spirit, and not to concrete historical reality.[47] Such was the way of a faith that had recently entered the political arena and become a power, in contrast to that of a faith long absent from that same arena.

A third stage in the Christian theory of war developed in the Middle Ages—that of the holy war, as manifested in the Crusades.[48] This, too, has a partial converse parallel in the development of Jewish tradition. The Jewish collective memory indeed recalls the biblical commandment to wage a holy war against the seven Canaanite peoples. The rabbinic sources had, however, neutralized this commandment with respect to the present and future day.[49] (Note also the story regarding the messages of peace sent by Joshua to the land's inhabitants.) Therefore, according to Maimonides, the notion of an obligatory war can refer today only to war waged to "deliver Israel from an enemy that attacks them"; this may be compared with the Christian concept of the "just war," but not with that of the "holy war."

The Zionist revolution has restored the Jewish people to the international arena and granted it political and military power. It has also fused national and religious motivations. Jewish religion has been called upon to demonstrate whether the process undergone by other cultures under these conditions has been an inevitable, deterministic one. That is, it remains to be seen whether the balance will now move from "just war" to "holy war" or, conversely, toward a sharper distinction between a just war of defense and prohibited war.

Notes

1. Maimonides, *Mishneh Torah, Hilkhot Melakhim* 6.1.

2. Cf. Shlomo Goren, *Meshiv Milhamah* (Jerusalem, 1986), 3:259.

3. Yeshayahu Karelitz, *Hazon Ish: Be'urim ve-Hiddushim 'al ha-Rambam*. Printed in Maimonides, *Mishneh Torah* (Jerusalem, 1957), *Melakhim* 5.1.

4. Expressions of this approach already appear among the Tosaphists. See Jacob Katz, *Halakhah ve-Qabbalah* (Jerusalem, 1986), 291–310.

5. Rav A. I. Kook, *Iggerot ha-Re'ayah* (Jerusalem, 1966), 1: 140. Cf. Yehudah Amital, "The Wars of Israel According to Maimonides" (Heb.), *Tehumin* 5 (1987), 461.

6. Maimonides, *Mishneh Torah, Melakhim* 5.1.

7. Mishnah, Sotah 8:7; Maimonides, *Mishneh Torah* 7:4.

8. Ramban, Hasagot *'al Sefer ha-Mizvot la-Rambam* (printed in Maimonides' *Sefer ha-Mizvot*), *Mitzvot 'Aseh she-hishmil hu-Rambam*, no. 3. For a detailed discussion, see Shaul Yisraeli, *Erez Hemdah* (Jerusalem, 1957), nos. 1–2; M. Z. Nehorai, "The Land of Israel in the Teachings of Maimonides and Nahmanides" (Heb.), in M. Halamish, ed., *Erez Yisrael be-Hagut ha-Yehudit bimei ha-beinayim* (Jerusalem, 1991), 129–36; Aviezer Ravitzky, *'Al Da'at ha-Maqom: Mehqarim be-Toldot he- Hagut ha-Yehudit* (Jerusalem, 1991), 42–46.

9. Shaul Yisraeli, "In Answer to a Query," in *Af Sha'al: Mizvah min ha-Torah?* (Jerusalem, 1978), 4; also Yisraeli, *Erez Hemdah*, no. 1. Rabbi J. J. Reines, the founder of the Religious Zionist movement, likewise advocated a stand unequivocally opposed to the conquest of the land of Israel by warfare. However, his position was based upon the oath taken by the people of Israel (according to the Talmud and Midrash) that they would not rebel against the gentile nations during their period of exile! Or *Hadash 'al Zion* (Vilna, 1902), 18; also Rabbi Samuel Mohliver, *Sefer Shivat Zion* (Warsaw, 1900), 1: 9. This approach is deeply rooted within Jewish literature. It depends, however, not upon ethical but upon theological considerations, which go beyond the scope of our present discussion. Cf. Bahya ben Asher, *Perush 'al ha-Torah* (Jerusalem, 1958), to Gen. 32:7; R. Isaiah Horowitz, Shenei Luhot ha-Berit (Jerusalem, 1963), 3: 48. See the appendix to my book, *Messianism, Zionism and Jewish Religious Radicalism* (Chicago, 1995).

10. Nahum Rabinowitz, "The Approach of Nahmanides and Maimonides to the Commandment of Inheriting the Land" (Heb.), *Tehumin* 5 (1984), 184.

11. See, for example, the comment of Rabbi Yaakov Ariel, *Tehumin* 5 (1984), 174–79.

12. Rav A. I. Kook, *Orot* (Jerusalem, 1976), 14. Cf. the commentary of Rashi on Deut. 1:8.

13. R. Levi Gersonides, *Perush la-Torah*, to Deut. 7:9.

14. Aharon Lichtenstein, "Human Ethics and Divine Ethics" (Heb.), *'Arakhim be-Mivhan Milhamah* (Alon Shevut, 1982), 18. Cf. Yaakov Blidstein, *'Eqronot medini'im be-mishnat ha-Rambam* (Ramat Gan, 1983), 216–20.

15. Blidstein, *'Eqronot medini'im*, 220 n. 18. See the remarks of R. David Bonfil (thirteenth century): "It is not just to steal the portion of other nations; God did not give Israel their land save for the fact that it was in the hands of the Canaanites, who did not themselves merit it." *Hiddushim 'al Sanhedrin, ed. Lifschitz* (Jerusalem,1968), to b. Sanh. 91a.

16. Maimonides, *Mishneh Torah, Melakhim* 4.10. Compare the above mentioned papers by Rabinowitz (note 9) and Amital (note 5); also J. Blidstein, "Holy War in Maimonidean Law," in J. L. Kraemer, ed., *Perspectives on Maimonides* (Oxford, 1991), 209–20.

17. According to one interpretation of Maimonides, he permitted a deterrent war, not a war for expansion alone. See R. Abraham de Boton, *Lehem Mishneh* (printed in standard editions of Maimonides' *Mishneh Torah*), to *Melakhim* 6.1. Cf. Efraim Inbar, "War in Jewish Tradition," *Jerusalem Journal of International Relations* 9 (1987), 86–87.

18. *B. Shevuot* 35b.

19. Maharsha (R. Shmuel Edels), *Hiddushei Halakhot va-Aggadot*, ad loc. Cf. Naftali Zevi Berlin's Torah commentary, *Ha'amek Davar* (Jerusalem, 1984), to Gen. 9:5; Deut. 20:8.

20. Moshe Sofer, *Hatam Sofer* (Vienna, 1865), 1:208; cf. Yehudah Shaviv, *Bezir Avi'ezer* (Alon Shevut, 1990), 102; Yosef Ahituv, "The Wars of Israel and the Sanctity of Life" (Heb.), in Y. Gafni and A. Ravitzky, eds., *Qedushat ha-Hayyim ve-Heruf ha-Nefesh* (Jerusalem, 1992), 263.

21. Yehudah Gershuni, "On Boundaries and on War" (Heb.), *Tehumin* 4 (1983), 59.

22. Amital, "The Wars of Israel According to Maimonides," 460.

23. Shaviv, *Bezir Avi'ezer*, 85 (emphasis added).

24. Rav Shlomo Zevin, *Le-or ha-Halakhah* (Jerusalem, 1978), 10.

25. Shaul Yisraeli, *'Amud ha-Yemini* (Tel Aviv, 1966), 77. Cf. Ahituv, "The Wars of Israel and the Sanctity of Life," 265.

26. Rav Kook, *Iggerot ha-Re'ayah*, 1:140. In the halakic realm as well, Rav Kook understood the permission to shed blood in war as a temporary measure; see *Mishpat Kohen* (Jerusalem, 1966), 153–54. For this reason, all of the opinions presented in this section draw extensively upon him. Rav David Fraenkel, the great nineteenth-century exegete of the Jerusalem Talmud (author of *Qorban ha-'Edah*), linked the permissibility of war to the halakic requirement that one protect an individual being pursued: if the Torah commanded one to save him from his pursuer, and in the absence of other options even permitted one to inflict mortal harm to the pursuer, how much more so to save an entire nation! See *Sheyarei Qorban* on J. *Sotah* 8:10; cf. Shemaryahu Arieli, *Mishpat ha-Milhamah* (Jerusalem, 1972), 13.

27. *Babylonian Talmud, Yoma* 22b.

28. Of course, this distinction is also related to the demonic image of Amalek and the commandment to obliterate him.

29. Yitzhak Aramah, *Aqedat Yizhaq*, nos. 81, 105.

30. A. M. Haberman, ed., *Gezerot Ashkenaz ve-Zorfat* (Jerusalem, 1960), 30, 97.

31. Eleazar ha-Rokeah, *Sefer ha-Roqeah* (Jerusalem, 1960), Hilkhot 'Eruvin nos. 196, 85.

32. R. Abraham ibn Ezra, Commentary to Zech 9:9–16.

33. Abraham ibn Daoud, *Divrei Malkhei Bayit Sheni* (Mantua, 1514), 62.

34. Eliezer of Beaugency, Commentary to Haggai 2:7–9.

35. The late historian H. H. Ben-Sasson reveals many interesting facts of this type in "The Singularity of the People of Israel According to Twelfth-Century Scholars" (Heb.), *Peraqim* 2 (Jerusalem, 1969), 166–68, 177, 214–16.

36. The following remarks are based upon my article "Peace in the Jewish Tradition," in A. Cohen and P. Mendes-Flohr, eds., *Contemporary Jewish Religious Thought* (New York, 1987), 691–92.

37. *Targum Onqelos* to Gen. 48:22; *Tanhuma, Beshalah*, ch. 9; cf. *Mekhilta de-Rabbi Yishma'el* 14.10; *Babylonian Talmud, Baba Batra* 123a.

38. *Babylonian Talmud, Hagigga* 14a; *Babylonian Talmud, Megilah* 15b.

39. *Midrash Tehillim* 45.4.

40. *Yalqut Shim'oni* 2: 141.

41. *Babylonian Talmud, Mo'ed Katan* 16b; cf. Shlomo Goren, "Heroism in Jewish Teaching" (Heb.), *Mahanayim* 120 (1969), 7–13; Reuven Kimelman, "Nonviolence in the Talmud," *Judaism* 17 (1968), 316–34; D. S. Shapiro, "The Jewish Attitude towards Peace and War," in L. Jung, ed., *Israel of Tomorrow* (New York, 1946), 220ff.

42. Goren, "Heroism in Jewish Teaching."

43. See, for example, R. Ya'akov Antoli, *Malmad ha-Talmidim* (Lyck, 1866), fols. 22b, 31b, 85b; Moses Ibn Tibbon, *Perush 'al Shir ha-Shirim* (Lyck, 1874), fol. 14b, etc.

44. See, for example, Joseph Gikatilla, Sha'arei Orah, pts. 3–4 (interpretation of the name *zeva'ot*).

45. See G. F. Nuttal, *Christian Pacifism in History* (Oxford, 1958); John Ferguson, *War and Peace in the World Religions* (London, 1977), 101–22, and the extensive bibliography on pp. 122–23.

46. Augustine *De civitate Dei* 19; see also the studies by L. B. Walters, *Five Classical Just-War Theories* (Hartford, CT, 1971), and J. B. Hehir, "The Just-War Ethic and Catholic Theology," in T. A. Shannon, ed., *War or Peace* (New York, 1980), 15–39.

47. See F. H. Russell, *The Just War in the Middle Ages* (London, 1977), 16–39; cf. Walters, *Five Classical Just-War Theories*, 61–62; Nuttal, *Christian Pacifism in History*, 106 (on parallels in Aquinas).

48. On the revival of the holy war approach among seventeenth- and eighteenth-century Protestants, see Michael Walzer, *The Revolution of the Saints: A Study in the Origins of Radical Politics* (London, 1966), 270ff.; Nuttal, *Christian Pacifism in History*, 115–16; and John Hick, "Christian Doctrine in the Light of Religious Pluralism," *International Religious Foundation Newsletter* 3 (1988).

49. See *M. Yadayim* 4:4; Maimonides, *Sefer ha-Mizvot, Mizvat 'Aseh*, no. 187; cf. Mordecai ha-Kohen, "Peace and the Wars of Israel" (Heb.), *Halakhah va-Halikhot* (Jerusalem, 1975), 180–203.

12

Judaism and the Obligation to Die for the State

GEOFFREY B. LEVEY

I

Dying in the state's behalf, and at its request, is a matter that one might expect to be of obvious concern to the Jews throughout their history. Twice in bygone eras (roughly 1000–586 B.C.E. and 140–63 B.C.E.), they have been ensconced in their own sovereign land faced with preserving that sovereignty against hostile neighbors and ambitious empires. Elsewhere, in the diaspora, they have been forced to define their relations and responsibilities to the host powers under whose authority they have variously been classed as aliens, residents, and citizens. And now, again, they are reestablished in their own sovereign state of Israel, in whose short history the call to arms has been unfortunately all too frequent. Yet the obligation to die for the state is not a question that enjoys special treatment or ready resolution in Jewish sources. In part, this is because the Jewish tradition is not in nature a philosophical tradition, given to abstract systematic treatises in the manner of the ancient Greeks, to whom Western thought has ever since been indebted. It is, rather, a legal tradition, given over to the interpretation and application of legal minutiae in keeping with divine edict. Still, it would be wrong to conclude that Judaism and the Jewish tradition lack a coherent position on there being (or not being) an obligation to die for the state. Such, anyway, is what I wish to argue in this essay.

But I also want to argue that the Jewish approach to the question of dying for the state has wider importance for political theory. Classic Western treatments of the question of the obligation to die have typically been caught in an enduring dilemma. On the one hand, as has been said, any theory that, like Hobbes's, Locke's, and Kant's, begins with the absolute independence of freely willing individuals and goes on to treat politics and the state as instrumental to the achievement of individual purposes would seem incapable of justifying an obligation upon individuals to lay down their lives for the state.[1] So, too, would it seem incapable of providing a sense of active community. On the other

hand, any theory that, like Rousseau's and Hegel's, begins with a notion of the state as an ethical institution representing shared values and
common sacrifices over and above individual interests, and that goes
on perhaps to regard the significance of war to be precisely that it en-
ables the primacy of the state to be reasserted over private concerns,
cannot hope, in turn, to preserve the individual's liberty to safeguard
his life and property.[2] The Jewish approach to the question of dying for
the state, I will contend, demonstrates *one* way this dilemma may be
overcome.

At once, however, a possible confusion needs to be averted. It has often been noted that the concept of the state is problematical, if not alien,
in relation to classical forms of Jewish government. Thus, Roland de
Vaux, in his masterful study of ancient Israelite institutions, concludes:

> Clearly we cannot speak of one Israelite idea of the State. The federation of
> the Twelve Tribes, the kingship of Saul, that of David and Solomon, the
> kingdoms of Israel and Judah, the post-exilic community, all these are so
> many different regimes. We may even go further and say that there never
> was any Israelite idea of the State.[3]

It may appear, therefore, that the very question of whether there is an
obligation to die for the state according to and within Jewish tradition
is ill-conceived. One, of course, may still want to inquire as to how
Jews faced this question as communities in the diaspora, under foreign
rule. But as regards how they did so under their own sovereignty, so
goes the argument, the answer ought to be plain: there is no question
of an obligation to die for the state in classical Jewish thought because
there is no idea of the state governing classical Jewish life.

Now, the confusion here consists in the semantic use of the term
"state." For in asking whether there can be an obligation to *die for the
state*, the issue is not what constitutes a coherent conception or practice
of statehood. The issue is whether one can be bound to sacrifice one's
life for the security and well-being of *any* broad and inclusive political
association of which one is a part because the political authority decrees it. That is, at stake is the nature and extent of individual obligation to the broader social unit or body politic. It is in this sense, then,
that the convenient phrase "dying for the state" may be applied to the
various regimes (as de Vaux puts it) characteristic of ancient Israel and
Jewish self-government.

The precise nature and extent of an individual's obligation to the
state may in turn, of course, depend upon the considered nature of the
state itself. This is the approach characteristic of Western theorizing
about the problem of political dying.[4] By being (or not being) obligated
to die for the state, it is meant that one is (or is not) bound by the state's

general and acclaimed end or purpose, the act of its foundation or the relationship to it among its members. Hobbes, for example, asserts the end of the state to be nothing else than the security and well-being of the individual, which, indeed, constitutes the individual's sole reason for contracting to form the state, and enthrone Leviathan, in the first place. For Hobbes, therefore, political obligation vanishes at the point at which an individual's security becomes compromised: there can be no obligation to die for the state.[5]

Rousseau, too, ultimately determines the case for the obligation to die for the state upon consideration of the state's basic purpose—though for him, unlike Hobbes, there *is* an obligation to die, since the state represents a shared moral life from which each citizen gains, and therefore owes his own. But Rousseau also suggests political dying to be obligatory in terms of the act of the state's foundation. The social contract includes, as it were, a "willingness to die" clause: "He who wishes to preserve his life at others' expense," states Rousseau, "should also, when it is necessary, be ready to give it up for their sake . . . and when the prince says to him: 'it is expedient for the State that you should die,' he ought to die, *because it is only on that condition* that he has been living in security up to the present."[6]

Again, Plato, in the trial of Socrates, suggests an additional reason, beyond the end and foundation of the state, generating an obligation to die. What leads Socrates to believe in the rightfulness of his drinking of the hemlock, as sentenced, is his long-standing acceptance of the state and its laws *as expressed* by his public commitments and prolonged participation.[7]

In classic Western treatments, then, the question of there being an obligation to die for the state typically turns upon a particular political theory. Now, this marks the point of departure for the Jewish approach to dying for the state. For in Judaism, one's obligations to the social compact, like one's obligations generally, are determined not according to political relations or some elaborated theory of the state but according to laws understood as divine commandments, or mitzvoth. It is true that these commandments became binding for the Jews after they entered into a bilateral covenant with God, a founding act of consent resembling at least one of the ways Western theorists attempt to ground political obligation.[8] It may even be said that, because Jewish tradition understands the Sinaitic covenant as historical and literal (as it does the covenants of Abraham and David), the ancient Jewish commonwealths provide a more convincing case of political obligation than do the so-called liberal democratic states, for which liberal theorists have found it necessary to invoke the *fiction* of a social contract.[9]

Then, too, the similarities do not end with the founding act of consent. They also relate to the (problematical) fact that the Sinaitic commandments are undertaken by a particular community at a particular time and are yet considered obligatory for all who are born into the covenantal community. For there are commentaries in scripture and elsewhere that seek to explain how succeeding generations can be bound to the covenant that very much resemble the modern liberal theories of tacit and hypothetical consent.[10] But for all the similarities, parallels, and historical connections, there is one difference unequivocally separating the Jewish and Western theoretical approaches to the issue of obligations to the body politic. The agents to whom consent is respectively rendered by the people in social contracts and in the biblical covenants are of completely different orders.

The "social contract" is generally formulated by political theorists to be an unwritten agreement among all contracting persons creating a sovereign. Consent, in this case, is rendered to *political* authority, and thus the institution of the state is central to the whole series of relationships binding citizen to sovereign and sovereign to citizen. The bilateral covenant at Sinai, on the other hand, is between a people, Israel, *and* the sovereign and creator of all things, God. In Judaism, if consent is meaningfully rendered at all, it is rendered to *divine* authority. The institution of the (Jewish) state, far from being the source of, and basis for, its members' obligations, is according to Judaism, merely a necessary instrument in the fulfillment of obligations established elsewhere.[11] This fact, moreover, helps explain de Vaux's observation, cited above, that there never was any Israelite concept of the state but only a series of regimes governing Jewish collective existence. It is conformity to God's commandments that is the measure of a Jew's obligations and not any given political institution, structure, or arrangement.

The question of dying for the state in Jewish tradition is not therefore the question of political obligation it is for so many classic Western thinkers. There is no attempt in Judaism to ask (or to answer) in the abstract whether there can be an obligation to die for the state at all, under any circumstances. In Judaism, dying for the state is instead a question of what the commandments betoken in terms of an individual's relationship to the body politic when the supreme sacrifice may be involved.

In the remainder of this essay, I want to examine closely those commandments that are of direct relevance to the question of dying for the state. For the most part these are the commandments concerning the declaration and prosecution of wars. There are, in addition, some commandments dealing with self-sacrifice and self-defense that will require some treatment in passing. All of these various precepts I will consider only in the context of the biblical Jewish commonwealths (a context that, anyway, most of them presuppose). This is not to say that the "working principles" by which Jews traditionally determined their obligations to the foreign states in which they were resident are not instructive too. Only that, because such principles necessarily depart from the experience, and hence the challenges, of an authentic Jewish polity, they are best left to separate inquiry.[12]

Furthermore, we recognize here that there is a difference between fighting for the state and dying for the state, especially inasmuch as the subject is war. But to note the difference is to note that nothing much is changed by it either. Being bound to fight for one's country implies, in most cases, an unnaturally high risk of death (or, what is maybe worse, mutilation). And it is this implication and not the eventuality that is important in considering the question of ultimate obligation. Accordingly, "to fight" and "to die" will be used as synonymous expressions. It is important to recognize, too, that in Judaism, just what the commandments do indeed betoken is not always a straightforward matter. While scripture constitutes the source and foundation of Jewish ethical teaching, it is in fact the exegeses supplied in the classical rabbinic material of the Talmud and other commentaries that represent normative Judaism as such. For this reason, we will begin first with an analysis of the relevant biblical passages before trying to elucidate the Jewish approach to the question of dying for the state implicit in the classical rabbinic literature.

II

The Bible contains numerous references to the nature of the expectation associated with the call to risk one's life in the service of communal goals.[13] Especially in the premonarchic period, the common feature of biblical wars is their sacred character. God marches along with the Israelites and is considered by Israel to be not only sovereign, but guardian. Thus the sacred character of biblical war ought not to be confused with the modern designation of "holy war." For, in de Vaux's words, "it was Yahweh who fought for Israel, not Israel which fought for its God. The holy war, in Israel, was not a war of religion," but of existence.[14]

Even so, it might be thought that the sacred quality of these biblical wars bore a distinct duty to participate in them. And in an important sense this is so. When the tribes of Gad and Reuben request of Moses that they be permitted to settle their cattle east of the Jordan rather than participate in the fight for Canaan, Moses rebukes them sharply: "Shall your brethren go to war, and shall ye sit here?" (Num. 32:6). He warns them that their proposed course of action would "augment the fierce anger of the Lord toward Israel" (Num. 32:14). Later, when the tribes of Gad and Reuben indicate their willingness to cross the Jordan in battle, Moses warns them that to refuse to participate in this war would be to sin against the Lord, and "be sure your sin will find you out" (Num. 32:20–23).

But the effect of the sacred quality of biblical wars with respect to a duty to participate is very much a two-edged sword. The fact that God is both the legitimator of Israel's wars and its guardian in battle meant that participation had to be infused with the requisite faith. "Fear not!" is the exhortation of God to Joshua and of Joshua to the people in the face of battle and danger (Josh. 8:1, 10:8, 25). Prior to battle against the Midianites, Gideon is commanded by God to go "Proclaim in the ears of the people, saying, Whosoever is fearful and afraid, let him return and depart early from mount Gilead" (Judg. 7:3). True, the reason God gives Gideon for this instruction is that the Israelite forces are too numerous, and hence there is a danger that in victory they shall pride themselves that "Mine own hand hath saved me" (Judg. 7:2). But it seems a mistake to see in this merely a device employed to reduce Israel's battle strength: there is always the question why *this* means should be adopted, and adopted in the first instance.[15]

Perhaps more significant, though, is that this same emphasis on faith and consideration for the "fearful" is repeated and extended in Deuteronomy 20. Here, the sequence of events reveals dramatically the crucial regard in which a correct religious disposition is held as a condition for participating in Israel's wars. The chapter opens with a series of restatements of the *need* for having faith in God.

> When thou goest out to battle against thine enemies, and seest horses, and chariots, and a people more than thou, be not afraid of them: for the Lord thy God is with thee, which brought thee up out of the land of Egypt. And it shall be, when ye are come nigh unto the battle, that the priest shall approach and speak unto the people, And shall say unto them, Hear, O Israel, ye approach this day unto battle against your enemies: let not your hearts faint, fear not, and do not tremble, neither be ye terrified because of them; For the Lord your God is he that goeth with you, to fight for you against your enemies, to save you. (20:1–4)

Next is specified a number of conditions of exemption from battle. However, surprisingly, the first exemptions have nothing obviously to do with a lack of faith in God or a fear of battle. They apply to individuals who, it seems, could well be ardent believers and accomplished warriors.

> And the officers shall speak unto the people, saying, What man is there that hath built a new house, and hath not dedicated it? let him go and return to his house, lest he die in the battle, and another man dedicate it. And what man is he that hath planted a vineyard, and hath not yet eaten of it? let him also go and return unto his house, lest he die in the battle, and another man eat of it. And what man is there that hath betrothed a wife, and hath not taken her? let him go and return unto his house, lest he die in the battle and another man take her. (20:5–7)

It may be that having these other unrealized concerns on one's mind was taken to suggest that such an individual would naturally not be of the "right" religious temperament for battle. Or, more likely, it may be that against war such concerns simply represent conflicting duties and, as one commentator has put it, "a premature breach in a man's involvement in life was explicitly prohibited."[16] Whatever the case, the final exemption, explicitly referring to the "fearful," seems to take on extra force for having been preceded by other legitimate conditions of military exemption where any simple "crisis of faith" is *not* the issue. "And the officers shall speak further unto the people, and they shall say, What man is there that is fearful and fainthearted? let him go and return unto his house, lest his brethren's heart faint as well as his heart" (20:8).

The Bible, then, displays a central tension over the question of there being a duty on the part of the Israelites to risk their own lives in battle on behalf of their people. On the one hand, the sacred quality of Israel's mission and military pursuits suggests a responsibility of "equality of sacrifice" devolving upon each individual.[17] On the other, this very same sacred quality requires that the duty to fight be undertaken with "proper" faith or not be undertaken at all. Nowhere perhaps is this tension better played out in the Bible than in the Song of Deborah.

In this, one of the most poetic and dramatic of all biblical passages, there is the familiar call to arms, the familiar invocation of God as both witness and judge, the familiar and awesome pressure to plunge into battle. Yet Deborah exalts, not the fact of participation, but the fact that such participation was freely entered into. "Praise ye the Lord for the avenging of Israel, when the people *willingly* offered themselves" (Judg. 5:2). And again: "My heart is toward the governors of Israel, that offered themselves *willingly* among the people" (Judg. 5:9). But what, to bring the tension to the straining point, of those who exercise their will and opt not to fight? How shall they be judged? As independent souls due respect or as betrayers of duty? When the crunch comes, the tension is resolved by Deborah in favor of the independence of those who refrained. There is certainly the expression of reproach and regret (though nothing stronger), as de Vaux notes.[18] "Why abodest thou among the sheepfolds, to hear the bleatings of the flocks?" chides Deborah (Judg. 5:16). But, more crucially, there is the ultimate deference to the integrity of conscience: "For the divisions of Reuben there were great searchings of heart" (Judg. 5:15–16).

On the face of it, the advent of the monarchy seems to confound this picture of "ultimate voluntarism" before any duty to risk one's life for the commonwealth. De Vaux has, characteristically, put the problem best:

> This strictly sacred character of war disappeared with the advent of the monarchy and the establishment of a professional army. It is no longer Yahweh who marches ahead of his people to fight the Wars of Yahweh, but the king who leads his people out and fights its wars (I Sam. 8:20). The combatants are no longer warriors who volunteer to fight, but professionals in the pay of the king, or conscripts recruited by his officials.[19]

The basis for the monarch being accorded these powers is found in a controversial passage in the first book of Samuel:

> And Samuel told all the words of the Lord unto the people that asked of him a king. And he said, This will be the manner of the king that shall reign over you: He will take your sons, and appoint them for himself, for his chariots, and to be his horsemen; and some shall run before his chariots. . . . And he will take your menservants and your maidservants, and your goodliest young men, and your asses, and put them to his work. . . . And ye shall cry out in that day because of your king which ye shall have chosen you; and the Lord will not hear you in that day. (8:10–18)

What ethical significance one attaches to these proffered royal prerogatives has tended to depend upon whether they are understood as divine dispensations, precipitated and agreed to by the people themselves, or rather, and only, as dire prophetic warnings of the sort of despotism a monarchy invites. Each interpretation has its notable protagonists.[20] It is perhaps reasonable, therefore, to see the merit in a third (although not necessarily exclusive) alternative: the Bible reveals a basic ambivalence toward the institution of the monarchy. After all, additional to the ambiguous passage cited above, there are others both evidently favorable to it (1 Sam. 9 and 11) and suspicious of it (Hos. 7:3–7, 8:4, 13:9–11).[21] And yet, to highlight the ambivalence with which the kingship is regarded in the Bible can hardly be to sustain the view that its establishment preserved the on-balance, premonarchic value on individual willingness before one's life is put at risk doing battle. One side of the ambivalence is always that the king has the right to conscript for battle almost anyone he pleases.

The crucial consideration is not therefore the kind or degree of legitimacy that the Bible accords to the kingship. It is that the king, though he may obtain certain prerogatives (like initiating wars not necessarily part of the "Wars of Yahweh"), is nevertheless bound to abide by God's laws. Once he sitteth upon his throne, states Deuteronomy (17:18–20), the king

> ... shall write him a copy of this law [which] he shall read therein all the days of his life: that he may learn to fear the Lord his God. . . . That his heart be not lifted up above his brethren, and that he turn not aside from the commandment, to the right hand, or to the left.

The king of Israel remains God's agent, as do indeed all the people of Israel. It follows that even in the monarchic period respect must be accorded the Deuteronomic provisions exempting certain "classes" of individuals elaborated earlier. Of course, it may be argued that with the lack of sacredness associated with some of the king's military ventures goes too the relevance of the Deuteronomic stress on having faith in God as a precondition for participation in war. Nevertheless, the further Deuteronomic concern for those who are "afraid" and "fainthearted" effectively preserves into the monarchic period the principle that individual willingness *precedes* being duty bound to fight.

The idea that the will to fight precedes the duty to do so is a radical one. Just how radical can be seen by reference to a contemporary political theorist. Michael Walzer has argued that "there is a crucially important sense in which the obligation to die can only be stated in the first person singular." Moreover, Walzer insists that this is so even though it "comes dangerously near to suggesting that a man is obligated to die only if he feels or thinks himself obligated."[22] Now, there is a crucially important sense in which this is precisely what the biblical concern for the fearful and the fainthearted does represent. For the fourth exemption effectively makes any obligation to die for the state self-constituting. Perhaps, then, the term "exemption" is not the best way of referring to or understanding the fourth Deuteronomic provision. With it, one is not so much excused from an obligation as there is no obligation until it is personally recognized. Yet, however one conceives of the fourth Deuteronomic provision, whether as dissolving a standing obligation or as helping create one, the conclusion remains the same. As the text stands, if the Bible advances any obligations to die for the state, they are "loose" obligations indeed.[23]

III

The significance of the Deuteronomic exemptions was not lost on the rabbis of the classical period. Nor, in particular, was the radical voluntarism implied by exempting from battle the "fearful" and "fainthearted." The Mishnah records that Rabbi Jose the Galilean understood the fourth exemption to refer to those fearful of having sinned and of having not yet repented.[24] This, he explains, is why it is juxtaposed with the exemptions of the newly wed man, the man who has built a house without dedicating it, and the man who has planted a vineyard but not redeemed it: they provide dignified pretenses under which a transgressor may discreetly return home. Rabbi Akiba, however, insists upon a literal interpretation of the fourth exemption: it refers to the coward, those "unable to stand in the battleranks and see a drawn sword."[25] But genuine cowardice is a condition not easily foretold: anyone may seemingly lay claim to it. Why then should the "coward" be so readily exempted? The Bible offers a psychological reason: "Lest his brethren's heart faint as his heart." This, however, assumes that genuine cowardice is involved, and does not treat the problem of decided noncowards abusing the provision.

An alternative, and more cogent, explanation is suggested by Rabbi Akiba himself. In another formulation, he maintains that the mention in the fourth exemption of *yareth*, or "fearful," refers to the coward, while the additional reference, *rakh halevav*, or "fainthearted" is to the compassionate. He who is "hero among heroes, powerful among the most powerful, but who at the same time is merciful—let him return."[26] There is some dispute among contemporary commentators as to whether this last entails something of the modern notion of conscientious objection.[27] Whatever the case, the inclusiveness of this formulation of the exemption effectively dismisses the need for determining genuine cowardice. Indeed, it seems to recognize the great difficulty in determining the real motivations of those not wanting to fight as against their stated reasons for not wanting to do so. Both the cowardly (or those fearful for their own lives) *and* the compassionate (or those fearful for the lives of others) are thus exempted. Such an argument, it may be noted, is even more radical than that of Hobbes. In his theory, only the genuinely cowardly—men of "feminine courage"—are esteemed to flee from fighting "without injustice."[28] As Rabbi Akiba appreciated, the fourth exemption is far more accommodating. It provides wide, almost open, opportunity to exempt oneself from duty on the battlefield.

But if the rabbinic interpreters recognized this, they were also moved to constrain its effects. This was done chiefly in the classification of biblical wars. The rabbis asked to which wars the exemptions applied. Except for one response where the terms are differently employed (entailing a peripheral dispute), the sages replied: "To discretionary wars [*milhamot reshut*], but in wars commanded by the Torah [*milhamot mitzvah*] all go forth, even a bridegroom from his chamber and a bride from her canopy."[29] This interpretation has stood as the more authoritative. But there are commentators who held differently. Maimonides and Rabbi Ishmael both ruled that the exemptions applied to all the wars engaged in by Israel. And the sixteenth-century talmudic scholar Rabbi David ben Abi Zimra maintained that while the first three Deuteronomic exemptions applied only to discretionary wars, the fourth, exempting the "fearful" and "fainthearted," applied to both discretionary and commanded wars.[30] Clearly, if the radical fourth exemption can be invoked in *both* commanded and discretionary wars, it is reasonable to conclude that there can never be an absolute obligation to fight for the state in Jewish law. If, on the other hand, the fourth exemption (along with the other three) were restricted solely to discretionary wars, it is possible that commanded wars constitute a class of war in which an absolute obligation to fight *might* exist. In either case, further questions must be faced before the full measure of any obligation to die for the state in Jewish law can be established. I propose therefore to broach the problem of the extensiveness of the exemptions according to the relative strength of case that can be made for any such obligation.

IV

It seems clear that the obligation to die for the state is most compelling in the context of *milhamot mitzvah*. Such wars are explicitly ordained by God, and, as we have seen, at least one authoritative rabbinic version claims that no exemptions are permissible here. The sages agreed that the wars expressly mandated by God are those waged against the Amalekites and the idolatrous Seven Nations in the pursuit and conquest of the land of Canaan. Some differences arise over whether the obligation involved here attaches specifically to vanquishing the paganism of the Seven Nations and not instead to the conquest of the land of Canaan, the promised land, itself.[31] These issues, however, do not affect the commanding or obligatory nature of the wars in question.

There is one ruling by Maimonides, though, that does importantly qualify the nature of the obligation to fight with respect to war against the Seven Nations. Maimonides posited that both a communal obligation to wage war against these nations and a personal obligation to eliminate their members applied.[32] But, of course, a personal obligation to fight is certainly not the same thing as being bound to fight for the community (or state). One would be simply fighting, as it were, for one's own sake. This difference is made no less significant by the claim of later commentators that Maimonides meant the personal obligation to be dependent upon the communal one: that an individual can be obligated to endanger himself in the discharge of his personal obligation only if the community has itself first fulfilled its obligation to wage war against the Seven Nations.[33] For it remains that once war has been declared by the community as a whole, the standing obligation to fight comes from a commandment addressed *directly* and *specifically* to the individual.

Important discriminations must then be made among *milhamot mitzvah*, or "commanded wars," before an obligation to die *for the state* is asserted. In war against Amalek, where the individual's obligation to fight derives from the general obligation of the community to wage war, it is entirely fitting to speak of an obligation to die "for the state." But in war against the Seven Nations, where individuals are bound to fight, not through the community, but on account of a personal commandment, the notion of dying for the state is inappropriate.

Still another discrimination must be made. It arises, again, from an important codification made by Maimonides and this time raises a more general problem. In his *Mishneh Torah*, Maimonides posits another variety of "commanded" war in addition to war against the Amalekites and the Seven Nations. This is the defensive war, a war "to deliver Israel from an enemy who has attacked them."[34] The difficulty is that, unlike the wars against Amalek and the Seven Nations, no biblical injunction or apparent talmudic reference exists for this kind of war. The question is thus raised on what basis a defensive war can be deemed obligatory when no divine commandment warrants it.

One answer that seems possible from rabbinic sources is the so-called law of pursuit, or *rodef*. Under this law, a bystander is obliged to help save the life of an intended victim, although the life of the aggressor may only be taken if that is necessary for this purpose. Defensive wars might therefore be obligatory on the grounds that one must render assistance to victims of military aggression. The halakic scholar J. David Bleich has recently posited this explanation, but only to dismiss it.[35] Bleich offers a number of convincing objections to this use of the law of rodef, but certainly the most "damaging" is that "there is no obligation to eliminate a *rodef* [pursuer] if it is necessary to risk one's own life in order to do so." Since this risk is precisely what war entails for the individual combatant, the law of rodef can hardly serve as the basis for there being an obligation to participate in defensive wars.[36]

Of far more interest, therefore, is Bleich's own argument for the obligatory character of defensive wars. They are obligatory, he claims, because they are undertaken by the monarch. Indeed, such wars explain, in part, the very need for a monarch. While "Jewish law recognizes that society has inherent power, albeit limited in nature, with regard to the expropriation of the resources of its members," says Bleich, "only the sovereign enjoys the power to compel his subjects to endanger their lives."[37] Clearly, the issue of dying "for the state" is involved here. In the absence of a divine commandment sanctioning defensive war, the obligation to die, or to endanger oneself, is now linked to the power of the state, as represented in the sovereign.

Still, the state's having the legitimate power to conscript individuals does not necessarily mean that there is an obligation for them to "enlist." A right to induct is not necessarily correlative with a duty to fight. One commentator has pointed out, for example, that on the basis of the prophet Samuel's proclamation of the prerogatives of the king (as quoted earlier), "a citizen does not have to voluntarily pay his taxes or surrender to the military . . . [but rather] the king or government would be obligated to bear the burden for enforcing their taxation and draft regulations."[38] What is missing with Bleich's reliance upon the power of the sovereign is, then, an adequate explanation of why the individual should be obliged to fight in defensive wars.

In fact, the missing step is easily enough to be found in rabbinic sources. A number of commentaries assert not only that the king may compel his subjects to do his bidding but that his directions must be obeyed. Anyone not obeying a royal decree, or who rebels against it, was considered *mored bemalkhut*, or treasonous (strictly, "rebellious against the kingdom"), and could thereby incur the death penalty.[39] Of course, this in turn only raises the question of why one is obliged to obey the king's command. One rabbinic response, it may be recalled, is that the prophet Samuel's description of the king's rights represents divine commandments consented to by the people. And there are others.[40] But rather than rehearse them here, it is perhaps more apposite to reflect, for the moment, on a somewhat different literature.

It is often enough recognized among political theorists that the very nature of defensive war harbors its own imperatives. When a society's survival is threatened through no fault of its own, even the most liberal theorists, those championing the near-absolute freedom of the individual, seem to want to reserve for the state supremacy over the interests of its individual members. "When the Defence of the Commonwealth, requireth at once the help of all that are able to bear Arms, every one is obliged," writes Hobbes uncharacteristically, "because otherwise the Institution of the Commonwealth, which they have not the purpose, or the courage to preserve, was in vain."[41] One might easily suppose, then, that the same sort of concern is what led Maimonides to include defensive war within the obligatory category of *milhamot mitzvah*. Or, as Maurice Lamm has put it, "If the conquest of the land is an obligation, then it stands to reason that the protection of that land is also an obligation."[42] But then again, perhaps it need not stand to reason alone. Commenting upon the Deuteronomic verse (26:17–18), "Harass the Midianites and smite them; for they harass you," an oft-quoted Midrash states: "On the basis of this verse our sages said, if [someone] comes to slay you, arise and slay him."[43]

V

While the foregoing may explain why defensive wars are obligatory in the absence of a direct commandment by God, it remains the case that they fall within the category of *milhamot mitzvah* for no other reason than that Maimonides legislated them so. This is important to emphasize, since discretionary wars, too, may be waged only upon the initiative of the monarch and yet constitute a completely separate classification to that of commanded wars. Rabbinic sources agree that "discretionary" wars are in general those waged by the House of David for the purpose of territorial expansion.[44] Beyond this, they are variously characterized as wars to "eradicate pagan wickedness," wars to "enhance the monarch's greatness and prestige," and wars conducted for economic reasons.[45] But, as outlined earlier, the distinctive feature of discretionary wars is that all four of the Deuteronomic military exemptions are acknowledged to apply. Some rabbis contended that the exempt were nevertheless obliged to assist with noncombat duties in the service of the war effort, though here, as well, it is not entirely clear whether this also includes those exempted under the fourth provision.[46] But whatever the range of these other duties, it is clear that ultimate obligation, the obligation to sacrifice one's life, is, by virtue of the exemptions, severely and significantly circumscribed in discretionary wars.

A number of rabbinic authorities ruled that a war initially waged as a "discretionary" could become a "commanded" war under the threat of defeat. Accordingly, those who were previously exempted from fighting are no longer so and must take up arms with the rest.[47] Certainly the circumstance in which one's forces appear to be on the verge of being overwhelmed, and one's country vanquished, has the semblance of a defensive war, and it is easy to appreciate the logic of the rabbis' ruling. But it is also true that dire consequence, or its anticipation, is a feature common enough to any war, at least at some stage, in one or another battle. This ruling by the rabbis thus seems to seriously detract from the significance of the exemptions. It seems to suggest that even in discretionary war the presumption in Jewish law is in favor of the body politic over the life of the individual, insisting, so to speak, on an obligation to die for the state.

Thus it is important to see that such a presumption is actually less encompassing than it might appear. For the explicit elaboration of exemptions in connection with "discretionary" war carries with it an obligation on the part of the *monarch* to refrain from engaging in (discretionary) wars when he is not confident of victory and thus may require the conscription of persons who would ordinarily be exempt. It is, in part, for this reason that discretionary wars can only be embarked upon with the consent of the Sanhedrin, or Court of Seventy-one, and the confirmation of the *urim ve-tumim*, or "priestly oracles."[48] The task of the Sanhedrin was to assess the need and likelihood of success of a proposed war, while the role of the *urim ve-tumim* was to confirm or deny divine legitimization for the intended military activity. The net effect of these procedures is to safeguard that only "winnable" wars are attempted, thus ensuring that those exempt remain exempt. Only where a war has gone "badly wrong," confounding, as it were, all the intelligence reports, do the exemptions become legitimately waived.

The question remains whether apart from those exempted there is an obligation to die for the state in discretionary wars. After all, like defensive wars, discretionary wars require the initiative of the sovereign, and this suggests that the monarch's declaration of war might similarly generate an obligation on the part of most to fight. Now, if it were only for the first three Deuteronomic exemptions—exempting, as they do, certain objective and definite types of individual status—such a case might be made. But, of course, there is the fourth exemption; as we have seen, a radical and open-ended exemption to the extent that anyone may seemingly invoke it. It may well be asked, then, just how meaningful it is to speak of there being an obligation to die when virtually anyone can exempt himself from it. This is, of course, another way of putting our earlier point that application of the fourth exemption effectively means that the obligation to die for the state is self-constituting.

In any case, the way in which the so-called exemptions take force clarifies that there is no obligation to die as a result merely of the sovereign's declaration of (discretionary) war.[49] It needs to be remembered that prior to announcing the various military exemptions to the assembled people, the "priest anointed for war" spends some emphatic moments counseling them on the need for faith and against the need to be afraid (Deut. 20:1–4). Commenting on this address, Maimonides says that it is designed so that "their hearts be aroused to war and he bring them to endanger themselves."[50] Bleich, curiously, claims this passage as evidence for the contention that the king has the power to compel his subjects to risk their lives.[51] But, in fact, the function of the priest's address suggests not compulsion but persuasion: the people are *brought* to endanger *themselves*. What we find, then, is not the existence of an already standing obligation, the binding force of which the people are being told to remember, but rather the process whereby the commitment or obligation to fight is being made.

The proclamation of the exemptions, and the opportunity for the people to invoke one or another of them, is what constitutes this process. According to Maimonides, two stages are involved.[52] The first is "on the frontier, when they are about to set out, just before the battle is started," where those who have planted a vineyard and not yet enjoyed its fruit are asked to return home. The second opportunity to affirm a commitment to fight is presented to the people when "the battle lines are drawn up, and they are drawing near the attack." At this point, the "priest anointed for war" counsels further against being afraid but proclaims that the newlywed man, the man who has built a house without dedicating it, and anyone who *is* afraid may also return home. The consequential nature of these pronouncements is dramatized, moreover, by their successive repetition by officers assisting the priest. All told, in Maimonides' account, the people have impressed upon them the impending battle together with the opportunities for individual retreat no less than seven times.

Once the last condition of retreat has been issued, however, and "when all those entitled to return home have gone back from among the troops," those remaining on the field are presumed to have committed themselves to fight. An obligation to fight, if not to die, has been created. Accordingly, any soldier now seeking to withdraw from the military effort is considered to be reneging on an obligation that he himself willingly undertook. And, as the Mishnah and other commentaries agree,[53] at the moment of battle such an attempt poses an unpardonable threat to the success of the entire military operation.

And it shall be, when the officers have made an end of speaking unto the people, that they shall appoint captains of hosts at the head of the people. And at the rear of the people they station guards in front of them and others behind them, with iron axes in their hands, and should anyone wish to flee, they have permission to smite his thighs, because the beginning of flight is falling.

An obligation to risk one's life fighting for the state is thus neither automatic nor necessary in discretionary wars; it is contingent upon the individual's willingness to do so. But the process whereby the individual may indicate whether he will fight or not is not indefinite; it has limits. Beyond a certain point, the individual is deemed to have cast his lot, to fight or not to fight. After that, he who has elected to remain and fight is no longer free to indulge a change of heart or mind with impunity. In this, of course, the rabbinic formulation contracts sharply with Hobbes's general theory, in which an individual may legitimately renounce a commitment to fight *whenever* he is so moved by fear.[54] Yet it is worth noting that in practice the rabbinic formulation is perhaps no more restrictive than Hobbes's. The people, after all, are not forewarned of battle and of the conditions for participation in the secure and removed environment of their homes or city. They are informed of such things on the edge of battle itself, where the clamor of shields and the ground-beating of horses' hoofs ought to impress upon all the deadly seriousness of what is in store.[55] The likelihood is increased, therefore, that those assuming a commitment to fight are those most prepared to carry it through to the end. The Hobbesian need of permissible individual retreat, midbattle, is minimized.

VI

To complete our picture of the classical rabbinic varieties of war, consideration must finally be given to the case of preemptive war. First introduced in the Gemara as wars "to diminish the heathens so that they shall not march against them," preemptive wars were designated a form of "discretionary" war by the sages.[56] As such, most of what has been said about the nature and extent of the obligation to fight in discretionary war in general is true of preemptive war in particular. The applicability of all four of the military exemptions limits any obligation to fight by the process of its very creation. There are, however, a number of aspects peculiar to preemptive war that bear on the issue of the obligation to fight.[57]

One has to do with what actually constitutes a preemptive war in the rabbinic understanding. In Jewish law, a preemptive war is one that is waged solely as a preventive military operation. Whether this be to forestall an imminent or only future danger is of no consequence to its status of preemption. Yet a war that is solely conducted to prevent anticipated danger is not regarded as preemptive if it should be in response to a prior attack. This is so even if there has been an intermittent cessation of hostilities. Jewish law, rather, designates such a war to be of the order, "to deliver Israel from an enemy," that is, a defensive war in the category of *milhamot mitzvah*. There thus exists the possibility that a war begun preemptively can become, through a conflation of enemy response and counterresponse, a strictly defensive war. The relative extent of the obligation to fight will then vary respective to the status of the war at any given time.

Certain preemptive military operations have warrant in Jewish law quite apart from the regulations and categories pertaining to war. In the face of imminent danger, and where innocent life is not put at risk, preemptive operations may be initiated on the basis of the principle, "If [someone] comes to slay you, arise and slay him."[58] The principle differs in this context from that of defensive war in that a preemptive war presupposes that no overt aggression has yet been visited by the enemy. Thus, however imminent such aggression may be or seem, preemptive action is deemed to be permissible only, and not obligatory. That there is a difference between danger being imminent and danger seeming imminent helps to explain this halakic ruling. The nonobligatory classification accorded preemptive war allows for the opportunity that alternative courses of action be tried, possibly averting the need for war or the exhibition of hostilities at all. Insofar, though, as preemptive action is deemed necessary, there is no obligation upon an individual to participate in it, just as the operation itself is not permitted should innocent lives be jeopardized.

All this changes should a preemptive action develop into a defensive war. As before, a preemptive action that is met by an aggressive enemy response has the effect of rendering any counterresponse a defensive, and no longer a preemptive, war. In these circumstances, the limiting conditions that attach to preemptive war sanctioned by the principle "If someone comes to slay you" will no longer apply. Instead, the war regulations as determined by the respective categories of "commanded" and "discretionary" war will, once again, come into play.

VII

In Jewish law, the type of war and the willingness of the individual are not all that is required for an obligation to fight for the state to be established. Such an obligation becomes truly binding only if certain conditions and institutions are fulfilled. Some of these have been mentioned already; for instance, the requirement that a discretionary war may be waged by the monarch only after the Sanhedrin and the *urim ve-tumim*, the priestly oracles, have, in their respective ways, determined that it is legitimate. Of course, in our day the Sanhedrin and the *urim ve-tumim* have no institutional existence. It thus follows that any obligation to fight requiring these institutions should be conceived in formal terms only.[59] Further such special provisions might now be noted.

While there is no need for the Sanhedrin in "commanded" wars (since such wars are divinely ordained and hence require no "independent" decision), there is need for the *urim ve-tumim* to pronounce upon their putative divine character.[60] Without the consultation of the *urim ve-tumim* or, what is perhaps less likely given their express sanction, without their confirmation, no obligation to fight in behalf of the state could exist. At least, no obligation could exist to fight the Amalekites and the idolatrous Seven Nations. For in defensive war, the third variety of *milhamot mitzvah*, the requirement of the *urim ve-tumim* does not apply. Just why defensive war should be exceptional in this regard is not all that clear, though Bleich, after elaborate consideration, suggests that it has to do with the role of the *urim ve-tumim* being to establish a state of war in which innocent lives are put at risk.[61] Because in defensive war innocent lives have already been endangered, and the harmony shattered by the aggressor, the legitimating function of the *urim ve-tumim* is no longer necessary.

One way of understanding these various provisions at a more general level is as a kind of "covering law" that sanctions war "only when there is sound military reason to assume that Israel will be victorious."[62] In the case of the explicitly commanded wars against Amalek and the Seven Nations, "sound military reason" for expecting victory would presumably entail little more than popular expression of faith in God as the legitimator of, and guardian in, these wars. Hence the special requirement in these wars that the *urim ve-tumim* be consulted, an institution whereby divine sanction for the proposed war may be established and the individual's faith reassured. In the case of defensive war, where, of course, the aggression has been perpetrated by the enemy, the precaution for Israel's likelihood of victory becomes superfluous. Neither the *urim ve-tumim* nor the Sanhedrin, accordingly, need be consulted in defensive wars. Finally, in discretionary wars, because they are *discretionary*, "sound military reason" had to be "publicly" assessed. Along with the need for divine sanction mediated through the *urim ve-tumim*, therefore, an intended discretionary war had to be appraised and ultimately determined by decision of the Sanhedrin, a body independent of the monarchy and concerned with the life and welfare of the community.

Though the satisfaction of these special provisions is necessary for an obligation to fight to be established, it should not be thought that it is, in this respect, sufficient. What the respective provisions really determine is, in Jewish terms, the justice of an intended war venture. If the provisions are satisfied, Jewish law bestows legitimacy upon the intended war. But the justness of a given war is not, in Jewish law, what determines whether or not an *individual* is obligated to fight for the state. This reposes in a separate process. As elucidated earlier, it is that process whereby in relation to the proclamation of the so-called exemptions an obligation on the part of each individual to fight is either created or rejected. The sole possible exception to this separation of the justness of war and the obligation to fight occurs with "commanded" wars precisely because, according to the sages, the exemptions do not apply here. Still, it bears reemphasizing that some notable rabbinic authorities disagreed on this. And this disagreement is significant enough to conclude that Jewish law understands the justness of war and the obligation to fight to be essentially separate, albeit related, issues.

VIII

Compared with that of the classic Western thinkers, the Jewish approach to the question of the obligation to die for the state undoubtedly appears complicated and involved. Most of the complexities, however, reduce to a few simple principles, and these are what lend the Jewish approach its coherence and importance. Of course, to isolate such principles from the amalgam of Jewish laws, conventions, and institutions for the purposes of theoretical elaboration is, in some sense, to part from one of the most fundamental of all principles animating the mode of traditional Jewish thought. There is certainly irony in this, perhaps even a paradox, but I do not see that any further implication follows from it. This being understood, it is perhaps not too bold to claim that the Jewish approach to the issue of the obligation to fight suggests a certain "theory," what might be called a theory of "graded ultimate obligation." At the general level are the gradations in obligation that Judaism posits *between* categories of war. These vary from "commanded" wars, in which the legal and conventional pressures upon the individual to fight are extremely compelling, to "discretionary" wars, where, because of the process by which the so-called military exemptions take effect, each individual determines for himself whether he will assume an obligation to fight.

At another, more specific, level Judaism asserts there to be gradations in the obligations to fight *within* each of the war categories. Within "commanded" wars, the most obligatory kind of war seems to be defensive war. Though lacking the express divine sanction in the manner of the wars against Amalek and the Seven Nations, the fact that they are yet included in the same category attests to their overriding power in their claim upon the military support of all members of society. That neither of the traditional Jewish checks upon the justice of a proposed war encounter, the Sanhedrin and the *urim ve-tumim*, are required in defensive wars, is further testimony to their compelling nature.

The wars against Amalek and the Seven Nations represent in Jewish history, if not the founding, then the "grounding" of a nation. Ordained as they were by God Himself, their obligatory character is commanding. Only in the case of wars against Amalek, however, is the obligation to fight actually in behalf of the state, the wars against the Seven Nations being properly the concern of a personal obligation, the duty, that is, of each individual qua individual in his direct relation to God. It may be that Maimonides' formulation of a personal obligation to fight against the Seven Nations is significant precisely in that the stakes in establishing the nation territorially are so high, and the historical and moral implications for the people so momentous, that it was held that an individual could not be bound to risk his life for any other reason than God's, and his own, sake. But it does not follow from this that the obligation to fight against the Seven Nations is any more or less "compelling" than the obligation to fight against Amalek. Both are, after all, divinely commanded, as both are, in our day, purely formal commitments. All that can be said is that while the latter represents an obligation to die for the state, the former does not.

As to "discretionary" wars, the undisputed applicability of all four types of military exemption makes differentiating the extent of the obligation to fight in such cases on the whole superfluous. The inclusiveness of the fourth exemption levels out any obligation to fight until, in the end, it is self-imposed. Yet Jewish law nevertheless insists upon one gradation when it comes to optional military ventures: certain preemptive actions, sanctioned insofar as they are in the face of danger and do not jeopardize innocent lives, cannot be obligatory at all. Outside of the formal regulations pertaining to war, such campaigns do not even witness the process whereby the exemptions are heralded and the obligation to fight can become self-assumed. They are completely voluntary throughout every stage of their execution.

Judaism, then, effectively grades the obligation to fight from its strongest to its weakest conditions. So whether or not there is an obligation to die for the state is a question not susceptible of decisive resolution in the sense of being either (and always) one way or the other: it is a question whose answer must depend on the context in which the problem presents itself. And the lines of division here do not, or do not only, fall between just and unjust wars. They also, and chiefly, fall between different kinds of just wars. The overall effect is to preserve the individual's freedom to protect his life and property in all but the most critical war situations. The first three Deuteronomic exemptions—treating of the man who has built a house, planted a vineyard, and is newly married—represent, in this regard, quite explicit safeguards of the individual's property and life affairs. Beyond this, the radical fourth exemption acts as the final guarantee of an individual's liberty to choose whether to commit himself to battle duty. Only where the very survival of the community is threatened can such individual liberties be overridden.

In this fashion does Judaism overcome the dilemma plaguing Western theories of the obligation to die. Against those liberal theorists who assert that the state exists for the sake of individual purposes, Judaism asserts that individuals can, at critical times, be rightly asked to subordinate their personal lives to the shared life and values of the community. And against those theorists who argue that, because the state represents a shared life and set of values, the individual owes his life to it, Judaism asserts that, in all but the most critical war situations, the individual has his own life to lead and his own choices to make. By not assuming the superiority of the individual or of the collective in terms of the state's foundation or purpose, Judaism is, consistently, able to safeguard the "lives" of both. The state gives way to the freedom of the individual, as the freedom of the individual gives way to the survival of the state. The individual, that is, may legitimately be called upon (as against volunteer) to risk his life for the state, not because the state so commands, but when it is genuinely imperiled. That leaves open the question of who is to decide such a matter, a function seemingly only performed by the state. But the distinction remains a crucial one nevertheless. For in a way that an obligation to die riding upon simple state decree does not, the condition of genuine state impediment at least allows for the possibility of contention. And when individuals' lives are at stake, that possibility assumes the utmost importance.

Notes

Work began on this study while I was a Visiting Graduate Fellow at the International Center for University Teaching of Jewish Civilization, Jerusalem, in 1983–84. I am grateful to two of my teachers at the Hebrew University, Professors Michael Walzer and Emil Fackenheim, as well as Dr. Michael Jackson of the University of Sydney, for comments on an earlier version of this article. An abbreviated version of this paper was read at the inaugural conference of the Australian Association for Jewish Studies, Melbourne, August 1987.

1. Michael Walzer, "The Obligation to Die for the State," in *Obligations: Essays on Disobedience, War and Citizenship* (Cambridge, Mass., 1970), p. 89.

2. The argument that it was Hegel's view that war "serves as a sort of civic education" by its ability to reassert state interests over private ones has recently been advanced by Steven B. Smith, "Hegel's Views on War, the State, and International Relations," *American Political Science Review* 77 (1983): 624–32.

3. Roland de Vaux, *Ancient Israel: Its Life and Institutions* (London, 1973), p. 98.

4. Walzer, "Obligation to Die," p. 77.

5. Thomas Hobbes, *Leviathan* (London, 1979), chap. 21. Hobbes does attempt to make certain exceptions to his principle that there cannot be an obligation to die, but with questionable success. See Walzer's discussion, "Obligation to Die," pp. 84–88.

6. Jean-Jacques Rousseau, *The Social Contract*, trans. G.D.H. Cole (London, 1975), bk. II, chap. V, p. 189 (emphasis added).

7. Plato, *Crito*, trans. Hugh Tredennick (Middlesex, 1969), pp. 90–94.

8. On the consensual aspects of the biblical convenant, see Daniel J. Elazar's essay, "Convenant as the Basis of the Jewish Political Tradition," in his edited volume *Kinship and Consent: The Jewish Political Tradition and Its Contemporary Uses* (Ramat Gan, 1981).

9. "The Biblical suggestion, for example, that covenant is the only moral, and therefore, the most durable root for a political community has in the form of the social contract, become a dominant, if not *the* dominant, metaphor for Western theory since the medieval period. While important social contract theorists do not always emphasize the Sinai Covenant some (i.e. Spinoza) make it their central focus and others (i.e. Hobbes) refer to it often." David C. Rapoport, "Moses, Charisma, and Covenant," *Western Political Quarterly* 32 (1979): 124. This article provides a good list of sources dealing with the relation between biblical covenants and modern notions of social contract.

10. These are cited and discussed in Michael Walzer's book, *Exodus and Revolution* (New York, 1985), esp. pp. 83–88. See also Gordon Freeman, "The Rabbinic Understanding of Covenant as a Political Idea," in Elazar, *Kinship and Consent*, pp. 68–73.

11. Pinhas Rosenbluth, "Political Authority and State in Jewish Thought," *Immanuel* 7 (1977): 101–13. For a more general discussion, see Isadore Epstein, *The Jewish Way of Life* (London, 1947).

12. The basic principle in this regard is *dina d'malkhuta dina* (literally, "the law of the kingdom is the law"), attributed in the Talmud to the third-century amora, Samuel. There is now a growing corpus or work investigating the application of this principle, although the specific question of the obligation to die for the state is mostly only implicitly rather than directly addressed. See Gerald Bildstein, "A Note on the Function of 'The Law of the Kingdom Is Law' in the Medieval Jewish Community," *Jewish Journal of Sociology* 15 (1973): 213–19; Leo Landman, *Jewish Law in the Diaspora: Confrontation and Accommodation* (Philadelphia, 1968); idem, "Civil Disobedience: The Jewish View," *Tradition* 10 (1969): 5–14; idem, "Dina D'Malkhuta Dina: Solely a Diaspora Concept," *Tradition* 15 (1975): 89–96; idem, "A Further Note on the Function of 'The Law of the Kingdom Is the Law,'" *Jewish Journal of Sociology* 17 (1975): 37–41; Aaron Rakefet-Rothkoff, "Dina D'Malkhuta Dina—The Law of the Land in

Halakhic Perspective," *Tradition* 13 (1972): 5–23; and Shmuel Shilo, "Maimonides on 'Dina D'Malkhuta Dina (The Law of the State Is the Law),'" *Jewish Law Annual* 1 (1978): 146–67.

13. All biblical references are to the King James Version.

14. De Vaux, *Ancient Israel*, p. 262.

15. When it transpires that the people remaining are still too numerous, God instructs Gideon to further "sift them" according to how they drink at a stream (Judg. 7:4–8).

16. Everett F. Gendler, "War and the Jewish Tradition," in *Contemporary Jewish Ethics*. ed. Menachem Marc Kellner (New York, 1978), p. 208. See also Johannes Pedersen, *Israel: Its Life and Culture*, vols. 3–4 (London, 1963), pp. 9–10.

17. The phrase is from James E. Priest, *Governmental and Judicial Ethics in the Bible and Rabbinic Literature* (New York and Malibu, Calif., 1980), p. 179, who, though employing it in the same context, fails to note that it represents but one side of "principles in tension."

18. De Vaux. *Ancient Israel*, p. 215.

19. Ibid., p. 263.

20. Tosefta, *Sanhedrin* 4:3; and *Sanhedrin* 20b. References to later rabbinic views on this issue are cited in Leo Landman, "Law and Conscience: The Jewish View," *Judaism* 18 (1969): 24 n. 46. Two recent views claiming Samuel's speech to be an indictment of monarchy are Louis Jacobs, "The Concept of Power in the Jewish Tradition," *Conservative Judaism* 33 (1980): 24–25, and Bruce Vawter, "A Tale of Two Cities: The Old Testament and the Issue of Personal Freedom," *Journal of Ecumenical Studies* 15 (1978): 266–67.

21. Gendler, "War and the Jewish Tradition," pp. 191–92. Cf. R. F. Clements, "The Deuteronomic Interpretation of the Founding of the Monarchy in I Sam. VIII," *Vetus Testamentum* 24 (1974): 398–410.

22. Walzer, "Obligation to Die," pp. 97, 98.

23. The expression is borrowed from Barrington Moore, Jr., in his summary (but apt) description of military obligations in the Old Testament. See his *Privacy: Studies in Social and Cultural History* (Armonk, N.Y., 1984), p. 188.

24. *Sotah* 44a.

25. Ibid.

26. Tosefta, *Sotah* 7:14.

27. For a statement of the affirmative and critical views, see, respectively, Landman, "Law and Conscience," pp. 25–26, and Maurice Lamm, "After the War—Another Look at Pacificism and Selective Conscientious Objection (SCO)," in Kellner, *Contemporary Jewish Ethics*, pp. 237–38.

28. Hobbes. *Leviathan*, chap. 21, p. 115.

29. *Sotah* 44b. The exceptional use of terms is Rabbi Judah's. The exemptions apply, he says, "to the wars commanded by the Torah [*milhamot mitsvah*]; but in obligatory wars [*milhamot hovah*] all go forth." The Gemara explains that there is no real dispute between the sages and R. Judah about the kinds of wars meant by these terms, the latter's novel use of terms representing rather a dispute about whether involvement in a given type of war exempts a soldier from the performance of other commandments.

The suggestion here that in commanded wars women can be conscripted to fight ("even brides go forth") is actually a far more complicated issue. So, too, there are complicating rabbinic rulings about the valid age limits within which males can be conscripted (the most commonly cited being ages twenty to sixty). In speaking throughout this article of "individuals" being obligated to fight, such conditions attaching to age and sex should thus be borne in mind.

30. See respectively *Maimonides' Mishneh Torah. Book XIV: Judges*, ed. and trans. Philip Birnbaum (New York, 1967), Kings 7:1; Rabbi Ishmael, quoted by *Midrash Tannaim* 20:1 and 20:19; and Rabbi Zimra (Radbaz), *Hilkhot Melakhim* 7:1.

31. Cf. *Sotah* 44b and Maimonides, Kings 5:1; idem, *Sefer ha-Mitsvot, mitsvot aseh*, addenda, no. 4.

32. The communal obligation is formulated by Maimonides in Kings 5:1 and in *Sefer ha-Hinnukh*, no. 425, and the personal obligation in Kings 5:4 as well as in *Sefer ha-Hinnukh*, no. 425.

33. See, for example, Shlomoh Goren, *Torat ha-Mo'dim* (Tel Aviv, 5714 [1954]), pp. 180ff.

34. Maimonides, Kings 5:1. I have quoted the translation given in Bleich, n. 35 below, p. 7.

35. J. David Bleich. "Preemptive War in Jewish Law," *Tradition* 21 (1981): 23. The various talmudic references associated with the law of *rodef* are cited by Bleich, p. 39, nn. 32–37.

36. Ibid., p. 18.

37. Ibid., p. 23.

38. Rakeefet-Rothkoff, "Dina D'Malkhuta Dina," p. 13.

39. *Sanhedrin* 49a; Maimonides, Kings 3:8–9.

40. These include the view that the king "owns" the land and has the right to expel noncompliant citizens (R. Asher ben Yechiel, R. Nissim Gerundi, and R. Shlomoh ben Aderes to *Nederim* 28a); the view that a pact exists between subjects and their king, whereby they agree to follow his ordinances (Rashbam's commentary to *Baba Bathra*); and the view that the Noahide precept of "Laws" ordains the "rule of law" and the king's right to execute it (*Even haEzer* to Maimonides, *Nizkei Mammon* 8:5, based upon Rashi's commentary to *Gittin* 9b). It must be noted, however, that these arguments are mainly addressed to the matter of obedience to non-Jewish kings.

41. Hobbes, *Leviathan*, chap. 21, p. 115.

42. Maurice Lamm, " 'Red or Dead?' An Attempt at Formulating a Jewish Attitude," *Tradition* 4 (1962): 185.

43. *Midrash Tanhuma, Parshat Pinhas*, sec. 3. See also *Sanhedrin* 72a and *Berakhot* 58a, 62b.

44. *Sotah* 44b.

45. See respectively Lamm, "Red or Dead?" p. 182; Maimonides, Kings 5:1; *Berakhot* 3b and *Sanhedrein* 16a.

46. Writes Maimonides: "All those who went back home from among the troops, after hearing the priest's proclamation, return now and provide water and food for their fellow soldiers and fix the roads" (Kings 7:9). See also *Sotah*

43a (in which there is also the statement that those returning home do *not* supply the army with noncombat assistance), and Tosefta, *Sotah* 7:15. Despite Maimonides' inclusive description, all mishnaic references are to variations only of the first three Deuteronomic exemptions; the fourth *appears* to be excluded.

47. R. Avraham Yeshaya Karelitz, and R. Haim ben Atar, *Moed* 114:2.

48. *Sanhedrin* 2a; *Berakhot* 3b, and *Sanhedrin* 16a.

49. Cf. Maurice Lamm, "After the War," p. 237: "But there is a sleeper in this affirmation of Jewish selective conscientious objection. It is true only on a *national* level, not on a *personal* one. Determination of the justice of a war was never left to individual decision. That burden devolved upon the state" (emphasis in original). Lamm is, or course, talking of conscientious objection and not directly of the obligation to fight. But he tends to assume that an individual is obligated to fight inasmuch as a war is pronounced (at the national level) just. Conscientious objection—and hence a judgment about the justice or morality of war (or selective conscientious objection, a judgment about the justice or morality of certain wars)—is not, however, the only ground upon which an individual may dispute the call by his country to enter battle. He may simply reject the state's command for him to risk his life, irrespective of his or the state's views about the justice of the proposed war. I discuss the distinction in Jewish law between the question of the justice of war and/or the obligation to fight in section VII below.

50. Maimonides, *Sefer ha-Misvot, mitsvot aseh*, no. 191.

51. Bleich, "Preemptive War," p. 23, and n. 47 (p. 40).

52. Maimonides, Kings 7:2–4, from which the following quotations are drawn. A similar account is given in the Gemara, *Sotah* 42a–b.

53. *Sotah* 44a–b. See also Maimonides, Kings 7:4; and *Pentateuch with Rashi's Commentary*, trans. M. Rosenbaum and A. M. Silbermann (London, 1934), at Deut. 20:9.

54. Hobbes, *Leviathan*, chap. 21.

55. Rashi comments that the four scriptural admonitions in the face of battle correspond "to four things which the kings of the nations do *in battle*: . . . LET NOT YOUR HEARTS FAINT—through the neighing of the horses . . . FEAR NOT from *the noise made* by the clashing of the shields. . . . AND HURRY NOT PRECIPITATELY at the sounds of the trumpets. . . . NEITHER BE TERRIFIED by the noise of the shouting (Siphre: Sota 42a, b)" (*Rashi's Commentary*, trans. M. Rosenbaum and A. M. Silbermann, at Deut. 20:3).

56. *Sotah* 44b.

57. My discussion here is based on Bleich, "Preemptive War," esp. pp. 18–30.

58. Ibid., pp. 24–25, 29–30.

59. The respective obligations to fight against Amalek and the idolatrous Seven Nations would, in any case, appear nowadays to be purely formal ones, given the impossibility of identifying the descendants of these ancient peoples. See Maimonides, Kings 5:4–5, and the discussion of this issue in J. David Bleich, *Contemporary Halakhic Problems* (New York, 1977), pp.17–18.

60. Ramban (Nahmanides) in his addenda to Maimonides' *Sefer ha-Mitsvot*, no. 17, and Maimonides, *Sefer ha-Mitsvot, shoresh* 14, cited in Bleich, *Contemporary*

Halakhic Problems, p.16. There is some question among commentators whether the war against Amalek requires the intervention of the *urim ve-tumim*, but this appears to relate to Amalek as a symbol of evil rather than to the Amalekites as a specific nation. See Bleich's discussion, ibid., pp. 16–18.

   61. Bleich, "Preemptive War," pp. 28–29.

   62. Ibid., p. 25.

Contributors

DAVID BIALE teaches at the University of California, Davis, and formerly directed the Center for Jewish Studies at the Graduate Theological Union. He is the author of *Gershom: Kabbalah and Counter-History*, listed by the *New York Times* as one of the best books of 1979, *Power and Powerlessness in Jewish History*, for which he received a National Jewish Book Award, and *Eros and the Jews: From Biblical Israel to Contemporary America*, and editor of *Cultures of the Jews: A New History*. He is also a contributing editor to *Tikkun Magazine*.

ROBERT M. COVER was the Chancellor Kent professor of law and legal history at Yale Law School, and a committed social activist, until his untimely death in 1986 at the age of forty-two. His publications include *Justice Accused: Antislavery and the Judicial Process*, which received the Harvard Law School Ames Prize for significant books in law, *The Structure of Procedure* (with Owen Fiss), and *Procedure* (with Judith Resnik). His research also included important work in Jewish legal history.

MENACHEM FISCH is professor of history of the philosophy of science and chair of the Graduate School of Philosophy at Tel Aviv University. He is senior fellow at the Shalom Hartman Institute for Advanced Judaic Studies, Jerusalem, and is president of the Israel Society for History and the Philosophy of Science. His published works include *William Whewell, Philosopher of Science* and *Rational Rabbis: Science and Talmudic Culture* as well as many journal articles on the history and philosophy of science, philosophy of language, and philosophical aspects of legal and theological rabbinic discourse.

GEOFFREY BRAHM LEVEY coordinates the Program in Jewish Studies at the University of New South Wales where he is also senior lecturer in politics and international relations. He is the editor (with Philip Mendes) of *Jews and Australian Politics*, the author of numerous articles in modern Jewish studies, and a contributor to *Essential Papers on the Talmud*, *Encyclopedia of American Religion and Politics*, *National-Cultural Autonomy and Its Contemporary Critics*, and *the Oxford Companion to Australian Politics*.

DAVID NOVAK is the J. Richard and Dorothy Shiff Professor of Jewish Studies at University College, University of Toronto. He is a founder of the Union for Traditional Judaism, vice president of the Institute on Religion and Public Life, and a fellow of the Academy for Jewish Philosophy, the Jewish Policy Center, and the Woodrow Wilson International Center for Scholars. His books include *Natural Law in Judaism, Covenantal Rights, The Jewish Social Contract: An Essay in Political Theology, The Theology of Nahmanides, Jewish-Christian Dialogue*, and *Jewish Social Ethics*.

AVIEZER RAVITZKY is the Saul Rosenblum Professor of Jewish Philosophy and chair of the Department of Jewish Thought at the Hebrew University of

Jerusalem. He is also a senior fellow of the Israel Democracy Institute. A specialist in medieval Jewish philosophy and contemporary Jewish thought, he is the author of *Messianism; Zionism, and Jewish Religious Radicalism; History and Faith: Studies in Jewish Philosophy*; and, most recently, *Freedom Inscribed*.

ADAM B. SELIGMAN is professor of religion and research associate at the Institute for the Study of Culture, Religion, and World Affairs at Boston University. He has also taught in Israel and Hungary, where he was a Fulbright scholar from 1990 to 1992. His books include *The Idea of Civil Society, Innerworldly Individualism, The Problem of Trust, Modernity's Wager*, and *Modest Claims*. With colleagues in the Balkans and Israel he directs the International Summer School on Religion and Public Life.

SUZANNE LAST STONE is professor of law at Cardozo Law School, Yeshiva University, and director of the Program in Jewish Law and Interdisciplinary Studies. She is a specialist in Jewish law and comparative legal theory and recently held the Gruss Visiting Professorship in Talmudic Civil Law at Harvard Law School. Her publications include articles in the *Harvard Law Review, Israel Law Review*, and *Yale Journal of Law and Humanities*, and contributions to the *Jewish Quarterly Review, Commentary, The Jewish Political Tradition*, and *Women and Gender in Jewish Philosophy*. She is on the editorial board of the *Jewish Quarterly Review*.

MICHAEL WALZER is a permanent member at the Institute for Advanced Study, Princeton. He is the author of *The Revolution of the Saints, Just and Unjust Wars, Spheres of Justice, On Toleration*, and *Politics and Passion*. He is co-editor of *The Jewish Political Tradition*, co-editor of *Dissent*, a contributing editor of *The New Republic*, and a member of the editorial board of *The Ethikon Series in Comparative Ethics*.

NOAM J. ZOHAR is a member of the philosophy department at Bar Ilan University where he teaches moral and political philosophy, rabbinical thought, and courses in ethics and halakah, and is director of the graduate program in bioethics. He is a research fellow at the Shalom Hartman Institute and has taught at both Princeton University and the University of Pennsylvania. His published works include *Alternatives in Jewish Bioethics* and several articles in related fields. He is co-editor (with Michael Walzer and Menachem Lorberbaum) of *The Jewish Political Tradition*.

Index

Abel, 86
Abi Zimra, Rabbi David ibn, 77
Abner, 156
Agudat Yisrael, 53
Akiba, Rabbi, 150, 158, 191
Amalekites, 156, 161, 192, 200, 202
Amasa, 156
apocalypticism, 51, 131–32. *See also* messianism
Aquinas, Thomas, 139
Arabs, political status of West Bank, 72
Aramah, Rabbi Yitshak, 176
Aristotle, vii, 40, 57
Artson, B. S., 119n13
aspiration, and duty, 8
Assyrian king, 160
Augustine, 178
authority, political, 93–94
autonomy: Jewish tradition versus, 78–79, 100; liberalism and, 122–23

Babylonian Talmud, 126
Bar Kochba revolt, 150, 154
bar mitzvah, 5
bat mitzvah, 5
Ben-Gurion, David, 49n21
Bentham, Jeremy, 7
Berlin, Rabbi Naftali Tzvi Yehuda, 115
Bible: dying for the state and, 186–90; families and individuals in, 40–41; human community in, 84; ownership in, 59–61; Torah as, 139
Bleich, David, 154, 163, 193–94, 197, 200
Bleich, Rabbi, 126
Blidstein, Gerald, 29, 159
Blidstein, Yaakov, 172
Bloch, Ernst, 143n5
Bodin, Jean, 125
borders. *See* boundaries
boundaries: and access to natural resources, 88–89; communal versus territorial, 79, 83–85; Jewish social, 89; and mobility, 77–78; ownership and, 58–62; significance of, 57
Buber, Martin, 62

Cain, 59–60, 86
Calvin, John, 139
Canaanites, 160, 161, 178, 192, 200, 202
Catholic Church, 123, 159
Chazon Ish. *See* Karelitz, Rabbi Abraham Yeshayahu
chosenness, 14
Christianity, 123–24, 177
citizenship: Israeli, 71; Judaism and concept of, 41–42, 52, 71
civil society: future Jewish, 25–26; Jewish social order versus, 13–21, 50–51; Judaism and concept of, 12–13, 15, 21–22, 31; Western origins of, 15, 50–51
clothing, in court, 10
coercion, 72
Cohen, Hermann, 23, 71, 136
collectivism: individualism versus, 4, 50; Judaism and, 43
Colloquium heptaplomeres de rerum sublimium arcanis abditis (Bodin), 125
commanded war, 151, 154, 157, 159, 165, 166, 192–95, 202
communal associations, 21
conduct of war, 161–65, 167
conscientious objection, 158
Conservative Judaism, 96
constitution, Israel's lack of, 70
conversion: definition of, 72; emergence of, 69–70; Jewish identity and, 90–91; war of, as forbidden, 152
cosmopolitanism, 141–43. *See also* international society
covenantal community: basic principles of, 16–17, 73–74; as basis for coherent modern Israel, 79–80; contractual versus, 140–41; and dying for the state, 184–85; interpersonal relations in, 43; political versus, 44; prohibition of idolatry in, 43–44; ritual and, 43
creation: international society and the role of, 134; natural law and, 139
Crito (Plato), 140

Rokeah, Rabbi Eleazar ha-, 177
Rousseau, Jean-Jacques, 4, 140, 183, 184

Salanter, R. Israel, 124
Samson, Rabbi Solomon b., 177
Samuel, 64, 93, 152, 194
Sanhedrin, 155, 170, 171, 196, 199
Saul, 156, 157, 161, 174
School of Hillel, 6, 115–16
School of Shammai, 6, 115–16
Second Temple, 68
Second Vatican Council, 123
secular Jews: in ideal Jewish social order, 22; in modern Israel, 71–75, 90
Seven Nations. *See* Canaanites
Shalit, Binyamin, 72–73
shalom, 150–51
Shaviv, Rabbi Yehudah, 174
shehita, 107
sidrei bere'sheet, 133
siege warfare, 163–64
Sinai, 4, 13
single-sex unions, 119n13
slavery, 76, 137–38
Smith, Adam, 123
social contract, 4, 140–41, 184–85
social justice, 85, 87
Socrates, 184
Sofer, Hatam. *See* Sofer, Moses
Sofer, Moses, ix, 121, 173
Solomon, 151
sovereignty: Jewish communal, 78; of non-Jews in Israel, 77, 79; Orthodox Judaism and problem of, 105
Spinoza, Baruch, 58
state: authority of, 93–94; individual in relation to, 39–40, 183–85, 194, 203; Jewish community in relation to, 35–40, 45–47, 51–53, 104–5, 183; as liability, 38; Orthodox Judaism and, 97–99; resistance to, 156–59. *See also* Israel, modern
Stone, Suzanne Last, 126
strangers, 17–18
Strauss, Leo, 135
suicide, 119n12
Synagogue Council of America, 122

tacit consent, 86–87
taxation, 39–40, 92–93
territory. *See* boundaries; land
texts, political power of, 65–66

theology, and political discourse, 128–30
thought, priority of language versus, 142–43
thumim, 155, 196, 199–200
tohar ha'neshek, 162
tolerance: of ethical diversity, 97–98, 100–103; principles of, 100–101; and public discussion, 97–98, 101–2; value of, 113–17, 125–26
Torah: as Bible and tradition, 139; education and, 37–38, 45–46; and modern religious communities, 36–37; state law versus, 35–38, 45–47, 51
Tower of Babel, 84
Tractatus Theologico-Politicus (Spinoza), 58
tradition, making use of, vii–ix, 75
travel agents, *halakic* restrictions pertaining to, 104, 117–18n7
tribes, and distribution of land, 62–63
Twersky, Isadore, 7
tzedakah, 85, 93

ultra-Orthodox Judaism: and epistemic modesty, 126; in modern Israel, 103; and women's voting rights, 111
Uriah the Hittite, 52, 156
urim, 155, 196, 199–200
Uziel, Rabbi Ben-Zion Hai, 109–10

violence, ownership of land and, 86–87
voluntary association, of Jews and non-Jews, viii
voluntary associations, in Jewish community, 39, 51–52

Walzer, Michael, 27, 190
war: attitudes toward, 153; casualties from, 173; commanded by God, 151, 154, 157, 159, 165, 166, 192–95, 202; conduct of, 161–65, 167; defensive, 153, 154, 155, 171, 193–94, 201–2; emergencies in, and suspensions of law, 165; ends of, 171–73; exemptions from, 158, 187–88, 191–92, 196; grounds for, 153–56; holy, 178, 186; intention and, 159–61; Jewish theories of, 149–50; in Jewish tradition, 151, 167, 176–77; just/unjust, 155, 158–59, 166, 178, 202; neutrality in, 166; non-Jewish, 160–61; permitted, 151, 152, 154–56, 165, 166, 195–98, 202; preemptive, 198–99; prohibited, 151–52, 166;